The Food Fighters

The Food Fighters

DC CENTRAL KITCHEN'S
FIRST TWENTY-FIVE YEARS ON THE
FRONT LINES OF HUNGER AND POVERTY

ALEXANDER JUSTICE MOORE

iUniverse LLC
Bloomington

THE FOOD FIGHTERS
DC CENTRAL KITCHEN'S FIRST TWENTY-FIVE YEARS
ON THE FRONT LINES OF HUNGER AND POVERTY

iUniverse books may be ordered through booksellers or by contacting:

iUniverse LLC
1663 Liberty Drive
Bloomington, IN 47403
www.iuniverse.com
1-800-Authors (1-800-288-4677)

Because of the dynamic nature of the Internet, any web addresses or links contained in this book may have changed since publication and may no longer be valid. The views expressed in this work are solely those of the author and do not necessarily reflect the views of the publisher, and the publisher hereby disclaims any responsibility for them.

Any people depicted in stock imagery provided by Thinkstock are models, and such images are being used for illustrative purposes only. Certain stock imagery © Thinkstock.

ISBN: 978-1-4917-2791-1 (sc)
ISBN: 978-1-4917-2793-5 (hc)
ISBN: 978-1-4917-2792-8 (e)

Library of Congress Control Number: 2014905328

Printed in the United States of America.

iUniverse rev. date: 03/27/2014

Contents

Part I: Robert Egger and the Rise of DC Central Kitchen, 1989-2004

Part II: Mike Curtin's Kitchen, 2004-2012

Dedication

To my father, who taught me to love stories,

To my mother, who taught me to write my own,

And to my beloved wife, Kathryn, who is its moral, meaning, and happy ending.

Acknowledgements

Throughout this process, I was humbled by the generous support of so many people. The staff of DC Central Kitchen, past and present, opened their hearts, memories, and personal files, making this book possible. Kitchen leaders, including Mike Curtin, Glenda Cognevich, Brian MacNair, Cynthia Rowland, and Chapman Todd walked me through their many critical decisions. Marianne Ali, Jerald Thomas, Susan Callahan, and Ron Swanson revealed the secrets of the Kitchen's Culinary Job Training program. Dawain Arrington, Howard Thomas, Carolyn Parham, and the legendary Miss Dorothy Bell opened up about personal challenges and tremendous professional successes. Alex Tait, Tim Forbes, and Craig Keller dug deep into their memory banks to recall their experiences as early DCCK staffers. Stephen Kendall, Lindsey Palmer, Gregg Malsbary, James Weeks, and Jessica Towers offered vital programmatic insights. The great José Andrés shared his grand schemes and rich recollections of the Kitchen, while Brian Ray and David Carleton offered frank outside assessments of the organization's strengths and weaknesses.

This book also owes its existence to Robert Egger, who founded DC Central Kitchen, wrote a book that brought me to its well-worn front door, and responded promptly, fully, and fairly to one information request after another, even when time zones made things difficult. Above all, thanks for the inspiration, amigo.

Thank you also to my incredible personal editor, Sonja Pedersen-Green, and my publishing world trail guides, Deborah McBride and Ed Quigley. Ann McCarthy and Russell Burmel of ThinkFoodGroup, Carla Hall, and Kirsten Bischoff deserve my thanks as well. And Ezra Gregg's remarkable photography appears on the cover.

I owe further thanks to everyone who taught me how to read, write, and think. Any failures to adequately do such things in this work are reflections only of my abilities as a student, not the tremendous work of my many teachers. The lessons and values of my Ithaca mentors Patricia Spencer, Naeem Inayatullah, Marty Brownstein, Barbara Adams, Michael Smith, Jim Swafford, and Marlene Kobre permeate this work. And to my graduate school advisors, Tom O'Toole, Ronald Krebs, and Michael Barnett, I'm sorry I never finished. Hopefully this book helps explain why.

Finally, I am forever indebted to several people named Moore. My parents, John and Marsha, have patiently and lovingly supported me for 28 years. And my wife, Kathryn, had the unenviable challenge of living with a first-time author for the past year, a task she handled with her usual grace and kindness.

Thank you, all.

Introduction

Half a mile north of the US Capitol sits a crumbling blue and grey building. The length of a full city block, its four floors are carved up between a shelter, a drug rehab program, and a medical clinic. Around back, past the litter-strewn gravel lot, is a dark hallway open to the outside air. A battered old owl decoy perches on an even older radiator, trying in vain to ward off the pigeons that flutter in looking for a break from the weather.

The pigeons aren't scared, but many people might be. Those who step into that poorly lit hallway, hang a sharp right, and lean into the heavy door marked 'DC Central Kitchen' are looking for something. Some are homeless adults looking for a meal. Others are former felons who heard about a job training program that would give them a fair shot, despite their records. Many are volunteers hoping to do a little good, or earn a little redemption. A few have been US presidents, first ladies, cabinet secretaries, and Nobel Prize winners—sometimes seeking photo opportunities, other times searching for solutions to problems that no white paper could answer.

This book is not a triumphalist tale of one plucky nonprofit defeating all comers. Rather, it is a story of the men and women who chose to lean into that heavy door each day, plunging into a kitchen packed with shouting chefs, clanging pans, boiling kettles, and second chances cooked from scratch. These people made bold choices and big mistakes as they built a nonprofit organization that defied every lazy stereotype and demeaning assumption associated with the individuals and organizations in the business of doing good. Far from being simplistic martyrs, this story's 'heroes'—such as they are—include addicts, egoists, and convicts. Yet by working together, they have engineered a model that turns the rough raw ingredients of leftover food and unemployed adults who have known little else besides failure, crime, and drugs into a liberating enterprise designed to not just fight hunger, but to defeat it.

There have been many nonprofits and social enterprises founded upon compelling ideas. Few of them have turned those concepts into tangible, lasting results. The difference, it seems, is less the intended model—though that certainly matters—than the skills, decisions, and steadfast commitment of those charged with implementing it. This book is entitled *The Food Fighters* because, ultimately, it is about the people who made DC Central Kitchen possible.

Everyone depicted in this work is a real person. I have worked to corroborate each of their accounts to the best of my ability. Human memories are imperfect things, and when memories of specific dates or events have become blurred, I have deferred to written records from those periods. External events that have affected the Kitchen, especially ones involving other organizations or individuals from outside DCCK, have been documented through open-source research. Some individuals referenced on the margins of this account, especially when those references might be viewed as unflattering, have had their first names changed and last names dropped. This is the only instance in *The Food Fighters* of intentional misdirection.

DC Central Kitchen—often called DCCK or simply 'the Kitchen' by those who know it—was always intended to offer new directions to the wider nonprofit sector. In 2004, Kitchen founder Robert L.E. Egger penned a book entitled *Begging for Change: The Dollars and Sense of Making Nonprofits Responsive, Efficient, and Rewarding for All*. His written broadside sought to slay the sacred cows of the nonprofit sector and shock it into new and better forms of action. Like its author, *Begging for Change* was impassioned and impossible to ignore. Because this book is about DC Central Kitchen, Egger's vision is critical to its narrative—but this work has no pretensions of being *Begging for Change II*. The pages that follow are dedicated not just to the big ideas underpinning the Kitchen's work, but the daily efforts of the diverse men and women who helped make those bold concepts a reality.

In the interests of full disclosure, eight years ago, I read *Begging for Change* and became one of the many precocious college students looking to learn at the feet of Robert Egger and DC Central Kitchen. After several attempts to become a respectable, sufficiently disinterested academic researcher, I am a full-time employee of DCCK, where I receive the bulk of my annual income. For some readers, this fact may call into question my credibility as a narrator.

When I began this project, I asked for and received full permission from the Kitchen's leaders to interview anyone, ask any question, and exercise my own judgment in disclosing my discoveries. This work is not intended to be a promotional item for DCCK, and the input of those leaders in the writing process has been limited to fact-checking assistance rather than editorial oversight. My status as a DCCK 'insider' has given me an unparalleled level of access to information regarding the organization. While the Kitchen prides itself on its transparency, no entity can be thrilled at the prospect of exposing its internal politics and decision-making to a critical investigator looking to publish his findings publicly. The Kitchen gave me *carte blanche* to tell its story as I saw fit and I have done so without censoring any relevant information that would have made my colleagues, my superiors, or me uncomfortable or appear in an unfavorable light.

In interview after interview, the women and men I spoke to described working for DC Central Kitchen in seemingly contradictory terms. They found it invigorating and exhausting, uplifting and heartbreaking, liberating and frustrating. This book aims to capture, as best it can, those struggles and successes in ways that advance our shared understanding of nonprofits, the people they serve, and the people who, in the words of Martin Luther King, Jr., have made a career of humanity.

Part I: Robert Egger and the Rise of DC Central Kitchen, 1989-2004

Chapter 1   Grate Expectations

The heavy rubber bottoms of Robert Egger's boots clomped along a tired tile floor as he headed into his office for the final time. 'Office,' perhaps, is a generous label. Almost 24 years after he founded DC Central Kitchen (DCCK), Egger and his nonprofit organization had developed a reputation for redefining some less-than-glamorous things. There, windowless mop closets became executive offices, wasted food became balanced meals, and homeless ex-convicts became dedicated employees. Robert's six-by-six foot room, with its sagging, dropped ceiling and white cinderblock walls, had little in common with most workspaces belonging to people with titles like CEO or President. A clunky metal desk sat to the left and those white walls were nearly papered over with pictures and posters of his heroes, from Frederick Douglass and Harriet Tubman to Elvis Presley and Bruce Springsteen. The cramped closet hid its significance well. In Robert's desk drawers, Kodak prints and press clippings told a grander story. Bill and Hilary Clinton toured the Kitchen twice. Barack Obama brought his whole family. George H.W. Bush named Robert his 275th Point of Light. Oprah gave him an adoring hug on national television.

Robert was a young man when he started the Kitchen. His hair, once wavy and parted, eventually grayed and thinned slightly. He decided to crop it short. The angular jaw he used to shave daily was eventually covered, in part, by a silver goatee. After packing away his picture of The King and an oversized cardboard check from The Boss, Egger picked up his iPhone and handed it to a colleague, who snapped a photo of him standing in front of the stripped-down walls spotted with masking tape. Egger posted it to Facebook. Twenty-four people liked it instantly.

In the photo, he leans on a chair, smiling slightly. Aside from his pale skin and light hair, his figure is all black, from his tight t-shirt and jeans to his leather belt and biker boots. Robert has worn black for almost as long as he can remember. It was the appeal of a black robe that first inspired him to become an altar boy.

"Back then," he recalls, "the altar boy uniforms were really cool. Black with white trim. It was a great costume." Waiting in line before class began at his California Catholic school, Egger got a tap on the shoulder from a teacher, who asked him if he was interested in helping out at the poorly attended 6 p.m. mass. "Next thing I know, I'm up on the altar, with no training." His audiences, one earthly, one celestial, wracked him with nervous emotion. It was a young Robert's first experience with a stage, a high-stakes show fraught with complex implications for right and wrong, good and evil. He was part of a production that was designed not to entertain, but to enrapture, to make an audience think along life-changing lines.

Despite his gig moonlighting at church, Egger was never much for authority figures. As a third-grader, he and his friends had ambled into a nearby canyon, away from prying adult eyes, to screw around with some matches. The dry brush caught fire quickly, and soon a good swath of the canyon was ablaze. By the time the boys emerged from the smoke, a row of disapproving parents and firemen had assembled, alerted by the flickering lights on the horizon. "We were so busted," he says, chuckling. The local fire chief visited Robert's school the next day and summoned the boy to the principal's office. Dressed in full regalia, the chief told Egger he was to write a three-page report on the dangers of playing with fire. "I went home, grabbed the pencil with both hands, and wrote this report. I saw that this authority figure wanted it, so I wanted to do a really good job. I made a cover for it out of construction paper and everything. I was so ready for this fire chief to say 'Son, you've done great work.'" The fire chief never came back. The experience of having a good idea, working hard, and, in return, receiving nothing but disregard "really pissed off" Robert. "That was the first time I questioned authority," he says.

A military brat, Egger found himself periodically hauled across the country by his parents. After California, he attended middle school in Quantico, Virginia, began high school in Louisville, Kentucky, and finished it outside Washington, DC. Egger found stability in two great pillars of pop culture: movies and music. His favorite film was *Casablanca*. Robert idolized Rick Blaine, the coolest dude in the coolest nightclub on Earth. Rick never had to advertise his American Café. Everyone knew it was the place to be, whether it was for the show that happened out front, or the shady deals and sultry indulgences that took place in its backrooms. The more he watched Casablanca, the more Egger began wondering about the backrooms in his own life. The killings of two Kennedys and a King during his formative years only fueled his irreverent sense of inquiry. His favorite music liked to stick it to the status quo as well. He loved the later work of the Beatles, the music of Woodstock, and, later on, the "Fuck this, fuck that," mantra of the Sex Pistols.

Egger graduated high school in 1976, but says that he "was always the worst student. Organized thinking was not my bag." His parents moved to Indiana shortly thereafter. Robert followed but quickly tired of the place. Six months later, he was back in DC, learning to tend bar across the Potomac River at the Fish Market in Alexandria, Virginia. After a year of building up his skills, he nabbed a gig at the legendary Childe Harold in DC's Dupont Circle neighborhood. "This was the place where the Ramones played their first show in DC, where Springsteen played, Emmylou Harris, man," Egger says, still awed by his proximity to history. Beyond the names that showed up on stage, one of Childe Harold's most popular regulars was the cocaine on its bathroom counters. Egger followed its savvy, short-tempered manager like a shadow, taking notes for his own club, modeled on Rick's American Café. He bought a motorcycle and leased a one-bedroom apartment. "I was 22 and felt like I was on top of the world."

In the spring of 1982, Robert was enjoying another average day of the high life. He slept late, strolled down the sweeping green space of the National Mall to play a round of pick-up soccer, headed home for a nap and a bite to eat, and then hit the Childe Harold early to set up. The Clovers, an R&B band, were about to perform. A small contingent of especially eager fans trickled in, and while Robert handed them a few clinking glasses filled with gin, tonic, and ice, his head snapped over to the doorway on his right. "I looked over to the door and there was a silhouette, surrounded by light." In walked a lithe blonde woman, dripping with self-confidence. "I had this weird sense of 'I know you,'" says Egger, but they had never met. He went about learning everything about her he possibly could, starting with her name: Claudia.

"Claudia was exotic, and had that beautiful blonde hair. She was from Albuquerque. She drove a silver Camaro and wore a leather jacket. I thought she was righteous." They were both smitten, but seeing other people. "We didn't see each other for nine months," Robert recalls. After their respective relationships had ended, the two bumped into each other at an art gallery and have been together ever since. To this day, whether he is chatting with close friends or total strangers, Egger almost exclusively refers to her as his "beloved Claudia."

With the blessing of Claudia's mother, June, the pair moved into an efficiency apartment in Georgetown. Robert phoned his mother, and asked her to mail him his grandmother's engagement ring. "It was so weird going to pick it up at the Post Office," he says. Robert and Claudia set about painting their new place one evening, working on a bottle or two of champagne while they were at it. Robert dropped to one knee and proposed.

Once engaged, Robert and Claudia had to pick a place to get married. Dismissing the church down the street from their apartment as "too snooty," the couple found an Episcopal church around the corner from Robert's latest place of employment, a high-end jazz club called Charlie Byrd's. The two decided they liked Grace Church's priest, Father Steve, and his $100 price tag for a marriage ceremony beat the hell out of his sacrament industry competition. Robert was also impressed by the church's participation in a program called the Grate Patrol. Seven local churches took turns preparing 125 nightly meals, driving to a number of spots across the city, and serving soup and sandwiches to homeless people. The program got its name from the sidewalk grates where homeless people slept, trying to capture some of the heat rising up through their metal slats. "It was the first time I'd seen a church do something besides talk," he says. Robert and his beloved Claudia had found their wedding venue.

"I hadn't been to church for years, and I was Catholic. But I was impressed. They were so open," Egger remembers. Robert and Claudia became dutiful attendees, and the Grate Patrol seized on their new faces. "I liked the church, but I wasn't about to go out on Grate Patrol," declares Egger. "It scared me to death." For years, he dodged their requests, always grabbing his wife and whispering "C'mon baby, time to go."

At the time, Robert was totally invested in preparing to open his own nightclub. He treated his time at Charlie's "like college," sponging up every drop of industry knowhow he could. He even bought a white sports coat, hoping that looking a little more like Rick Blaine would speed along the process of actually becoming his Hollywood hero. "I was 27 years old, and spent two-and-a-half years of my life trying to raise $3 million to start up my nightclub." Egger wanted his club to revitalize a fading and increasingly tired, corporate scene. Once built, The Blue Circle would be romantic, mysterious, classic, and unpretentious all at once. "We had seen the end of the big band, and then the end of the rock combo. The DJ set was king, but I knew there was all this undiscovered musical talent on the B and C lists of DC. I wanted to reveal all that local talent and turn it into a scrappy little team that'd take the pennant," he says. The planned décor was "straight deco," right down the glass brick bar. And as it was at Rick's, the audience would be a primary part of the show, as Egger eschewed the usual central stage for a series of "performance niches" throughout the venue. He hoped the club's "air of savoir-faire" would eventually speak for itself. "I wanted the sign out front to have no words—just a big granite slab with a blue circle on it, so people could hop in a cab and say 'take me to the blue circle.'" He had crafted a detailed vision, but found no backers.

Finally, in the spring of 1985, the Eggers found themselves backed into a corner by their fellow congregants at Grace Church. Robert reluctantly agreed to commit one of his evenings off to the Grate Patrol. That Tuesday night, they headed into the basement of their church, finding four batches of lentil stew simmering atop an electric stove. Along with two other regulars, Robert and Claudia dumped the stew into one big pot and loaded it into a well-worn step van along with some loaves of white bread and a few cases of oranges. Egger asked the Grate Patrol veterans where they had gotten the food. As someone who had managed the food costs of restaurants and clubs, Robert was shocked to learn that the volunteers shopped at a ritzy Georgetown supermarket, better known for its social scene than its savings.

"Why oranges and not apples?" asked Egger.

"Because many of the people we serve have bad teeth and can't chew," one of the regulars responded. The choice made obvious sense to Robert once he took a second to think about it. He had just never taken a second to think about anything like that before.

At dusk, the van departed. Along the way, Egger could not see out the van's windows, and he realized he had actually never noticed where DC's homeless people congregated. As the van approached its first stop, Robert contorted himself to finally catch a glimpse outside. In the drizzling rain, a line formed before the vehicle came to a halt at the corner of 21st Street and Virginia Avenue, near the US Department of State headquarters. "It was a bizarre, Pavlovian reaction, like a bus stop," he remembers. Nervous, Egger suggested Claudia take off her gaudy hoop earrings. His streetwise wife curtly told him where else he could put his energy. Grabbing some Styrofoam containers, he began serving food and surveying the crowd.

"When we got there," he recalls, "it was a long line of men, with a few women. Some were clearly mentally ill, but there was an equal number of men who, outwardly at least, looked like everything was okay. In a prophetic moment, I told Claudia, some of these guys look like they can work."

"It's none of your business," responded Claudia, out of the side of her mouth. "You're here to serve a meal. You shouldn't judge over a cup of soup." Egger went back to ladling lentils, but continued to process what was happening in front of him. The Grate Patrol team never got down from the van, staying elevated above the people reaching up to them for cups of soup until they drove on to the next stop. Whenever the van pulled away, several piles of trash were left behind by clients who had cast aside their cups, utensils, and orange rinds.

At the third and final stop across from the World Bank, a few of the men from the first stop on Virginia Avenue had caught up, looking for another round of food and coffee. Handing out seconds caused the Grate Patrol to run short on supplies. One man snapped at Egger, "You shouldn't come out here if you're not prepared."

In fact, Egger had really not been prepared for that evening. He had swallowed the peace and love rhetoric of his Sixties-era upbringing whole. Racism repulsed him. Robert had become a faithful attendee of the ultra-tolerant Grace Church. He called everyone he met at Charlie's 'friend' and 'brother.' Yet when it came time to help people who were different in so many ways from himself, he had proven to be uneasy, suspicious, and even fearful. "That's where I drew the line, and became aware that if I wanted to know the true meaning of friendship, I had to go out there and experience it first-hand."[1] That night, Robert realized he had been more or less full of shit for as long as he could remember. Each day since, he has described himself as a "recovering hypocrite."

As he stewed on the experience, Egger did not limit his criticism to himself. "On one level, [the Grate Patrol] made sense. It was very compassionate and very real. What they were doing, they were doing for all the right reasons, but they weren't doing it the right way." Claudia was less conflicted, seeing significant

---

[1]   Egger, Robert, *Begging for Change: The Dollars and Sense of Making Nonprofits Responsive, Efficient, and Rewarding for All* (New York: Harper Business, 2004), 175.

value in a group that wanted to do good going out and actually doing it. She went to bed and suggested he do the same. Egger kept running through the experience over and over in his mind. "Looking out at that rag-tag line of people, I thought, 'there's got to be more than this,' but there wasn't."

Robert was troubled most by two things. First, he recalled the men who seemed like they could, under the right circumstances, hold a job. "I still believe that you shouldn't judge that because someone looks a certain way they should be working," says Egger, "It was more that I was curious. Was this all we did? No partnerships, no social workers?" Second, he hated the inefficiency. Each week, this tiny operation was buying groceries at expensive retail prices and spending hours in a church basement to prepare a limited number of low-quality meals. "There had to be a better way." That night, he drew his first distinction between the concept of 'doing good' and 'doing right.' The Grate Patrol was unquestionably good in its intent and purpose, but, in practice, what it was actually doing did not seem to be what was right for those it served.

The next day, Egger threw on his white jacket and headed to Charlie's. He couldn't shake the memory of his night on the Grate Patrol, though, and even his favorite distraction—planning for his nightclub—could not keep his mind occupied. Robert decided to become a regular at the Grate Patrol until he could figure out how to make it better. He agitated for the program to think bigger and sat down with volunteers from other churches, trying to get them to do the same. What if there was a central kitchen that the groups could share, creating some sort of economy of scale?

The response was not promising. If the operation grew and became more professional, the church members feared they might lose the fellowship of cooking together. The social atmosphere of the Georgetown grocery store was appealing and fun. They liked things just the way they were.

Egger was shocked. All this work, night after night, was not, primarily, for the people eating the meals. It was for the people serving them. "That was when I learned that too much of what we call 'charity' is more about the redemption of the giver than the liberation of the receiver," says Robert.

Before long, Robert became the leader of the Grate Patrol, where he gained full knowledge of its excessive food costs. It was the height of the Eighties' economic boom. Reaganomics was the toast of DC, and Charlie's was tossing out pounds upon pounds of lobster, steak, and shrimp every night. Egger realized the Grate Patrol did not need first-hand food. He could use leftovers. Robert called some of his hospitality industry colleagues. The caterers, chefs, and restaurant managers he knew said they would be happy to donate surplus food to a good cause, so long as they were not liable for spoilage or food-borne illness. While any waste of product equaled lost profit for such businesses, at least having a viable partner for donations meant they could write off the value of that food as a tax deduction. Using leftovers meshed perfectly with Egger's plan for a central kitchen. That facility could serve as a hub for recovering a wide array of excess food items and creatively turning them into real meals.

He discussed the idea with a number of DC's nonprofit leaders. "You can't take food from restaurants and feed people with it," said one. "It violates DC health codes."[2] There were no such codes, but the DC nonprofit establishment was in no mood to be corrected by a twenty-something nightclub manager with a high school diploma.

Dismissed by each person and group he spoke with, Robert flashed back to that fire chief from the third grade. He had an

---

[2]   Egger, *Begging for Change*, 33.

idea, a good one, and the relevant authorities would not give him the time of day. He told Claudia he wanted to put The Blue Circle on hold. In the past year, no one had given his nightclub pitch much consideration either. Sick of having his visions trampled, Egger decided to go into business for himself. "I *knew* I could do the central kitchen. And if people could see that, maybe in a few years, I could get the nightclub off the ground."

By the time Robert Egger arrived on the scene, America's latest round of hunger games had been playing out for the better part of a decade. After so much of the country had gone hungry during the Great Depression, an aggressive public sector significantly increased its role in how the United States grew, harvested, and distributed its food. At the height of the Great Society reforms, acute hunger looked to many like a thing of the past. It wasn't. The Seventies brought economic decline. The Eighties, government retrenchment. An uptick in household need, coupled with a diminished public sector, inspired a revival of the American instinct, first documented by Alexis de Tocqueville in 1835, to form private associations in response to public crises.[3]

Three types of entities emerged in response to the rising tide of hunger. The soup kitchen—a Depression-era holdover that served prepared meals to assembled groups of hungry and homeless citizens—witnessed a modern renaissance. The food pantry, meanwhile, specialized in pre-packaged, non-perishable items and distributed them directly to clients. Both groups were fueled by a new innovation: the food bank. Initially pioneered in Arizona in the late Sixties, these warehouses emerged in the

---

[3] In New York City alone, the number of emergency food providers exploded, from just 30 in 1979 to 600 just 10 years later. For more, see Janet Poppendieck, *Sweet Charity? Emergency Food and the End of Entitlement* (New York: Penguin Books, Ltd. 1998).

Eighties as critical regional aggregators of food stuffs, much of it excess farm product subsidized by the federal government. The food banks allowed front-line providers, the soup kitchens and food pantries, to 'withdraw' food items at little or no cost, bringing unprecedented efficiency to the process of putting food in struggling homes.

Other groups employed some hybrid of these three models, and as more people took up the cause of hunger, a few entirely new methods gained traction. In 1982, a New York City-based group called City Harvest started recovering food from restaurants and caterers and dropping it off at area homeless shelters. In a critical move, City Harvest brought leftover food out of the dumpster and into the conversation about how to best address hunger in America. Robert Egger wanted to go beyond addressing hunger, though. He wanted to take on its root cause: poverty.

Robert sought to blend the efficiency of a food bank with the resourcefulness of City Harvest to mass produce meals that small groups like the Grate Patrol could serve to their clients, saving everyone time and money. Instead of handing out food in a vacuum, he would empower other nonprofits to direct their existing resources to support services instead of meal preparation. With their food expenses covered, DC's shelters, halfway houses, and rehabilitation programs could focus on liberating their clients from the conditions that were causing them to go hungry.

As much as Egger hated seeing leftover food tossed aside, the discarding of people to lives of permanent dependency troubled him far more. Robert set out to determine just how many of those men and women who looked like they might be able to work actually could. Instead of merely cooking the meals at his kitchen, he would "teach homeless people the basics of food service as a part of a modest job training program."[4] Egger would thus go beyond handing food to homeless folks and actually recruit them to help prepare the meals that they and people like them relied on each day. Charlie Byrd's and every other dinner spot in town had a constant need for entry-level workers. Robert figured he knew most anyone who mattered in DC's culinary scene anyway, and that those relationships would only get stronger if his organization allowed them to write off their food waste. He could use those connections to help his trainees find jobs, and complete the path from the streets to self-sufficiency. "It was never as much about fighting as hunger as it was about exposing opportunity," he says.

For Robert, "This wasn't a left-wing or right-wing thing. This wasn't a God thing. It was about feeding and empowering people."[5] He had his political leanings and his spiritual beliefs, but he was primarily motivated by what he saw as the unassailable logic underpinning his operation. At first, he wanted to call the program Lazarus Kitchen, because it gave food and people new life. He worried about the sectarian overtones, though, and settled on something more ecumenical. "The name had to be smart and accessible for everyone," Egger concluded.[6] He picked DC Central Kitchen.

Egger phoned his old art director from a free arts magazine he used to edit called *The Unicorn Times*. He needed a logo: "Nothing fancy, something as simple, clean, and industrial as ACME," he says. His friend sent him back a mock-up of a black circle with plain lowercase letters reading "d.c. central kitchen." In the upper right-hand section of the circle were four long, thin triangles, slightly separated and parallel to one another. Together, they were a reductionist rendering of a fork's tines, as

---

4   Egger, *Begging for Change*, 33.
5   Egger, *Begging for Change*, 36.
6   *Ibid.*

if they had been pressed into the circle from behind. Egger loved it. To this day, the bare-bones logo has never been changed.

For the latter half of 1987, Robert and Claudia immersed themselves in the details of launching DC Central Kitchen. He found an office in what once was a dentist's operating room, nestling his desk on a tile floor in between old, exposed nitrous oxide lines that still jutted out from the wall. From that converted row house, Robert would head to a nearby library to learn everything he could about philanthropy, nonprofits, and foundation grant-making. While writing, Robert kept a Merriam Webster's dictionary, once given to him by his parents, on his desk at all times. "I am the world's worst speller. I was so scared of looking stupid," he admits. He did a lot of typing, and even more editing in red ink. Claudia, who worked as a legal assistant by day, ended up taking a good deal of dictation. Together, the couple wrote and submitted a dozen grant proposals to local foundations, attaching a letter with the signatures of 10 restaurant and catering company managers indicating their support.

By the end of 1988, Egger was sick of receiving rejection after rejection from the city's foundations. "I tried to keep my spirits up by telling myself that if a nightclub denizen and committed hedonist like me could see the possibilities, and if my colleagues in the biz were as open to helping as they suggested, somebody in the nonprofit side of this coin *had* to be ready to buy in."[7] The denials continued until one day in December, when he opened his mailbox and found an envelope that was slightly heavier than the others he had opened in recent weeks. He rushed inside and held it up to his ceiling lamp. The distinctive outline of a check emerged. Afraid to jinx anything, Robert ripped open the envelope and, without looking at it, tucked the check under his thigh as he sat down to read the letter.

---

[7]   Egger, *Begging for Change*, 34-35.

On the fine, textured stationary of the Abell Foundation was a brief typewritten note. "The Board of Trustees has considered your proposal for a grant of $15,000 to aid your new project . . ." it began. Egger could not wait. He whipped the check out from beneath his leg. The foundation had fulfilled his request and then some. The check was for $25,000, "in the hope," said the letter, "that it will give added impetus to aid in starting up the program."

He exhaled slowly, and his mind began to race. Robert had never seen that much money in one place, but this whole venture was inspired by a fight against profligacy. "I knew it wasn't going to last me six months if I didn't spend it carefully." He secured a used, white Ford Econoline van with a three-on-the-tree stick shift affixed to the steering column. He popped its temperamental clutch and drove it to Atlanta, where another hunger-fighting group had offered to outfit it with a refrigeration unit in the rear for cheap, and doubled back up I-95. Then he started calling his catering buddies, telling them it was time to serve up or shut up.

After just one go-round with the foundation grant cycle, Robert was already tired of chasing down individual contributions. He wanted the money to come to him. To achieve that rather ambitious goal, he needed do something big, something flashy, something that would attract lots of attention and inspire people to give and get on board. Robert needed a stage. One that might be televised, say, throughout the free world.

The timing of the Abell Foundation grant, just before New Year's, 1989, forced Robert to "immediately adapt and take advantage of the opportunity." A buddy of his from Charlie Byrd's had snagged an event management gig with the Republican National Committee, planning some of the ins and outs of George H.W. Bush's inauguration. He offered

Egger a few leads, and Robert began burning up the landlines of everyone involved with the festivities, trying to find the caterer-in-chief. As soon as he heard a 'hello' on the other end of the line, Egger launched into his 15-second spiel, describing the Kitchen, his refrigerated truck, and the public relations value of donating the leftovers from an inaugural ball to a good cause.

Most folks hung up. Others gave him additional numbers to call. But one person, the elusive top caterer, finally said, "This is a great idea. We'd love to be involved." The heads of other inaugural balls caught wind of the plan and wanted in too, including Republican Senator Dan Coats of Indiana. Republican officials and lobbyists began notifying the media of Egger's plan.

"I didn't need to pitch the story," recalls Robert. "The idea was irresistible. Food recovery had been done elsewhere, but never in DC and certainly not with the backdrop of lobbyist parties." On Inauguration Day, *The Washington Post* ran a story about Egger's plans. Between recovery trips to each ball, Robert alternated taking calls from journalists and radio shows, on the one hand, and interested food donors on the other. The donations were distinctive. Robert hauled one barrel-sized vat of lobster bisque inside the doors of the city's largest homeless shelter. By the time an exhausted Egger staggered into his apartment, DCCK's grand opening had captured the imagination of a public desperate for new solutions to old problems.

The calls from media members and political players were not the ones that stuck with him, however. He immediately began receiving messages from men and women across the District asking for food. They were single moms, working dads, and adults calling on behalf of their elderly parents living on fixed incomes. "For the first time, I was exposed to the extent of hunger. It wasn't just homeless people," he remembers. "The DC Central Kitchen hadn't been open for even one full day before I reached the bittersweet realization that my program, no matter how innovative or how sexy it was, could never solve hunger."

For the first six months of DC Central Kitchen, the operation was fueled almost entirely by Robert's energy and Claudia's patience. Her contributions were especially remarkable, given that she gave birth to their daughter, Julia, shortly after the Kitchen opened for business. In those early days, when it operated out of the old dentist's office, DCCK behaved a lot like New York's City Harvest, taking leftovers from one place and dropping them directly at organizations with need for some extra food. Donations were spotty and unpredictable. And without a refrigerator, late-night pick-ups posed something of a problem if none of his recipient agencies were open to accept them. Robert figured out he could run an extension cord from his office and plug his truck in at night, maintaining sufficiently cold temperatures for the food he kept in the back of the vehicle. He would roust himself two or three hours later, unplug the truck, and begin another pre-dawn delivery run. One night, four homeless men discovered the curious set-up and snagged the cable, running it into an abandoned building across the alley. "Here they were at 4 a.m., still awake and using my juice to power up their appliances and radio. I offered them some of my food in exchange for that extension cord. They agreed."[8]

The loquacious Egger talked up his new venture to anyone who dared engage him in conversation, including a bright young Dartmouth graduate named Alex Tait. Egger met Tait at a pick-up soccer game, where Tait's searing foot speed stood out immediately. "Have you ever seen someone so fast that their

---

[8]   Egger, *Begging for Change*, 39.

stride just looked different from a normal human being? Alex was that fast. He could fly," recalls Robert.

Alex had just finished a two-year stint at National Geographic and an extended trip through Europe before heading back to DC to play casual soccer and look for his next job. "Robert's a talkative guy, so it wasn't hard to find out what he was doing," remembers Tait. "He told me to come down to the Kitchen and be his driver." DCCK had its first full-time employee, and the fleet-footed geography major set about mapping his routes across Washington.

"I would drive from the glitziest areas of town to the deepest, darkest parts of DC in the middle of the night," says Tait. In that refrigerated 'reefer' van, Alex picked up Robert's handy shortcuts around the District, visiting high-end catered events and heading to the smaller shelters, group homes, and halfway houses that first signed up for DCCK deliveries.

Meanwhile, Robert was freed to focus on fundraising, giving talks and managing the grant cycle he quickly came to hate. In practice, though, job descriptions did not mean much. "That was the 'band of brothers' period of the Kitchen," says Robert.

The small number of true believers in the fledgling operation took on new responsibilities and met new crises as they emerged. Working for the Kitchen "was an 18-hour-a-day thing," remembers Tait. Even Tait's small Ford pick-up was drafted into service when the reefer headed into the shop.

Despite his devout belief in the Kitchen's principles and promise, Robert still saw DCCK as a short-term gig. On slow afternoons, Egger and Tait would slip out to the alley behind their office to toss around a baseball and Robert's plans for The Blue Circle. Robert turned out to be much better at selling the ideas behind the black circle of the Kitchen's logo. "Instead of getting B and C list musicians, I was promoting the D and

F list citizens," he says. For all the seductive opulence of his dream nightclub, it was the elegant simplicity of DC Central Kitchen that would ultimately prove irresistible to so many high-rolling contributors. He put away the white jacket. In a nonprofit sector littered with self-proclaimed white knights, Robert Egger became the man in black.

Chapter 2 Scraps

Robert Egger was not the first person to think of using leftover food to fight hunger, but DC Central Kitchen broke new ground in turning that seed of an idea into a full-blown engine of food recycling and meal distribution. There are two reasons the Kitchen succeeded where others had fallen short. Its people were dedicated, and they were good with details.

A sense of dedication and eye for detail are rarely found in the same person. Each year in America, nearly 40,000 new nonprofits declare themselves open for business.[9] Many, if

---

9   Dym, Barry, Susan Egmont, and Laura Watkins, *Managing Leadership Transition for Nonprofits*, (Upper Saddle River, NJ: Pearson Education Inc., 2011), 5. In 2010, more than 59,000 groups applied for tax-exempt status, and that figure represented a *decline* of 30 percent over the year before. See: Chiu, Lisa, "IRS Figures Show Charity Creation May Be Slowing After Years of Fast Growth," *The Chronicle of Philanthropy*, April 3, 2011, accessed October 21, 2013, http://philanthropy.com/article/Charity-Creation-Appears-to/126962/.

not most, fail.[10] Individual nonprofit founders, often long on passion but short on follow-through or relevant expertise, struggle to balance vision with execution. In the Kitchen's case, its energetic sense of commitment fueled its ability to tend to small particulars. This successful cycle was embodied by the unique relationship between Robert Egger and the man who became his alter-ego, Chapman Todd.

Chapman was born near Cincinnati, Ohio and fell in love with politics early on. After college, he followed the inexorable path of most young policy wonks. "Where else would I go but Washington, DC?" he asks. In his first job at the Council of Mayors, Todd developed an interest in homelessness issues but quickly tired of the circular debates he found in the public policy realm. At the time, Todd vowed to himself that he would not reach his "mid-forties and still not understand this issue." A friend turned him on to a volunteer opportunity at a local soup kitchen. In his spare time, Todd began picking up surplus items from area grocers late at night and handing them out to people living on the street the next day. In a matter of months, a position opened up driving the truck for that program, and Todd eagerly traded in his high-minded desk job for a minimum wage gig that put

---

[10] Due to some of the quirks of nonprofit tax law, tracking organizational failures, closings, and bankruptcies within the nonprofit sector is extremely difficult, but it is likely not a pretty picture. Nonprofits can voluntarily dissolve in many US states, and organizations with annual budgets below $25,000—and, by definition, one that's nearly out of money—does not need to file a 990 with IRS. One of the few studies to attempt to quantify this issue claims that 17 percent of nonprofits 'exited' the sector from 1998 to 2003. For more, see Vance, Danielle L. "Government Funding and Failure in Nonprofit Organizations," MA Thesis, Department of Philanthropic Studies, Indiana University, (Bloomington, IN: IUPUI Scholar Works, 2010), accessed October 15, 2013, http://hdl.handle.net/1805/2502/.

him on the front lines of a crisis he had embraced as his central cause.

Initially, Todd was thrilled with his choice. "What could be better than giving food to folks out on the street?" he asks, brightly. After six months, however, Chapman had an Egger-like epiphany: "Wait, it's the same guys every day! I knew all their names." Meanwhile, Egger's Kitchen was nearing its first anniversary, and Robert started calling Todd's employer, looking to chat with the person running its grocery store recovery operation. Mishearing Chapman's unique first name, Robert expected to meet a holy man called *Chaplain* Todd.

Infected by Robert's energy, Todd soon left his employer to work alongside Robert as his second-in-command. Lean, with a lazy haircut, soft features, and a softer voice, Chapman Todd was the Yin to Egger's Yang. Robert loved cheeseburgers and leather jackets. Chapman was a vegetarian whose rumpled suits always seemed a size too big. Egger talked about receiving his education "on the streets of DC" while Chapman attended college on an idyllic campus in Connecticut and later earned a law degree while working full-time at the Kitchen. Where Robert was pushing 'that vision thing,' Todd was an operator who had spent years learning the intricacies of DC's nonprofit landscape. Chapman was an eager networker and careful diplomat, skills that proved essential when Robert's rhetorical flourishes tweaked and piqued the old guard of DC's social service sector. When Egger railed for the creative destruction of failing nonprofits, Todd countered by saying "this is not a competition. There's room for all kinds of different models. [DCCK was] trying to improve the system, not devalue other organizations." Robert was out front, distinguishing the Kitchen and raising money. Chapman followed in behind, massaging the behind-the-scenes partnerships that allowed the Kitchen to function programmatically.

While their differences strengthened the fledgling Kitchen, what they shared was even more important: relentless professionalism. "Beyond Robert's enthusiasm and ability to sell sand in the desert," remembers Todd, "we showed we were for real by showing up at the Corcoran, or Natural History Museum at 1 a.m. to pick up the leftovers from a banquet . . . We weren't a bunch of flakey do-gooders." What set DC Central Kitchen apart was, in Todd's words, "the reliability and the accountability" of its people and programs.

Egger and Todd had pagers permanently affixed to their hip. Three times each week, one of them was on call overnight. "For eight years, I was part of the driving team," says Egger. "We all were." Caterers and restaurants quickly learned that the Kitchen could walk its talk, and its tools—from pagers that never turned off to trucks that always turned up early—indicated a level of professionalism that 'the flakes' could not match.

The Kitchen's competence escalated further once it secured its second home, a row house on Florida Avenue NW. It was cramped, but it had a kitchen. The new space allowed DCCK to go beyond the City Harvest model of redistributing surplus food and begin turning donated prepared foods into new meals within the confines of a commercial kitchen. In fact, meal service was now a mandatory operation, since the place came rent-free so long as the Kitchen could handle daily deliveries to three transitional homes run by the building's owner, a local nonprofit named the Coalition for the Homeless. For the first time, the organization needed someone who knew how to cook. They hired Abdul Raheem, the Coalition's night manager who became a drug counselor in DC after a restaurant career in Seattle. "Chef Abdul was a straight up hustler," says Chapman with a knowing smile. When he was not wearing multiple hats at the Kitchen, Raheem, a practicing Muslim with dark skin and a wiry frame, tooled around in a tricked-out Pontiac Grand Prix with chronic maintenance problems.

The added work of meal production should have drained the Kitchen's small staff, but "it actually made things a lot easier," reports Alex Tait, the Kitchen's first delivery driver. "We could prepare food people would actually eat." When DCCK was limited to direct distribution, it would sometimes find itself leaving a dish of broccoli at one agency and a pile of pork tenderloin at another. "What do you do with 15 suckling pigs? Just drop them off the homeless shelter?" muses Tait. Having a kitchen allowed Abdul to blend more or less complementary ingredients, improving the diversity and nutritional quality of DCCK's offerings. When funding allowed, the Kitchen even purchased some ingredients. A valuable partnership with the local food bank helped DCCK obtain some basic, non-perishable food stuffs. The Kitchen's partner agencies "really appreciated the improvement and what we served became much more consistent," Tait recalls.

Tait was not the only Kitchen staffer to grapple with the problem of suckling pigs. After a Smithsonian event on Caribbean history flopped, the caterer phoned DCCK just before midnight, looking to hand off 50 of them. Egger took the call, climbed into DCCK's used Ford van, and headed down to the National Mall. On that "night of a hundred pig eyes," Robert zipped through the flashing yellow lights of downtown DC, pondering just how he would goad the Muslim Abdul into preparing the unclean creatures. "I asked myself what the hell I was doing, and why I wasn't running a warm, inviting nightclub where you didn't have to depend on the kindness of strangers," says Egger. "I wondered how my life in Casablanca had transformed to life in Bedford Falls."[11] The next morning, Egger brought the pigs, eyes and all, into the kitchen, bracing for a power struggle with his

---

[11]   Egger, *Begging for Change*, 39.

devout chef. He need not have worried. That day, and on many days since, Robert says he found inspiration in "the willingness of people to bend barriers in order to help the hungry. Those suckling pigs were one of the best meals Abdul ever served." His faith restored, Robert redoubled his commitment to his fledgling organization, and pushed his dreams of a nightclub further into the distance.

As committed and as professional as Robert and his team were, they could not keep up with DC Central Kitchen's growing workload on their own. They began welcoming volunteers who could lend their time and talents to the organization. Most of these well-meaning men and women discovered the Kitchen through the press, as major media personalities like Katie Couric, Ted Koppel, and Ed Bradley began covering DCCK's exploits.

Like any shoe-string nonprofit, the Kitchen appreciated the free labor, although Egger saw each new visitor as more than an extra set of hands. "I wanted to fight hunger on the most important battlefield, the brain," he says. Robert wanted to help volunteers reach some of the same conclusions he had during his time with Grate Patrol. But Egger knew better than to outwardly assail the assumptions of good people willing to work for free. He needed a way to challenge his audience without alienating them. Before he could change the way they thought about hunger and handouts, he needed his volunteers to voluntarily open their minds. Egger, a proud amateur historian, went back, way back, to the fall of Troy. And it took a heroin addict named Reggie to lead him there.

Clean for about three months, Reggie's drug treatment provider referred him to DC Central Kitchen, where he enrolled in the organization's very first Culinary Job Training program class in January 1990. Long, lean, and in his early thirties, Reggie was toeing the knife's edge between relapse and recovery, but showing some promise as he arrived at the Kitchen on time each morning. One day, "a group of white, middle-aged medical doctors came into the Kitchen to volunteer," inspired by a special feature about DCCK that Couric had run on the 11 o'clock news. "When they arrived," recalls Robert, "I asked Reggie to guide these volunteers through the morning routine." Reggie paused, wary of working with men so different from him. Robert glanced over at the doctors. They had the same unsure look on their faces. "I could feel an invisible barrier rising up between Reggie and the group. Everyone was hiding behind a mask to shield his discomfort."[12] Robert sharply told Reggie to get started, and walked away before anyone could protest—or he had time to rethink the rash move.

Robert busied himself for about 20 minutes, and checked back in on Reggie and the doctors. The doctors had admitted they had no idea how to julienne carrots, a skill Reggie had already learned through the Kitchen's training program. The men with medical degrees were deferring to the expertise of someone with an eighth-grade education, and Reggie gradually embraced his newfound position of authority. "The dynamics of the group had shifted," says Robert. "Reggie now spoke with confidence, and the doctors stood side by side with him listening attentively." The MDs started asking Reggie who he was, where he was from, and how he had ended up at DCCK. He opened up about his struggles with drugs, his three young daughters, and his dream of working in an upscale downtown restaurant. "The doctors were taking it all in, quiet, but visibly engaged and impressed."[13]

"*Eureka*," thought Egger. Under the guise of an unassuming nonprofit, Robert would turn over his volunteer program to the Kitchen's culinary students. He would put the inmates in

---

[12] Egger, *Begging for Change*, 13.

[13] *Ibid.*

charge of the asylum, and, instead of proclaiming his "crazy ideas" about how homeless people could feed themselves and others, he would let volunteers reach those conclusions on their own. Like a wooden horse left outside the gates of Troy, a generous offering—*'come down to the Kitchen and help feed others'*—would be embraced by unsuspecting volunteers. Once inside, however, Egger's Trojan horse would force the helpers and the helped to engage one another, and learn a thing or two along the way. Maybe not all homeless people were crazy, and maybe not everyone who was out of a job was lazy. Perhaps handing out food was less important than hiring people with checkered histories.

Most well-adjusted human beings will walk away from a volunteer experience with a case of the 'warm and fuzzies'— that effervescent feeling just south of the sternum that tells them they did something decent, even selfless. That sensation is temporary, however, and its impact fleeting. In contrast, Egger designed what he called a 'calculated epiphany' to kick in over the course of each three-hour volunteer shift. At 9 a.m. each morning, Robert could feel the tangible uneasiness among his volunteers as they realized just who they would be working alongside. By noon, however, the conversation would be percolating, and two very different slices of humanity would sit down together for lunch, breaking bread and stereotypes.

"*That's* how we fight hunger at the Kitchen," Egger would write, years later. "By changing people's views, maybe we can get the big-ticket changes further down the road. If we can get young kids, corporate citizens, and elected officials to see the logic of what we are doing, then they have to get off the pity bus and hop on the logic train."[14] Inspired by Reggie, Egger made the calculated epiphany a core element of the Kitchen's programming. "I began with a young man's fervor to do big

---

14   Egger, *Begging for Change*, 129.

things—serving elegant meals and placing our culinary students at the finest French restaurants. I learned, however, that it was much smarter to scale back and allow the calculated epiphany to work its magic," he says.

Egger founded the Kitchen because he believed that, in the right hands, food destined for dumpsters could become real meals and people headed for destruction could become contributing members of their community. He applied the same perspective to working with that community. He had a kitchen, a bunch of meals to get out, and an ample supply of willing volunteers. Instead of doing what most feeding organizations did with those same supplies—make more meals—he rearranged them to create a catalytic environment for changing minds. For 10 years, the Greeks left their ships on shores of Troy so they could escape if things went south. Odysseus scrapped those triremes and used the wood to build the weapon that allowed them to end the war in victory. Egger wanted to do the same thing, just with different scraps.

The Kitchen's hatred of waste did not limit itself to leftover food and devalued people. Egger's philosophy also extended to financial practices. Robert's original vision inspired a MacGyver-like approach to problem solving: *why buy new when an improvised solution of paperclips and chewing gum will do?* There were upsides to this approach. Part of it was inspirational. Volunteers and donors would visit the Kitchen and say *"Wow, I can't believe you're doing all this with such little resources."*

More pragmatically, all this improvisation kept the Kitchen's financial liabilities low during lean fundraising years. Robert was a natural with an audience, and he would ultimately become very good at pulling in individual contributions to DC Central Kitchen. In the meantime, he managed his operation's expenses carefully, ensuring that it remained, in Chapman's words, "an extraordinarily low-cost operation" throughout its first decade. Making payroll sometimes involved close calls, but the staff bought into their leader's belief they could do more with less. Unlike the thousands of organizations that fail each year, Todd recalls that "there was always the confidence that this nonprofit was different, that this was going to make it."

When the Kitchen did spend money, it focused on investing in new solutions. Applying his background in computer programming, Alex Tait built a rudimentary food tracking system in Hypercard on the Kitchen's bulky Macintosh SE. Tait rigged up the system in a week, while Robert temporarily shouldered his truck driving duties. Used to tracking their information in pen or pencil, visitors from other nonprofits were blown away by DCCK's detailed records of food donations and financial transactions.

And for years, says Todd, "the pager guy loved us."

"In those primitive days," recalls Tait, these now-extinct tools were essential to Kitchen business. During business hours, whoever manned the front desk that day would field calls from the companies looking to donate food, and then page a DCCK driver. The driver would find a payphone, call in, and take down the donor's address. The desk staff then called the donor back to confirm a time for pick-up—if they were still by a landline telephone. Each night, the last man left in the main office would record a new answering machine message stating who was on call and how to page them.

Pagers ruled, until one day when Robert walked in hollering "They hooked me *up!*" He had attended a promotional event where a local tech firm gave him a prototype cell phone for one cent. Egger excitedly waved the matte grey handset at Todd, but could extend his arm only so far. The receiver was connected by a cord to a bulky backpack. Strapped into this contraption, Egger looked an awful lot like a nonprofit Ghostbuster.

In time, cell phones dramatically improved the Kitchen's daily operations. "They made us more efficient," recalls Todd. "We could re-route on the fly and shift drivers around whenever a donor called." From today's technological perspective, some of these processes seem one step away from sending up smoke signals, but in the early Nineties, they felt like the sharpest point of the cutting edge.

Not every call to the Kitchen asked them to pick up food. In 1991, Todd received a call from the Jacksonville, Florida Police Department, saying that a DC Central Kitchen van had been recovered in a strip mall parking lot, and was waiting to be picked up from their impound lot. Chapman had already noticed he was short a delivery vehicle. After all, it was their only one.

The white Ford van had disappeared along with its driver, a bony fellow named Andy, three days earlier. In the meantime, Chapman volunteered his Ford Ranger to serve as "the official DC Central Kitchen delivery vehicle." While Egger tooled around town in the small, flat-black pickup, Todd, always ready to respond to an inopportune phone call, booked a plane ticket and headed to Florida. He found the van, entirely drained of oil, right where his employee had abandoned it. DCCK never heard from Andy again. Todd phoned the DC police, told them his stolen vehicle had turned up, and headed north along I-95 to Washington.

Evidently, Chapman's message did not reach the right person. Days later, Todd was driving that same van at the corner of M and 5th Streets NW, en route to a United Way function. A cop car flashed its siren, and four more quickly swarmed upon the soft-spoken Chapman and his battered vehicle. "They hauled me out of the driver's seat, pinned me up against the door, and cuffed me. Here I was, a guy in a suit and tie, in a hot van being taken to jail." The ordeal took place in front of Hannah House, a now-shuttered family shelter. One of the residents, a client of DC

Central Kitchen, came barreling out of the red brick row house, hollering "I know him! He didn't do anything!" The police officers were unmoved. Chapman spent the afternoon in lockup, and with Robert out of town on business, it was up to a confused Kitchen cook to bail out his boss.

After less than two years on Florida Avenue, DCCK was growing fast. It needed a bigger kitchen, one suited to commercial meal production and more professional culinary training. For many nonprofits, the decision to pursue bigger, better facilities is largely determined by their means. If they can afford to expand, they will. If not, they won't. Most share an underlying assumption that that securing more money, more staff, and more space are valuable pursuits that will invariably advance their mission.

Robert found this line of thought to be at best lazy and unexamined, and at worst greedy and self-interested. He viewed the nonprofit fundraising landscape as an integrated ecosystem. Every time an organization raked in five or 10 or 20 million dollars for its latest dream home, he believed that it drained that sum from the collective budgets of scores of other nonprofits. Egger would come to label the proliferation of these large-scale fundraising efforts—typically called 'capital campaigns'—"good intentions gone bad."[15]

To justify the size and scope of these campaigns, nonprofits must generally promise to serve more clients in more ways, often in response to some staggering level of need. This cycle creates a trap. In theory, a successful service organization should be able to show that, because of its effectiveness, it needs to help fewer people, not more. In practice, however, organizations are often rewarded by pointing to how much worse things are getting—in other words, how ineffective they are presently—while

---

[15]   Egger, *Begging for Change*, 53.

promising to do better with a larger building and broader client base. If Gordon Gekko was a nonprofit fundraiser, he might say that *"Need is good."*

Because of the Kitchen's relationship to food and hunger, Egger took particular issue with the 'food bank fallacy.' Then, as now, the major funding appeals made by food banks fell into two categories. The first was food shortage: *"There is so much need that we cannot meet because our cupboards are bare."* The second was limited capacity: *"With a larger building, we can distribute more food to meet all these needs."* But, Egger wondered, if these groups were always short on food, why were they constantly pushing for bigger, evidently emptier, buildings?

No one was much interested in answering his query. The model, as it was two decades ago and remains today, continues to serve the right people: donors looking to do something 'good' and food banks eager to accept their checks. To wit, in July of 2012, one major US food bank capped off its latest capital campaign to much fanfare, opening a brand-new $37 million, 120,000 square-foot facility with a dozen loading docks.[16] In November, it was back in the newspapers, bemoaning a 37% drop in food donations from the year before.[17] Its patrons were left with a cavernous monument to canned food and canned responses to hunger.

For Robert, a DC Central Kitchen capital campaign was out of the question. The Kitchen desperately needed an upgrade from its cramped home on Florida Avenue, but Egger and Todd had no plans to move until they could find an empty, idle kitchen available for free or damn near it.

---

[16]   Gowen, Annie, "D.C. food bank to open $37 million facility to combat 'growing hunger crisis,'" *The Washington Post*, July 29, 2012.

[17]   Gowen, Annie, "Cupboards bare at area food pantries as government donations drop and need rises," *The Washington Post*, November 21, 2012.

In the spring of 1992, Robert received a phone call offering him that kitchen. On the other end of the line was a most unlikely partner: Carol Fennelly, the head of the Community for Creative Non-Violence (CCNV). CCNV was founded by Father Ed Guinan in 1970 as an expression of anti-war Christian sentiment, but eventually evolved into a commune that sought to humanize homelessness. Staff and clients all lived together and everyone could stay as long as they liked. Formal case management was dismissed as paternalistic. And since the staff worked for no salary, they were effectively as homeless as the people they were serving. CCNV's passion seized the imaginations of many in DC and beyond before its rapid rise to national prominence in the 1980s under the equal parts volatile and visionary leadership of Mitch Snyder.

A former car thief who embraced a radical, egalitarian form of Christianity while in prison, Snyder was a master of political theater. His creativity and electric personality suited CCNV, which was unabashedly political in nature, in stark contrast to most other social service organizations. In 1984, when the American Conservative Union decided to bake and serve the world's largest apple pie—some 17 feet across—to depict the 'fruitful' benefits of trickle-down economics, Snyder gathered the homeless clients of CCNV, dressed them in business suits, and crashed the rally. His cohort stomped through the pie, making a huge mess and horrifying the assembled crowd of buttoned-up Alex Keaton wannabes.[18]

That same year, Snyder embarked on a 51-day hunger strike to goad President Reagan into handing him and CCNV control of the tired Federal City Shelter, an 180,000-square foot facility just a few blocks from the US Capitol building, and $5 million

---

18   Blais, Madeleine, "A Room of Her Own," in *The Heart is an Instrument: Portraits in Journalism*, (Amherst: University of Massachusetts Press, 1994), 99-100.

to renovate it. Consuming the better part of a city block on the corner of Second and D Streets in Northwest Washington, the facility was Snyder's greatest prize, greater even than the fawning media attention that followed his successful challenge of America's overwhelmingly popular president. The four-story building was home to thousands of beds and, in its basement, a 10,000 square-foot commercial kitchen. CCNV never had the programmatic wherewithal to do much with that kitchen, though. It served more to facilitate the informal, internal barter economy of CCNV staff than it did to feed genuinely hungry people.

In DC's direct service circles, Snyder was king. He had upstaged Reagan. He embarrassed powerful DC Mayor Marion Barry in a 1989 court battle over the condition of DC's shelters. He was even played by Martin Sheen in a made-for-TV movie. Through it all, Carol Fennelly was by his side. He and Fennelly had been inseparable for over a decade, romantic and philosophical soul mates running CCNV together. But Snyder's sudden death in 1990 triggered major changes in the shelter he ran and in the life of the woman he loved.

Fennelly was the natural choice to run CCNV in his stead, but without Snyder's charisma, the organization began to unravel. Snyder had been lax about shepherding people out of his shelter, refusing to set time limits on client stays. Worse, rumors of uninhibited drug use began streaming out of the fortress-like facility.[19] Now, his philosophical commitments were damaging the practical work of CCNV and the Community's high-minded theatrics seemed increasingly out of line with its day-to-day programmatic shortcomings. It was time for CCNV to start doing more and talking less, and that started with putting its kitchen to better use. Fennelly picked up the telephone and

---

19   Twomey, Steve, "The homeless are where her heart is," *The Washington Post*, January 20, 1994, B1.

called Robert Egger. If DCCK would pledge to serve meals to the upstairs residents of CCNV at no cost, they could have the space for free. All they had to do was ramp up their daily production from 400 meals to 2,000 with no additional financial resources. Egger did not hesitate in saying yes. He had gotten his kitchen, but instead of running a capital campaign, all he needed was a listing in the yellow pages.

Snyder's mystique continued to shroud his organization with an aura of importance for years after his death. Egger admits to feeling a little star-struck when he received his first permanent parking pass for the gravel CCNV lot. "We're legit now," he said to Todd the day they moved into the basement of the massive shelter, its right angles and concrete walls evoking the Belgrade School of Cold War Architecture. "It was the house Mitch Snyder built," says Egger. "I was awed by CCNV's sense of reckless, joyful revolution."

Chapman and Robert had a rough introduction to their new home. The first new 'neighbors' they met included a half-dozen CCNV residents who had ambled out to the lot, asking if they could help. "What they meant, evidently, was 'could they help themselves' to our stuff," Egger says, shaking his head with a smile. "We lost so much shit that day."

As Egger and Todd tried to dismiss their unwanted assistants and figure out what was missing, they realized the window air conditioning unit was shot. They headed across the musty, cluttered hallway to the CCNV maintenance shop. "Now, these guys were great, amazing, could fix anything," Egger remembers, "as long as you got them before 11 a.m., when they were too drunk to function."

"These guys were twisted," agrees Todd. "A serious beer drinking crew." They rousted Ned, a rotund character with a Santa Claus beard. "He really was amazing with air conditioners. That squad could fix anything with duct-tape, a screwdriver, and a can of beer," says Chapman. As Ned crouched over the busted unit, clutching a Steel Reserve in his off hand, Robert carefully addressed his new repairman.

"You can't drink in the kitchen," he said in a friendly voice.

"Well," replied Ned in an equally friendly, yet firm tone, "I can't give a shit about that." The Steel Reserve stayed.

Beyond Ned, the maintenance crew included Terrance and Mickey, "the Frick and Frack" of CCNV. Todd remembers poking his head into their office one day with a small question, only to find the inseparable duo skinning and gutting a deer they had strung up from the ceiling. Chapman thought better of interrupting them. He quietly ducked back out before he was compelled to figure out where and how they had obtained a dead deer in the middle of downtown DC.

Terrance and Mickey were also notorious for performing unrequested favors in exchange for cash when their beer money ran dry. Most common were ambush car washes. "I'd walk out at the end of the day, and one would sidle up to me, saying 'Man, I did good job on those rims. Now what's that worth to you?'" remembers Chapman. Sometimes, the work wasn't worth much. One day, Egger and Todd discovered Mickey had inexplicably taken steel wool pads and a caustic cleaning solution to the windshield of Todd's Ford Ranger. The glass was scratched and scored in big, sweeping circles. Robert was horrified.

"There are many reasons I respect Chapman Todd," says Egger, years later, "and one of them is his ability to let go of things I never could." After surveying the damage, Chapman turned and looked at Robert.

"It's just stuff," he said softly, and calmly headed off to his night class at George Washington University Law School. He still drives that Ford Ranger, though it has a new windshield. The CCNV parking sticker is still affixed to the back.

The Federal City Shelter and the enormous, poorly-kept gravel lot that ran along its eastern edge looked like a slice of Stalingrad dropped into the American capital. The essential trade that gave DCCK a home in the shelter's basement—free meals for free rent—was, in Egger's words, "good business." Robert quickly found that the Kitchen's new home offered other, less tangible benefits, too. The unsightly shelter was surrounded by valuable, well-developed real estate, readily accessible by public transit, and, for better or worse, known as something of a DC landmark. Dozens of the men and women staying in the shelter spent their days milling around outside the building. Their presence, while benign, was often enough to make pedestrians in power suits divert their eyes and quicken their step en route to their office buildings. For Egger, who craved a sufficiently dramatic stage for his show of calculated epiphanies, the setting was perfect. So perfect, in fact, that the Kitchen calls that crumbling building home even today, two decades later.

To enter the Kitchen, staff and visitors must pick their way through a cluster of unoccupied shelter residents, loop past a battered old Metro bus stop, and proceed along a narrow sidewalk littered with menthol cigarette butts. A small, rusting aluminum sign with DC Central Kitchen's logo hangs on the northeast corner of the building, an arrow pointing left down the parking lot. A hundred yards ahead and off to the right, an open, unlit truck bay serves as the Kitchen's front door. With shifting gravel crunching underfoot, volunteers push through the long, dingy plastic flaps that hang over the entrance and step into darkness. Their pupils rush to dilate. The dim hallways offer a few access points to DCCK, and many opportunities for wrong turns. Only the luckiest new visitors find their way to the Kitchen's front desk on the first try.

Volunteers looking for a heart-warming experience doing a little good for someone else often question their judgment in those first few moments. Soup kitchens, by their very nature, separate the helpers from the helped, usually by a Plexiglas sneeze guard. Some organizations even use the word 'others' in their name, implying a fundamental difference between those who serve and those who eat. DCCK's basement location throws volunteers—many of them corporate teams looking to give back, or out-of-town church and student groups—into the gritty trenches of America's war on poverty.

"A lot of times," says one Kitchen staffer with pride, "volunteers walk down that alley, and they freak." Sufficiently scared in the opening 15 minutes of their experience, volunteers are primed for Robert's production.

"In the Nineties, the shelter was even darker and scarier. It was like you were an extra in a movie," reports one long-time employee.

Once inside the Kitchen, visitors make their way past the front desk, head into the lunchroom, and find a folding chair. They shift uneasily in their seats. Eventually, a DCCK culinary graduate employed by the organization will enter and launch into a stern lecture on kitchen safety, demanding gloves, hairnets, thorough hand-washing, and the like. The graduate will start gruffly, but when the nuts and bolts of food sanitation have been covered, his tone softens. It's story time.

The specifics of each personal story are different, but the arc and rhythm are the same. The tale begins bleakly—in homelessness, prison, addiction, abandonment, abuse, or some combination thereof. Then, the graduate will talk about his first days at the Kitchen. How hard the work was, how long the days seemed, how doubt and the threat of self-sabotage plagued each waking moment. And then, something changes, and confidence and hope creep in as the rough but loving embrace of DC Central Kitchen takes hold. The story flashes forward to today, and the graduate speaks of gratitude and redemption. The story is consistent without seeming contrived. The volunteers realize they are not there to help 'the hungry' or 'the homeless.' They will be working beside them instead.

In a traditional soup kitchen, volunteers are an audience to the tragic dramas lived out by those in line. At DC Central Kitchen, volunteers are part of the show. And Egger the old nightclub runner wanted to put on a spectacular show every time. Convinced that complacency was "capable of screwing up all that's good," Robert demanded that his staff bring their full energy to his stage each morning, lest the corrosive effects of lethargy or apathy seep into the operation. "My approach is one of relentless incrementalism," he says. "It's doing the little things extremely well, day after day after day." Robert's management style might be best described as cheerleader-in-chief, leading by vigorous example and provoking those around him to keep up with his Roadrunner-like energy. Some leaders believe in MBWA—Management by Walking Around. Egger preferred Management by Sprinting Ahead.

In line with his showman's instincts, Robert also obsessed over the Kitchen's optics and messaging. Kitchen promotions were brash and bold. They aimed to provoke thought instead of guilt-trips. And they drew stark contrasts between DCCK's methods and achievements, on the one hand, and the sector's status quo, on the other. While what the Kitchen said in print was generally less provocative than the sorts of things Egger would say in person, even the slightest competitive tone flew in the face of a direct service sector comprised of organizations that make big public shows of just how nice, decent, and fundamentally good they are. Funders love to pressure these groups to partner with one another—generally speaking, out of a desire to save money and reduce redundancy. Nonprofits, as a result, play along and restrict their disputes to the backdoor channels of rumor and innuendo. The sweet-natured charade tends to suit them. Since there are only so many nonprofits that can stand out in the eyes of donors through the uniquely strong results of their programs, others elect to fall back on how 'good' their missions are and how 'needy' their clients must be.

Among nonprofits in the hunger space, there is no cause more 'good' than feeding children, no client more 'needy' than an innocent youth. Childhood hunger has long been described as a third rail of American politics. Even the most committed fiscal hawks will usually shy away from slashing funds designated for hungry kids. Aware of its untouchable status, hunger organizations play up their services for children, often featuring young, forlorn faces in their advertisements. Robert called this "playing the pity card," and refused to "pimp kids" in the Kitchen's promotions.

"The real face of hunger in America is a working mom with two children," Egger says. For every hungry child, there is a parent who is out of work or working but not earning enough to support that family. Get that parent a decent job and you fix the underlying problem causing the symptom of childhood hunger—but that's hard, and raising money with pictures of sad, starving kids is much easier. Ask Sally Struthers.

"We can't continue to propagate a caste system of needy people in which children are at the top because that implies there's someone at the bottom," declares Robert, "and it's usually the 'Big Uglies': drug addicts, convicts, and homeless people." Most of those Big Uglies were once cute kids in bad situations, fit for a food bank ad. Time and poor choices may have made them less sympathetic, but, in Robert's view, no less deserving. "We need to help them just as much as we need to help today's children." [20] If its professionalism was what distinguished DCCK in

---

[20]   Egger, *Begging for Change*, 123.

the eyes of its food donors, it was the Kitchen's distinctive tone—frank, principled, and solutions-oriented—that impressed the people writing checks.

With additional space, a larger staff, a little more money, and a growing roster of volunteers, the Kitchen began to see changes in the food it was using and the ways it used that food to advance its mission. Through the end of 1992, DCCK continued to run its pager-centric pick-up operation, relying on caterers and restaurants for food donations. But with more preparation and storage space in the CCNV basement on Second Street, the Kitchen could afford to think bigger and more strategically. In what Chapman Todd calls "a game changer," DCCK began a partnership with hospitality industry giant Marriott, which, at the time, was responsible for running the dining halls of American University. Thanks the efforts of one particularly insistent AU student, Marriott agreed to sit down with the Kitchen and see what could be done with their cafeteria leftovers. When Robert and Chapman rolled up with a climate controlled reefer truck and several years of technical know-how in the realm of food recovery, the on-site Marriott manager was shocked.

"We weren't expecting, you know, a business," he told them.

"Marriott would never work with flakes," Todd says, "so our professionalism got their attention and our reliability made sure we kept it."

At most US universities, meals are provided buffet-style in all-you-can-eat portions. This imprecise model creates tremendous quantities of food waste. The Kitchen realized it had struck a rich vein of potential resources. Better yet, the waste was predictable, and DCCK began picking up enough food from AU on Fridays to last it through the weekend. DCCK reached out to other nearby schools, including the University of Maryland and Catholic University, to snag their surplus as well.

These bulk recoveries allowed the Kitchen to send more uniform meals to all its partner agencies. Catering pick-ups after wedding receptions, by comparison, often meant that some agencies got the chicken, others, the fish.

With a powerful brand like Marriott upping their in-kind—that is, non-monetary—donations to DCCK and reaping the benefits of the ensuing tax write-offs, other large kitchens and firms took notice. Helping matters was the 1996 passage of the Bill Emerson Good Samaritan Food Donation Act. In his push for a national law that would spur the development of like-minded food recovery operations across the country, Egger found a kindred spirit and eager ally in the Clinton Administration's Secretary of Agriculture, Dan Glickman. Together, they led the effort on Capitol Hill to protect well-meaning food donors from legal liability in the event of spoilage or food-borne illness. From convention centers to pizza chains, institutional food service sites across Washington began making consistent donations of product to DC Central Kitchen. Scheduled, predictable pick-ups and drop-offs of donated food increased through the 1990s. By the end of the decade, the Kitchen was recycling nearly 1 million pounds of food annually from more than 1,500 food donation partners, 400 of whom provided regular contributions essential to Todd's treasured reliability and accountability. This second-hand bounty allowed the Kitchen to churn out 3,000 meals per day for nearly 100 partner sites in and around DC.

Egger knew from the first days of DCCK, however, that the leftover largesse he relied on would not last forever. "After all," he says, "donated food is lost profit." The large food service companies increasingly central to DCCK's model were not run by chefs. The people in charge had degrees in business administration. They understood inventory and supply chain management. The internet bubble of the 1990s had lots of people playing fast and loose with their capital. That bubble was going to burst someday, and those enterprising managers were going to find places to trim the fat. Unfortunately, that was the very fat fueling DC Central Kitchen's meal production. Change was coming, and the Kitchen rushed to get out ahead of it.

Chapter 3 | The Seeds of Social Enterprise

Robert Egger and Chapman Todd knew that the food sector partnerships they had worked so hard to cultivate in the past half-decade would most likely change, and not in ways that were good for DC Central Kitchen's bottom line. If food donations fell, the Kitchen would need to begin buying its own food in greater quantities. One response might have been to raise more money from the usual channels nonprofits look to: philanthropic foundations, government grant programs, and private donors. Egger, however, feared becoming dependent upon an annual application process that undermined strategic planning and sustainable growth. The Kitchen prided itself on its ability to creatively use food and people in ways that produced value for the organization and its surrounding community. Why couldn't it apply that same resourcefulness to its fundraising?

In its early days, Robert wanted DCCK to be the best nonprofit it could, rather than a half-baked business that divided its energy between making money and doing good and ended up doing a lousy job of both. He crafted a motto for the Kitchen that stressed excellence in service: "Cook as you would for your own family." But when his struggles around fundraising caught up with his ambitious, risk-taking temperament, Egger could hardly help being intrigued by the concept of social enterprise.

As the Kitchen grew, he became more confident in its ability to take on some revenue-generating activities in ways that would not crowd out its central purpose. "The idea of using purchased food to create real business opportunities flowed very naturally from the overall concept of the Kitchen," remembers Egger. In the mid-Nineties, Egger and Todd began fleshing out the details of an in-house catering company.

Referring to himself as a "righteous entrepreneur," Robert selected a second DCCK motto that began punctuating his public talks and private conversations: "Smart Business."[21] Together, *'Cook as you would for your own family'* and *'Smart Business'* formed "the yin and yang of the Kitchen," says Egger, a dual mandate of maximum social impact and unrelenting resourcefulness.

In light of that mandate, the Kitchen's new catering company had to earn money while advancing its mission. If they could pull it off, Egger and Todd hoped the two goals would reinforce one another. On the money side, catering gigs would generate unrestricted income, free from the strings and stipulations of many charitable donations, while helping meet cash flow needs that did not align with the usual cycle of grant-making and grant-chasing. That money could then feed the mission, as some of what they earned could be used to provide transitional employment opportunities to at-risk men and women who completed their Culinary Job Training program. While some graduates were ready to enter the workforce after 12 weeks, others could benefit from an entry-level job that afforded them a little more time in the supportive environment of DCCK. Instead of trying to drive down their labor costs to the bare minimum, the Kitchen's new catering operation would try to pay a decent wage to people that would otherwise be out of work.

---

[21]   Crowley, Elizabeth, "For-Profit Do-Gooder," *The Wall Street Journal*, November 29, 1999, 12.

The Kitchen's specific foray into the catering business was inspired, in part, by some of its loyal food donors. Several area companies had gotten to know Robert and Chapman by calling them after catered office functions and offering up the remaining leftovers. Eventually, these friends of the Kitchen started asking if they could just pay the organization to cater their meals instead of handing their money to someone else and sending DCCK the scraps. In 1997, the time seemed right for Todd and Egger to turn the rough sketch of a catering company into a functioning operation. To distinguish its catered meals from the reclamation projects they delivered to shelters, the Kitchen named the new venture 'Fresh Start Catering,' in recognition of the second chance it offered its culinary students-turned-employees.

As much as the Kitchen tried to embrace a 'Smart Business' approach in of its programs, some rules of the business world proved problematic for Fresh Start. While for-profit firms were expected and encouraged to compete vigorously with one another, DCCK had to be especially careful. "The caterers were some of our biggest donors. We couldn't risk taking away their clients," remembers an early Fresh Start employee. Forced to play especially nice in the sandwich sandbox, DCCK found that ready clients were in short supply. Already staffed with undesirable employees, the Kitchen began looking for undesirable customers.

Other nonprofits had plenty of need for catered gatherings, but did not offer the steady business that larger caterers coveted. "No matter how much food we gave out, every charity in town wanted more," says Egger. "The idea of creating a business to meet that need made loads of sense." The Kitchen consulted with its catering industry contacts, who responded that they would be glad to see someone, especially a group like DC Central Kitchen, step into that available niche. And instead of sending their limited funds to for-profit caterers, nonprofits could direct their resources to a fellow service organization, keeping their money 'in the family.'

In addition to earning money and creating jobs for DCCK graduates, Egger hoped that the small catering outfit would become an extension of his vaunted stage. The catering business is notorious for running on thin profit margins. Some of the best business, then, comes from fancy galas and events—weddings, bar mitzvahs, and the like—that include full spreads and plated meals and allow caterers to pass on more of their labor costs to their customers. At these types of functions, Egger figured he could "pop out from behind the curtain" to thank everyone for coming out, introduce DC Central Kitchen, and reveal that the people who had served them all night were among the Kitchen's many culinary graduates. Here was another forum for his calculated epiphany: *"You mean the person pouring my coffee was a homeless person and now she has a job through your training program? How cool!"*[22] The epiphany had to come after each meal. Otherwise, Robert feared his guests would "look at the servers with pity or, worse, suspicion, and not as professionals."[23] His vision was of a clandestine charity, call-sign *double-o-501(c)3.*

In practice, it was years before Egger found any curtains to hide behind. The nonprofit customers Fresh Start Catering relied upon just did not need very many plated dinners. Most of their orders were for boxed lunches. From an operational perspective, Todd decided these drive-and-drop meals were especially appealing. They were cheap to make, comparatively easy for inexperienced DCCK graduates to prepare, and Fresh Start could do a whole bunch of them at once. Galas, meanwhile, not only required more resources, but demanded 'front-of-house'

---

customer service skills. For many of the rough-edged culinary graduates employed by Fresh Start, interacting with well-to-do guests was intimidating and difficult. For their part, many attendees also probably suspected that their waiters were not formally trained *maître d's*. Fresh Start thus progressed in fits and starts, largely subject to the revenue streams of other nonprofits and when they felt they could splurge on a catered meal. "Fresh Start's business wasn't steady enough," says Todd. "We needed stable income, and so food service contracts offered the key to becoming a real job creator."

In the summer of 1997, the Kitchen secured a small contract providing 100,000 snacks and lunches to organizations serving low-income children whose families normally relied on free or reduced-price school meals to stave off their hunger. To keep its accounting straight, DCCK spun off this effort from Fresh Start and dubbed the program Contract Foods. When it came to getting these reimbursed meals out the door, Contract Foods did its job, but it lacked the resources to push the nutritional envelope. The biggest focus at the time was getting the right number of portions to the right place on the right day. "It was a lot of counting fish sticks," remembers Todd. One Contract Foods chef hired to support that summertime production agrees: "It was all mind-numbing counting." That chef, Marianne Ali, just could not seem to get the hang of tallying all those fish sticks and sandwiches. A few weeks in, after yet another error, she fully expected to be fired. Her supervisor smiled and told her to get back to work. It was a merciful choice that permanently shaped the future of DC Central Kitchen.

Born Marianne Giles, Ali grew up in nearby Landover, Maryland with both of her parents, two brothers, and five sisters. Her father, T-Bone Giles, had been a cop before entering the construction business and moving up the ranks to become a superintendent—no small feat for a black man in southern Maryland in the Seventies. Despite Jones' modicum of success in the face of virulent racism, he carried great hate in his heart. An alcoholic, he would stumble home drunk, looking for a fight and menacing whomever he found with his police-issued .38. "My older siblings were smart enough to stay out of the house," remembers Marianne, but she was too young to escape. She started hiding that .38 whenever he left in the morning and laying low once he staggered in at night, trying to assess his mood. Oftentimes, "after an episode, he would break down, and cry, and talk about his father abusing him," she recalls. "I went from wanting to kick his ass to being his mother."

One of the siblings that escaped was Marianne's older brother, Cush. He was handsome, athletic, and had a knack for writing poetry. "I idolized him," she says with a smile. "He played basketball, so I started playing basketball." After Cush headed off to college on the west coast, he got into serious drugs. "He started getting high, so I started getting high." At just 17 years old, she says, "I was introduced to intravenous drugs, and I loved it." Getting high became her primary purpose. At 19, she discovered she was pregnant, and managed to briefly break away from her addiction. A year later, however, Marianne became romantically involved with her drug dealer and starting using again.

For fully 20 years, Ali was a hardcore heroin addict. Her dealer beat her regularly. Somehow, matters got worse before they got better. For the last three years of her addiction, she got into crack cocaine. The drug accelerated her descent to rock bottom. "If I hadn't gotten into crack cocaine," she figures, "I might still be on heroin today." Today, Marianne is distinguished by her curvaceous hips and commanding presence. At the worst of her addiction, she was down to a sickly size two. Along the way, Marianne lost her mother to lung cancer. Nine years after her death, in 1994, Marianne looked at the calendar and realized that the next day would have been her mother's birthday. Overcome with a bitter mixture of grief and guilt, she decided to find a detoxification program. She had visited such programs before, but always walked right out of treatment to a nearby shooting gallery. "I knew I had to find a place to go after detox." She headed to a rehabilitation center where most clients were admitted for a few weeks. Marianne stayed for six months. Eventually, Ali figured she needed to find work. She ended up in DC's publicly-funded Vocational Rehabilitation program, where she decided to pursue a kitchen career. "At the time, drug addiction was counted as a disability, so Voc Rehab foot the bill for me to attend L'Academie de Cuisine."

L'Academie was, and remains, a high-end, boutique culinary school in suburban Maryland led by esteemed French chefs. Ali proved to be something of a demographic anomaly among its student population. Her best friends there turned out to be Carla Hall—who now hosts her own show on ABC—and a Harvard-educated lawyer who left the bar to find work in restaurants. "Here I was," muses Marianne, "riding along with these two and we're the best of friends."

After graduation, Marianne secured a job preparing meals for some highly ranked, yet entirely obscure federal officials, and stuck there for about a year. While working, she received a call. Her beloved brother Cush had been badly beaten. He fell into a coma and soon died. Marianne struggled to cope. At the lowest point in her recovery, another call came. Her former advisor at L'Academie tipped her off about a position in DCCK's Contract Foods operation supporting its summer meal production. Eager for a change, she seized the opportunity. "I was so early in my recovery, though," she recalls. "I just wasn't right." The mundane details of portioning those meals pushed Marianne to the edges of her capacity to focus. "Mentally, it was like a fog, mixed with panic and embarrassment, kinda like the adult who doesn't know how to read and tries to disguise it." Overwhelmed, Marianne kept peering around the corner of the kitchen to the students enrolled in the Culinary Job Training program. "Should I be over there with them?" she asked DCCK Culinary Instructor Frank McKinney, a retired Marine Sergeant. He did her one better, and moved her into a hybrid position, teaching skills to the homeless men and women enrolled in the training program while leading the Kitchen's daily conversion of donated food into full meals. The opportunity energized her and, gradually, the fog in her mind began to fade.

Per Robert's insistence, 'Cook as you would for your own family' was emblazoned on the wall across from the main production line. Marianne and her colleagues took it seriously. They did not skimp on effort, but they were chronically short on quality supplies. "Back then," says Ali, "calling what we did 'menu planning' is a . . . *strong term*." At times, the mish-mash of ingredients ended up averaging out to some shade of brown. Fresh produce was always in short supply. Heads of lettuce sometimes had to be peeled down to their core to avoid using wilted, discolored leaves. The Kitchen's search for healthier leftovers led Egger to discover new local sources, including a number of farmers' markets in nearby northern Virginia. Robert worried about the ramifications of sending a truck labeled 'DC Central Kitchen' to Virginia suburbs that had hungry and homeless people of their own, although they were far fewer in number than the District's. He swung a deal with a public relations firm to purchase and commission a new van named the *Virginia Express*.[24] The *Express* shuttled across the George Washington Bridge to recover farmers' market leftovers and

---

[24]   Greely, Alexandra, "Great Taste of Virginia," *The Connection*, October 13, 1993, 43.

drop DCCK meals at a number of Virginia homeless shelters and nonprofits, expanding the Kitchen's hunger-fighting reach along with its access to fresh fruits and vegetables.

Despite the addition of the *Virginia Express*, the majority of donated food coming into the kitchen at Second Street still consisted of pans and even pallets of prepared food from large culinary institutions, like universities and corporate cafeterias. These dishes were not just reheated and sent out. To stretch their supplies, Marianne's team would repurpose key ingredients—especially prized portions of protein—dice and cube them, and spread them over a far greater number of soup and stew servings. "When I first arrived in 1999," says a long-serving Kitchen employee, "there were a lot of soups and goulashes. Our meals were served in Cambro liquid containers, usually meant for coffee and drinks. When the food eventually came out of those Cambros, all the hard work we put in on presentation and color didn't always translate to the clients."

Distribution was also a work in progress. For the meals sent upstairs to CCNV clients, "we'd use vats that were three feet across, cover the top in aluminum foil, and wheel them out." While this saved time and packaging expenses, the Kitchen began hearing that residents were complaining about not receiving enough food. The vat, while enormous, left portion control up to whoever held the final ladle. When she was promoted and began overseeing DCCK's meal production, Marianne pushed the Kitchen to begin using aluminum delivery pans and place 25 portions of that day's dish, whatever it happened to be, in each of them. This innovation eliminated the guesswork for the scores of agencies receiving DCCK's meals and helped the Kitchen better understand how much food these partners actually needed. It also meant that the different food groups—proteins, starches, vegetables, and so on—did not need to be blended into the same soup container, allowing the Kitchen to branch out into more solid foods.

No matter how much progress its staff made on the margins, DCCK's relationship with its recipient agencies remained a regular source of contention and drama. Most agencies, on most days, were appreciative. Others were less so. "It was a fucking gripe-fest," remembers one DCCK staffer. The Kitchen's usual response was "It's free, it's what we have, and we're doing our best." Of course the menus lacked variation and presentation was lacking. After all, no one was paying DCCK for its services. At times, the alchemy of turning a smattering of leftovers and dry goods into thousands of meals in a matter of hours seemed nothing less than miraculous. As long as none of the Kitchen's partners seemed willing to pay for better service, the complaining was largely idle.

The one exception was DC Village, a now-defunct emergency shelter in Southwest Washington. DC Village approached DCCK, saying they wanted better meals and that they were willing to pay for them. Ali looked at her expenses and negotiated a per-meal price with the shelter. Production for DC Village moved over to the Contract Foods corner, and arrangement continued amicably for months, until the Kitchen's bookkeeper realized that they were actually making money on the deal. She demanded Ali alter the deal. "Cut the price to break-even," she said. "This isn't in line with our mission." Internally, the Kitchen had not yet reconciled where it was supposed to act more like a smart business and where it should be an open-source, generous collaborator for the good of the nonprofit sector.

Charging shelters may have crossed a symbolic line for some, but the general framework of the Kitchen's later success in the world of social enterprise had been sketched out by the end of the 1990s. A quarter of its 1999 budget, some $300,000, consisted of earned revenue rather than charitable contributions.[25] Catering income was important, but food service contracts were the key to ensuring steady income and stable job opportunities for DCCK graduates. And the fresh, local produce from across the Potomac had such strong appeal that its use helped de-stigmatize food coming out of DCCK, which had generally been associated with the unused and unwanted waste of others.

Some of these important gains were attributable to a new line of business: school food. The SEED School approached DCCK in 1998 looking for help with their food service. Marianne and her team were happy to oblige. SEED, an urban boarding school, started paying for breakfasts, lunches, and dinners from DCCK's Contract Foods division. The enterprise was not strong enough to last, however. After contracting with the Kitchen for its first year, SEED elected to bid out its dining services. DCCK simply could not compete with the offers from larger, for-profit school food providers. The idea of generating jobs and revenue through a school meal program was sound, even revolutionary—no nonprofit was beginning to touch that line of work—but doing school food right would require staff, systems, and expertise the Kitchen did not yet have.

While the Kitchen was long on ideas, it had a ways to go toward executing them. When Robert ran through the litany of active DCCK programs and projects, from food recycling and meal distribution to job training and social enterprise, he was being totally truthful. The Kitchen *was* doing all these things. That 'vision thing' pervaded the basement kitchen. Each activity, however, possessed plenty of room for improvement. Egger, the idea-generator with no off switch, had proven the early skeptics wrong. The Kitchen model could work safely, legally, and effectively. But as Chapman Todd would later put

25   Crowley, "For-Profit Do-Gooder."

it, "To go beyond the start-up phase, nonprofits have to be confident enough to broaden the vision and bring on people with more expertise . . . There comes a point when you have to stop laying groundwork and hire people with different skills who can take the organization to the next level." By the end of the Kitchen's first decade, colleagues within and outside DCCK started whispering in Robert's ear, "It's time to think about transition."

In the nonprofit sector, founder transitions are sensitive matters. It is hard enough for profit-seeking entrepreneurs to cash out to bigger buyers or shareholders. Since nonprofit leaders see little cash for their efforts, they often care much more about receiving adequate credit for their work, their ideas, and their sacrifices. Some founders never give up their position and, in many cases, damage their organization's ability to keep pace with changing conditions, respond to new opportunities, or simply maintain its energy level. Egger vowed to never become one of those founders. So he took the whispers seriously. "I was happy to hand over the operation of the Kitchen, and the first person I did that with was Chapman. I wanted to prove this wasn't 'The Robert Show,' that the organization could step up and do great work without me." Unlike some of his peers, Egger was willing to begin the process of handing the reins over to others—but those people had to be the right ones, and that hand-off had to be flawless.

For eight years, Robert had found balance and support in his relationship with Chapman. For external audiences, Egger was the man behind DCCK's achievements, but Todd was the man behind the curtain. Robert's willingness to step back and let his programming-savvy colleague run the operation on a daily basis was rare in a sector riddled with micromanagement. The two men's rapport made the give-and-take of daily decision making uniquely amicable and effective for the better part of a decade.

The Kitchen's rapid pace, uneven finances, and harsh working conditions, however, made staff burn-out a permanent fixture of its organizational culture. Eventually, Todd the nonprofit generalist decided he had done what he could at DCCK, and elected to make room for the specialists that could push the Kitchen forward. He resigned in the spring of 1998. Egger's yin needed a new yang. Promising growth in Fresh Start and Contract Foods encouraged Robert and DCCK's board of directors to seek out someone who really knew financial management, and maybe even a thing or two about making a profit.

Thumbing through a copy of *The Washington Post* shortly after Chapman's departure, Cynthia Rowland happened upon a small, two-inch-wide advertisement seeking a Business Manager. A native-born Texan, the auburn-haired, bespectacled Rowland studied finance and business administration in college before spending a decade at a multi-billion-dollar energy firm in Houston. "When I moved to DC, I knew I wasn't a politician. That basically left tourism and nonprofits," she recalls. Rowland ended up at a small arts organization, where she applied her financial acumen and had her first run-in with the nuances of nonprofit accounting. The tiny, cryptic newspaper ad she found a few years later did not say anything about working for a nonprofit, but Rowland was intrigued and fired off a resume.

Her first round interview with a DCCK board member left her conflicted. While she had no formal party affiliation, Rowland says her "political, social, fiscal leanings were far more conservative than anyone at DCCK or, more generally, that type of cause-related social service organization." Had the Kitchen fallen into the same vaguely liberal groove that typified much of the hunger and homelessness space, Rowland would have walked. Her interviewer handed her a small, tri-fold pamphlet describing the organization. On the back, it stated Robert's firm belief that "waste is wrong," and that unique twist resonated with Cynthia. "I had become appalled at the level of waste in America in many respects, but especially when it came to food," she says. That hatred of waste appealed to her fiscal conservatism, and warily, she agreed to meet with Egger.

It proved to be a most unusual vetting process. "To be honest," she remembers, "that first interview basically consisted of Robert talking and me listening. But he did what Robert does so well, and that's speaking with passion and insight. I kept thinking *'Wow, that's really smart!'* after each point." She left his office believing that DCCK was fundamentally different from other direct service nonprofits, and when Egger offered her the position of General Manager, she accepted. As Todd did before her, Rowland brought a level of operational know-how and management experience that complimented Egger's frenetic energy and penchant for charging at windmills.

Rowland relished the excitement she found at DCCK, a compelling messiness that stood in stark contrast to her prior experiences in corporate finance and at a sleepy arts nonprofit. The vague title she assumed allowed her to pursue her primary interests in organizational leadership and program design. She had a special finesse with fine details, and her exacting methods dovetailed effectively with Egger's principle-driven desire for his staff to do more with less. Staff members who exceeded their allotment of office supplies were sometimes told to bring pens from home.

At times, however, Rowland remembers wondering just what she had gotten herself into. "The A/C never worked in the summer, the heat never worked in the winter, and the 20 of us on staff had maybe five or six square feet of workspace each." Communication was challenging and recordkeeping spotty. Programs were segmented, with only a limited sense of how they operated within the Kitchen's larger context, especially when it came to finances. A businessperson to her core, Rowland described each program as a 'profit center. ' As such, she expected that each manager be responsible for maintaining some semblance of an operational budget and understanding her individual income sources and cash flow.

Of these profit centers, Fresh Start was the most promising at the time. As Rowland was beginning to settle in, her catering director quit and Cynthia, who had no kitchen experience, became a self-taught caterer on the fly. She ultimately hired a female chef named Chris Johnson, "who brought up Fresh Start Catering a huge amount," raves Rowland. "She took Fresh Start from doing staff lunches at the food bank to working the annual galas of big nonprofits." While Chapman had reached exactly the opposite conclusion in the early days of Fresh Start, Rowland saw an outfit that had quickly outgrown its existing market niche and led a strategic switch from boxed lunches to black ties.

"Oh my god, those boxes were awful," recalls Chef Jerald Thomas, who joined Fresh Start a year into Rowland's tenure. "When I came aboard," says Jerald, "we were using these thin cardboard boxes that took forever to assemble and couldn't hold anything moist, or they'd totally fall apart." On days with big lunch orders of 150 or more, Johnson had to assign one person to box assembling duty, a task that took the better part of six hours. "At 3 p.m., we would finally start counting all the finished boxes to see if we had the right amount, and only then could we start assembling the lunches. Last-minute orders were a nightmare and we couldn't do lunches on back-to-back days."

To really grow, Fresh Start had to develop its own delivery system, an independent inventory, and a better-funded bunch of nonprofit partners. Johnson developed a relationship with the Smithsonian, for example, in which Fresh Start provided buffet service at the opening of each new exhibit. Impressing these new clients demanded a change in Fresh Start's philosophy for hiring graduates of the Kitchen's job training program. While the catering outfit was originally envisioned as a transitional opportunity for graduates who were in some way behind the curve, Johnson began identifying the most promising students in each class and grooming them for Fresh Start upon graduation. The conversion, however, was never complete. Fresh Start still extended some of its full-time and part-time positions to DCCK graduates who wanted a job, but could not find one outside that basement kitchen. Inconsistency in its hiring process contributed to inconsistency in Fresh Start's services.

Despite its general arc of progress, Fresh Start's ambitions at times outpaced its capacity. Taking on a special lunch function for the Congressional Black Caucus at the Rayburn House Office Building, Chris, Jerald, and Executive Chef Gary Bullock tried to corral a squad of recent Kitchen graduates through Rayburn's intimidating security checkpoints and winding hallways. "Everything that could have gone wrong—delivery, timing, service, you name it—did. It was a total failure," says Jerald. "The three of us looked at each other and promised ourselves we'd never embarrass ourselves like that again."

Jerald Thomas was extremely hard on DCCK's culinary students and graduates, because he is one. Thomas spent nine years as a cook in the US Navy before losing a decade of his life to homelessness and addiction. Eventually, he ended up at Clean and Sober Streets, a recovery center that shared the Federal City Shelter with DCCK and received its meals each day. Several times over the course of 1997, Jerald ventured down to the basement, surveying a chaotic kitchen operation. "I wasn't sure I wanted any part of it," says Thomas. In 1998, he decided to enroll, expecting little. Due to his prior foodservice experience, he did not get much from the culinary curriculum. The Kitchen's unique version of tough love, however, resonated with him. His instructors challenged Jerald's attitude, demanding he take responsibility for his actions. "It was very simplistic, nothing magical, but it turned out to be profound for me. I took those lessons and chewed on them late at night." Upon graduation, he secured a job as the lead chef at a Central Intelligence Agency office facility in Virginia, where he stayed until the Kitchen lured him back with the opening at Fresh Start. "I was grateful for the second chance they gave me, and it seemed like Chris and Fresh Start were really trying to up their ante."

In time, Jerald rose through the ranks of DCCK. A tireless perfectionist, Thomas developed a close relationship with the similarly minded Robert Egger. "If Robert was the king of DC Central Kitchen, Jerald was the prince," recalls an admiring former colleague. While working full-time at the Kitchen, Thomas enrolled at nearby Stratford University, earning a degree in Culinary Arts. In 2005, he was named Director of Kitchen Operations, managing the production of thousands of meals for the city's shelters and nonprofits each day. And in 2011, as he began to think about retirement, he orchestrated another move within the organization. Jerald rejoined the Kitchen's Culinary Job Training program as its lead culinary instructor, getting tough with another generation of DCCK trainees.

Two decades earlier, Egger had imagined that his central kitchen would one day use the production of meals for other agencies—groups like Clean and Sober Streets—to attract people who needed a second chance. In that kitchen, those 'tough cases' would receive the training and support they needed to land steady work. Some, he hoped, would even find those jobs in his own organization, mentoring the men and women who came after them. He may not have envisioned those many concepts being so perfectly embodied in a single person like Jerald Thomas. While the biggest operation at the Kitchen was, and would remain, meal preparation, the organization's many pursuits in the years to come would each be tied to the Culinary Job Training program that constituted its core. Filling stomachs was fine, but changing lives was what mattered. Egger did not just want to fight hunger. He was looking to satisfy a deeper hunger among his clients, one that could only be filled by the self-confidence, self-worth, and self-sufficiency that comes with a real job.

Chapter 4 The Ones who Could Work

Robert Egger has never once referred to DC Central Kitchen as 'a feeding organization.' "We're not," he protests. "We're an empowerment organization." Fueled by his frustration on the Grate Patrol truck, Egger vowed to found an organization that would use food distribution not as an end, but as a tool. At the center of this plan was his vision for a Culinary Job Training program, one that recruited the types of men and women who relied upon programs like the Grate Patrol, enlisted them in preparing meals for other hungry citizens, and, in the process, taught them the basic skills they needed to find entry-level work at hotels and restaurants.

For many 'feeding organization' types, this all sounded crazy. Their responses to Egger's plans ranged from dismissive to dismayed. *"You want to train the homeless? No one will hire them." "Look, I know you mean well, but you're underestimating how hard it is for them to hold down a job." "Wait, you're giving these people knives?"*[26] Egger, through his lens of empowering the people he served, resented the implication that the only thing a homeless person could be any good at was standing in a soup line. "There's no dignity in free food," he once told the *Wall*

---

[26]   The first two quotes are reproduced in Egger, *Begging for Change*, 33; the final one he repeated in an interview with me in January 2013.

Street Journal, "This system is so pity-based. Pity creates nothing of substance."[27] In the insurgent spirit that came to typify DC Central Kitchen, Egger and his team went about trying to prove their contemporaries wrong.

The Culinary Job Training program (CJT) would eventually become the crown jewel of DCCK's activities. Its origins were somewhat more modest. Robert began training some students at the start of the Kitchen's second year, and a trial and error approach reigned. With spotty and inconsistent financial support, DCCK could not afford to hire a full-time culinary instructor. Chef Abdul Raheem, the Kitchen's primary production cook, took on double duty. "Abdul was good with the trainees. He knew when to be hard on them," says early staffer Alex Tait. Raheem had plenty of street smarts and sly charm but was hardly a pedagogical wonder. An average class consisted of about four people, almost always men, who were living in one of the city's shelters. Students spent their days working alongside Abdul and other volunteers to prepare that day's meals. As a result, culinary 'lessons' varied widely, based on what surprise ingredients showed up the night before.

In this early days, Egger and Chapman Todd shared many moments that caused them to say *"Oh yeah, I guess we have to account for that now, too."* Chapman recalls asking "a lot of dumb-shit questions back then." Written tests on culinary theory seemed like a good idea, until they realized how many of their students could not read. Eventually, the staff decided to give students a weekly stipend of $50 to cover their incidental expenses while in the program. No one on DCCK's staff or board of directors knew if handing out these stipends violated any labor laws, but they knew students needed enough money to get to the Kitchen each day without having enough to tempt

---

27   Crowley, "For-Profit Do-Gooder."

them into relapsing. Fifty bucks seemed like a reasonable number, so they rolled with it.

Before long, the District's Department of Employment Services caught wind of the stipend and initially determined that those small payments made each student an employee of the Kitchen, thus making the Kitchen liable to pay unemployment benefits and withhold taxes. This threat to the Kitchen's finances caused one foundation to panic and suspend its grant payments to DCCK. It took a year for city officials to conclude that the stipends fit a loophole for allowances that provide "no profit to the employee but is used . . . to meet the expenses of the employer's business."[28] The relieved foundation reopened its checkbook and DCCK went about its business, albeit with a new and acute awareness of how the good intentions of government could screw up the work of a private nonprofit testing out new solutions.

By the winter of 1990, the training program had begun to generate some good buzz across and beyond Washington, DC. Eager to share his model with other organizations, Egger spent the next year teaming up with a group of Cornell University hotel management students to put together a formal curriculum. Designed to run for 12 weeks, Robert "wanted a program that was more demanding and more instructive than a seminar, but not as rigorous as a cooking school."[29] The manual with an Ivy League school seal stamped on the front cover implied high expectations. "The perception changed. Now it was 'this is school,'" says Todd. They tried to create a model geared towards tactile learning and practical instruction. Each morning, the students learned through immersion, helping to

---

[28]   Correspondence from Michael A. Milwee, General Counsel of the Department of Employment Services to Michelle D. Bernard, Esq. of Shaw, Pittman, Potts & Trowbridge, June 10, 1994.

[29]   Egger, *Begging for Change*, 41.

dish out a growing number of meals. The afternoon was spent on straightforward, bare-bones skills training. Students learned how to hold a knife, at what temperature to keep poultry, and the like. The Kitchen's growing relationships within DC's culinary network inspired dozens of local chefs to offer free cooking demonstrations and tutorials to CJT students while opening up their own commercial kitchens for field trips.

One tradition was established early on. Since most new trainees were spending their nights in the shelters and halfway homes that relied on DCCK deliveries, they were already familiar with the Kitchen's meals. On the first day of the program, Robert would saunter in and ask, "How many of you have eaten our food?" Usually, at least three-quarters of the class raised their hands. "Now," Robert continued, "how many of you liked it?" The hands dropped. "Now, it's up to you to do better," he would say, bringing the meaning of those meals full circle.

A few years passed, and the Kitchen began to attract more money, more attention, and more students. It was time to hire a full-time culinary instructor who could use the organization's Cornell-approved manual to its full effect.

"There was a manual?!" Susan Callahan asks incredulously, 17 years later. Strong-jawed and bright-eyed, Callahan is prototypically Irish: straightforward and straight-laced until she grips an amber pint in her hand. Born to a military family, she spent the final years of her youth in DC when her father landed a lobbying job after Vietnam. When it came time to attend school, she quickly realized "there were no women chefs. You either became a dietitian or a 'home ec' teacher. I picked the former." She was more or less content, until she caught a television cooking show one afternoon, "and there was this *handsome* French chef. I said 'I wanna do that.'"

Susan enrolled at L'Academie de Cuisine, a well-regarded French culinary school in DC's Maryland suburbs. She excelled as a restaurant chef and later as an L'Academie instructor. Her path to professional success, however, was quite difficult. For more than a decade, Susan bounced from day job to day job, trying to find positions that would accommodate her young family. At one point, she worked in the Marriott test kitchen, where she was shocked at the level of food waste. "I started donating our food to a small Maryland nonprofit, not from being some sort of goodie-two-shoes, but just because it made sense." As she would later recall, however, being a woman in that industry, let alone a new mother, at that time "was incredibly hard, and I reached my breaking point." For the duration of Lent in the spring of 1996, Callahan wrestled with her future. Imbued with an Episcopal sense of social justice, she even considered becoming a priest.

On Holy Tuesday, a friend casually mentioned to Susan that an urban nonprofit was running a culinary program for homeless, hard-luck cases in the basement of a DC shelter. Callahan was intrigued. Her students at L'Academie were, almost universally, white children of privilege who had been pushed into liberal arts degrees by their parents, bottomed out by their late twenties, and decided to start over in chef's whites. The Kitchen's student population offered a welcome break from the fussy Frenchmen and suburban burnouts she had dealt with for more than a decade. She applied on Ash Wednesday, was hired on Good Friday, and started the Monday after Easter.

Callahan's faith was quickly tested. "I was scared to death my first year, this little white girl in a totally different environment. As soon as I started, I drew up all these lesson plans. And I threw them out just as quickly." While that Cornell manual collected dust on Chapman Todd's desk, a confluence of factors—an explosion of new nonprofits, safety net reforms, and increased competition for limited philanthropic resources among them—led more and more organizations to ask the Kitchen for free meals. DCCK never said no, so Susan and her students increasingly devoted their time and energy to morning meal production. "Yes, there was a general progression [to the course]—you start with soups and stocks and work your way up. But the reality was that we had all those meals to get out, so let's get that done and keep everyone safe. Whatever happened in the afternoon with the guest chefs was just fun." In her opinion, "the real learning took place in production anyway, and there wasn't enough money to do much else."

Doing so much with so little turned out to be an unwritten part of Callahan's job description. "You know the biblical story of feeding the multitudes?" she asks, a playful Irish spark in her bright eyes. "That was DC Central Kitchen every day. We fed thousands of people without fail, without ever having any food." Even when big donations rolled into the Kitchen's cavernous pantry or unreliable freezer, "we knew it wasn't a surplus. We had to act like we had no food so we could make it last until the next big donation."

Susan's counterpart was Frank McKinney, the thick-necked retired Marine who commuted in each day before dawn from Manassas, Virginia. "They were a great pair," remembers Chapman. "Susan taught the students how to hold a knife. Frank showed them how to get three thousand meals out the door, fast." Neither one was big on bullshit. "I was never real good at the social worker side of things," says Callahan. "I didn't care about their circumstances. I figured they all had circumstances, so let's keep them on task and get them a job." The Kitchen's 'professional development' curriculum consisted of a coffee can. "Every time someone swore, showed up late, or acted out, they had to put 50 cents in the can. At the end, the student with the fewest demerits won the contents," says Susan. When it came to cursing, the students probably didn't always have the best role models in a proudly profane organization. Almost 20 years later, a new Human Resources staffer attempted to implement a similar policy with the Kitchen's top executives. "Fuck that," said one, rifling through his wallet for a dollar bill. "I'm putting in a five now to cover my ass," said another.

Now teaching at an area university, Callahan remembers her years at the Kitchen "As so fun, so raw. There were so many times that whole operation should have been shut down." The Federal City Shelter was in constant need of repair, and Susan often had to work around areas of the Kitchen that were cornered off with tarps and duct tape. Maintenance issues had a nasty habit of cropping up at the worst times. In 1998, the Kitchen received word that the president and first lady, Bill and Hillary Clinton, wanted to volunteer in two weeks, preparing Bill's own lasagna recipe. Secret Service agents began prowling the building, thoroughly displeased with the President's selection of a place to do some good. Just a week before the visit, Callahan recalls, "it began raining sewage—actually raining sewage in the Kitchen." The pipes of the upstairs homeless shelter ran through DCCK's ceiling, and those pipes burst days before the leader of the free world was supposed to roll in. "We were horrified," says Susan. "We pleaded with the health department, and scrambled to get things fixed and the walls painted before the president showed up." On the upside, the great sewage storm of '98 did finally provide the impetus for the Kitchen to paint its walls white, instead of the unsightly brown they had been for years.

Even Susan's husband, Paul Dugard, got dragged into her efforts. With big, unblinking blue eyes and hands like catcher's mitts, Dugard was a natural fix-it guy, good with electrical gear and steering wheels. In 1997, he was the first person to wire the Kitchen for Internet connectivity. Later, Paul tore out its phone lines and installed superior ones the State Department had thrown away. And each fall, Robert and Susan dispatched him to nearby Virginia, where public lands would be overrun by deer. Many states elect to thin their deer herds before the onset of winter, when the herds' food supplies run short and, in nature's efficient cruelty, starvation trims the population anyway. Virginia, however, mandates that the killing be used to feed homeless people. On cold November nights, Dugard would head across the Potomac and meet up with a dozen SWAT team sharpshooters carrying silencers and spotlights. "They had to hit them in the neck, you see. Researchers wanted the jaw to determine the deer's age, and a torso hit might damage the stomachs, which they needed to test for parasites," he says with a sense of frank detachment most common among Animal Planet narrators. The game wardens would hand him the carcass, which he would skin, butcher, and bag for later use by Susan and her students. "I got so good I could do the whole thing in five minutes, and I'd bring back 25 or even 35 deer at a time." Susan stops him. "You didn't always have to butcher them," she says. "After all, sometimes I'd want to show my students where a chop or a tenderloin came from." Thanks to the couple's efforts, DCCK served a whole lot of venison chili, which CCNV clients derisively deemed "eating Bambi." As Robert remembers, "we did an eggplant and venison stew that, to this day, was the greatest meal the Kitchen ever served. [The People for the Ethical Treatment of Animals] hated it, but we were in no position to turn down fresh protein." Dugard did, however, have the good sense to decline a generous offer he received from Dulles International Airport, which was willing to hand over a thousand dead geese that had strayed too close to the runways, if only the Kitchen was willing to pluck and gut them.

Her doting husband was not the only person Susan Callahan introduced to her eventful place of employment. In fact, much of her legacy at DC Central Kitchen stems from the men and women she helped bring through its doors. While still teaching at L'Academie de Cuisine, she was assigned a new student advisee. At the time, L'Academie's student population was about 1% non-white. The intense Black woman with a curvy figure and straight spine that walked into her office in 1995, then, made an impression. "I need to be up-front with you," she said. "I'm in recovery and I suffer from depression."

"Who doesn't?" replied Susan.

They both laughed. Susan Callahan and Marianne Ali became fast friends. Once Callahan arrived at DC Central Kitchen, she knew Ali was a perfect fit. Thrilled to receive a call from her former advisor, Ali readily ditched a boring job cooking for high-level US Postal Service officials and joined DCCK a week later, supporting its new contract providing summer meals to low-income children at area youth programs.

Before long, Marianne slid over to work for Susan. "What drew me to the training program," says Ali, "was the connection between my history and the students' histories—the brokenness, being told you won't ever be nothing. I knew when I told my story the students would put a level of trust in me. I'd tell them about my days down on Division Avenue, using creek water to cook my dope. You can't make that shit up." Susan coached Marianne intensively, building up her confidence and giving her more and more responsibility. Ali says she could not wait to get to work in the morning, filling a totally unique role at the Kitchen: the formally trained chef with the weathered awareness of a lifelong addict. However, she saw her ability to relate to students in a knowing, genuine fashion as less of a counseling tool and more of a decoder ring for the self-defeating lies and half-truths those trainees would pull out when the going got tough.

Callahan and Ali were the same age and attended the same boutique cooking school. And they shared the same hard-nosed philosophy when it came to teaching the Kitchen's culinary students. "At 6:30 a.m.," declares Susan, "life sucks. But you have to have to get up and go to work, listen to authority, and do as you're told." When Ali first joined Callahan's program as a culinary instructor, she agreed. "I didn't see it as a social service program. I believed we should have only nuances of social services." Years later, when Ali succeeded her former advisor, she dismissed outsiders who suggested that the Kitchen hire a full-time social worker. "There were folks that thought we should really focus on case management and just try to find room for culinary training around that. My response was that we didn't have time to do that shit in 12 weeks." To this day, Ali is skeptical about the perfectionist aims of some social service providers. "The only things we fix here are meals, not people," she declares.

For nearly every Kitchen staffer associated with the Culinary Job Training program at some point in its history, the refrain is the same: *'We're not trying to perfect people. We're trying to get them a job.'* Not every student would overcome his or her demons. Many would never find work. Others would bail after their first or second paycheck, blowing that cash on a chance to get high.

No educational program bats a thousand. There is a tradition at Harvard Law School of professors telling crammed lecture halls on the first day of class, "Look to the left. Now look to the right. One of you three people won't be here by the end of the semester." The Kitchen offers a slightly different take on this one-in-three story. Thumbing through some old personal photos, a 2001 culinary graduate stopped and pointed at a shot of two old classmates working in DCCK's production line. "I made it. But him, he's out using again, I see him all the time. And her, she's dead." Drug addiction, prison, and death—these are the stakes facing the students of DC Central Kitchen. It is the kitchen of last resort.

All of the Kitchen's culinary instructors have, at some point, have grappled with the self-recrimination and guilt that follows a student's failure. Relentlessly optimistic, Robert was more comfortable with the program's imperfect outcomes. "We're planting seeds here," he told Susan Callahan after an especially hard day. "They'll go out into the world, and they may not make it on the first try. But the seeds are still there. Many more will figure it out in time." He was right. Dozens of graduates have bottomed out—some spectacularly so—only to turn up at the Kitchen a few months or a few years later, clean and looking for a second chance. Several graduates employed by the Kitchen have even been fired, forgiven, and re-hired over the years.

For outside observers, the Kitchen's statistics warrant skepticism. *"OK, so you have a 90 percent job placement rate, but do you have any idea how many people actually keep those jobs?"* In fact, over the years, Kitchen records show that about 80 percent of students who find work are still working six months later. For some metrics-oriented foundations, these figures are less records of achievement than indicators of a need for improvement. *"How can you employ the 10 percent who aren't finding work?"* is a common query. So is *"What about the 15 to 20 percent who aren't lasting in their jobs?"* The important thing to remember, Kitchen leaders often reply, is that the population they're serving, absent the aid of DC Central Kitchen, would have a success rate close to zero. If 30 percent of students succeed, the program pays for itself in spared welfare and prison costs. With a success rate in the neighborhood of 80 percent, as it stands today, the Culinary Job Training program has exchanged tens of millions of dollars in incarceration and safety net expenses for millions in payroll taxes and consumer spending by employed graduates. Forget about saving souls. The program makes sense if for no other reason than it saves money.

Internally, however, DCCK offers itself little quarter from criticism. While the hard-headed approach of 'put on your hairnet and get to work' had proved valuable in the program's early years, the continued struggles of many trainees and graduates eventually convinced Callahan and her team that maybe there was more need for social work than they initially thought. In 1997, they decided to add a one-hour session once each week that would let the students talk through some of their issues. At the same time, these meetings were supposed to offer trainees some unadulterated tough love. The Kitchen needed someone who had the empathy and emotional perceptiveness of an experienced counselor and the ability to stand up to defiant trainees in a way that commanded their respect. They were looking for a rare person indeed.

Barrel-chested with a cleanly shaved head and ruddy face, Ron Swanson's bulk and jaw line recall an aging Rottweiler not yet drained of his fight. Big, gruff, and tough enough to call out the hard-edged students of the Kitchen, Swanson might easily be mistaken for one of the many ex-offenders to become a DC Central Kitchen reclamation project. Yet he was no prisoner. In fact, Ron Swanson was a priest.

"I never was much of a priest," recalls Swanson with a smirk that fades quickly. "My real passion was social justice." This passion wasn't founded in the white, liberal do-goodery that surrounded him as a young man in the Pacific Northwest. For as far back as he can remember, he carried "an incredible amount of anger" in his heart, largely inspired by an emotionally distant set of parents. "They were good people," he repeats several times, "but they couldn't give me the love that I needed. And I knew that wasn't right. And the more I looked around, I saw things around me that weren't right either." Swanson turned his outrage outward, finding fault with the racial and economic injustices of the Fifties. A self-professed nerd, he studied art history before moving south to pursue a Masters of Divinity in the lefty hotbed of Berkeley, California.

For nearly 30 years, Swanson served in the Episcopal Diocese of San Joaquin in Central California, overlapping with the farm worker mobilization efforts of Cesar Chavez. His congregation was riddled with conflict and inequality. The Church's largest benefactors were wealthy white landowners. The congregants most in need of earthly assistance, however, were Hispanic farmworkers from Central America, trapped in brutal conditions at cheap wages—by the very people seated a few rows away. Swanson felt compelled to bring both aid and attention to the needs of his low-income congregants, but institutional politics and financial imperatives limited his ability to help them.

In time, his unresolved pain and resulting rage became too much. Swanson's remedy of choice was a punishing mix of alcohol and tranquilizers. For two decades, he lived the double life of an alcoholic priest. His struggles led him first to Alcoholics Anonymous, and then to an interest in small group counseling among his congregants. Now clean for 30 years, one might think Swanson had found a way to let go of his anger. Far from it. Unlike the gentle pacifism typically associated with Christianity, Swanson says anger is his central tool, both in bettering himself and fighting the wrongs he sees around him. "Anger was my road to sobriety and sanity, my motivation," he recalls, "But just being angry isn't enough. You have to channel it, and realize that is a part of you. I become angry at things that aren't right, take ownership of that anger, and then decide how to act with it."

Late in his career, Swanson was sent across the country to Washington, DC, charged with reviving a decrepit church and dwindled congregation in the historically black neighborhood of Anacostia. Once designed to limit the number of undesirable minorities calling it home—such as the Irish or, worse yet, freed blacks—the historic neighborhood of Anacostia in time became a tragic case study, first in white flight and then in the crippling effects of the crack cocaine epidemic. Today, the two DC Wards located east of the Anacostia River are home to some of the worst economic and public health conditions in the United States.[30] When Swanson arrived in 1992, matters were even worse. After a four-year stint that included successfully renovating a flood-damaged church that many neighbors had simply assumed was abandoned, Swanson retired.

He hated it. Alone with his anger and alcoholism, he started volunteering at a few nonprofits across the District, but nothing captured his energy until a former parishioner, Susan Callahan, suggested he visit DC Central Kitchen. She knew the Culinary Job Training program needed someone who understood addiction, was used to fighting for hopeless causes, and possessed a finely tuned bullshit detector. Who better than an alcoholic priest from Anacostia?

Drawing on his experiences in AA, Swanson assembled a list of discussion topics that would help students share their stories and connect with one another. "It was wild with that group," chuckles Swanson. "They were angry." Their malice pointed in every direction: at their families, their neighbors, themselves, and even at DC Central Kitchen. Some complained that their training program was really just a chance for the Kitchen to benefit from free labor. There was always plenty of wrath aimed at Swanson, who demanded that his students venture into dark memories and devastating failures. One early student said Ron was no different than the warden who had tormented him in prison. That barb stung, and it underscored to Swanson the

---

[30] A common mistake is to refer to the entire area of DC that is east of the Anacostia River, Wards 7 and 8, as 'Anacostia.' Anacostia is a small historic neighborhood in the heart of Ward 8, and is the community in which Swanson did his work.

critical importance of relaying to his students that they shared the same struggles.

The wounds of most Kitchen trainees run deep. They have been hurt, hurt others, and found ways to hurt themselves. Surviving in foster homes and housing projects, let alone shelters and prisons, forces these men and women to bury their pain, covering it with thick, coarse scar tissue. Anger, defiance, and detachment come easily. Openness and honesty are dangerous forms of weakness. And, in the words of one former student, "in comes this big old white dude asking you about your life. Early on, that relationship is very difficult." Swanson quickly found that one meeting once a week was not going to break through to his students. He had to get past their reactionary rage and down to the core issues, faulty thought patterns, and destructive behaviors that kept his students mired in hardship. Forget mock interviews; these folks needed full-scale interventions. After just a few weeks around the Kitchen, he began agitating to expand his class to an intensive daily session, spanning 90 minutes and nine weeks. He also told Susan that she should probably hire him.

Swanson convincingly argued that his work would give students a stronger foundation for long-term success. His students came around even faster than some of his coworkers. "Ron taught us about eye contact, approaching people we have problems with, and what our body language says. They don't cover that at employee orientation," says one graduate with a chuckle. "You gotta be there on time, at 8:30 a.m., dressed and ready to go. If you can't handle that for 12 weeks, you won't make things work at home or at a job. And if you can't handle Ron, your ass will be back in jail or on drugs." For Swanson, it's important to snarl at his students so they sit up straight. But most of his work involves helping students forgive others and forgive themselves so they can stand tall.

Swanson succeeds, in large part, because he finds a way to connect with his students. One former trainee who had been in and out of drug treatment programs for years before ending up at the Kitchen reports that "some other counselors rely on book stuff. Not that there's anything wrong with that, but Ron has a history. He comes from a place of caring."

"I've looked in the mirror and realized I needed to change," says Swanson. "All I bring is the insistence that my students do the same." He must walk a fine line, though, between relating to his students and placing himself at the center of the conversation. "I have to be careful that I'm not here for my own needs." In his view, this question of needs is centrally important. He says that he and his colleagues in the job training program "are not here for our own needs. If we make a mistake and hire someone who is, they don't last. Our team is here to carry out the mission of the Kitchen. Other organizations—whether they mean to or not—care more about their staff than the clients they're supposed to be serving."

Swanson's vision for his students is that they will no longer need him or DC Central Kitchen. This commitment to obsolescence is rare among nonprofits, and especially so among those fighting the seemingly timeless ills of hunger and poverty. In the Gospels of Matthew, Mark, and John, Jesus declares that "The poor will always be with you." The strategic plan of nearly every food bank, soup kitchen, and shelter facility in America is predicated on an unwavering belief in the persistence of poverty—the poor will always be with us and we will always need bigger, shinier facilities to feed, house, and clothe them. If an organization can't change its clients' fate, Swanson figures, it ends up just looking out for itself.

Even if many of his students no longer need the Kitchen, however, Swanson himself does. He tried retiring again in 2009. "I did not like it," he says, pausing deliberately after each word.

He was back as a volunteer in a matter of months, a move quickly followed by his return to the payroll. "There's something about being at DC Central Kitchen. This is the best job I've ever had in my life. This is what I was born to do." After shepherding more than 50 CJT classes through to graduation, Swanson is the program's longest-serving employee.

Swanson is still angry, but his ability to channel those feelings continues to grow stronger. On one unseasonably warm afternoon in October 2012, Swanson finished off a snack of popcorn, brushed the leftover crumbs and kernels off his desk onto the floor, and headed home to his Southeast Washington apartment. Without a porch to sit on, Swanson enjoys sunny days parked in his driveway, rolling down his car windows and leafing through a copy of *The Washington Post*. But on this day, as he reached the sports page, his phone rang. His supervisor, Marianne Ali, had spotted the mess under his desk, and told him to put his car in drive, return to the Kitchen, and clean it up. He calmly complied. "I could have gotten angry, but I knew I was wrong, and I knew that this is the type of responsibility we talk to our students about every day." The old priest smiles. He is a work in progress, an old Rottweiler open to learning a new trick.

Ron Swanson exudes respect for his younger boss. Despite their radically different upbringings and prior careers, Ron and Marianne share a unique bond, rooted in living much of their adult lives in recovery from substance abuse. The two have worked alongside one another for 15 years. "She's the real idea person," he says. "Marianne pushed for this program to grow in all sorts of different ways." Together, they overhauled the Kitchen's approach to recruiting students. In the early and mid-nineties, a typical class consisted of four to six students, usually men, most of whom were living in one of the residential support programs upstairs from DCCK, either CCNV or Clean and Sober Streets. Welfare reform brought radical changes. With the Department of Labor paying the Kitchen for 'welfare-to-work' services and shelling out hourly wages to jobless adults enrolled at DCCK, enrollment exploded. In the latter part of the decade, an average class began with between 30 and 40 students referred by a dozen or more agencies that Ron started collaborating with on a regular basis.

Larger classes invariably led to student retention problems. Driven off welfare by changes in federal legislation, many new students had never before held a job and were totally unprepared for the mental stress, physical rigors, and social norms of the workplace. Others might have been ready for some form of employment, but had little interest in a culinary career. In 1997, for example, just 33 men and women completed the program, less than a third of those who initially enrolled. In the years that followed, Marianne, Ron, and the rest of their growing department began devising ways to keep more of their students. One of the most common trainee complaints came from their prominent role in the Kitchen's daily meal production. Some students felt taken advantage of and quit in the program's second month. They never came around to Marianne's view that "each day's meal *was* the lesson. It was 'Oh, we have carrots? Today, we're learning ways to cut carrots.'" Marianne decided to break the monotony with special events. In the program's fourth week, she added a Heritage Day, when area chefs would demonstrate a particular regional or ethnic cuisine. In week six, she developed a Culinary Cook-Off in which students broke into teams and competed to develop the best take on a specified dish. The events also gave the Kitchen's many hospitality industry supporters more opportunities to interact with the organization while celebrating the students' continued progress.

Under Ali, the Culinary Job Training program embraced an organic approach to innovation. There were no five-year plans, just constant conversations about what was working and what was not. In certain ways, the Kitchen was a trend-setter. It was, for example, a leading pioneer of the now-popular 'sectoral employment model,' using industry knowledge and contacts to develop and refine a training program specifically suited to employers' needs.

In other ways, DCCK turned out to be a trend-responder. It is said that when white America catches a cold, black America gets pneumonia. If that's true, when black America gets pneumonia, DC Central Kitchen has to invent a new form of penicillin out of leftover food and low-skill labor.

Of the people who rely on the Kitchen's meals and job training services, more than 90 percent are black residents of Washington, DC. Robert Egger, in contrast, is a Caucasian male in cowboy boots from California. He is keenly aware of the complex racial dynamics at play at DCCK. In his many travels and talks, Robert often fields questions about the biggest challenges he has faced. "I always say, up front, that I have the unique fortune of being a white man in America. I have and have had every conceivable advantage. And when I'm frank and open about that, I see people of all races respond to me with that same level of openness." Racial distinctions are an unavoidable reality in DCCK's daily work. Marianne Ali regularly refers to Robert as "the coolest white guy" she knows, implying different color-based standards for coolness. At Robert's insistence, the Kitchen started publishing the percentage of its employees and supervisors who represent racial minorities, as well as those who are women and ex-offenders, on its website. Some figures are less impressive than others. Most of the Kitchen's top staff over the years has been white—from Robert and Chapman Todd through Cynthia Rowland and current CEO Michael Curtin. Nearly everyone employed at DCCK as a kitchen worker or delivery driver, meanwhile, is black. As such, maintaining a cohesive organizational culture has never been easy for the Kitchen. Yet Egger's charisma, credibility, and earnest commitment to a functional, productive form of workplace diversity—one that stressed internal promotions and second chances—allowed the organization to avoid both substantial infighting and the unseemly appearance of privileged, suburban do-gooders shouldering a modern version of the misguided 'white man's burden.'

DCCK's success in fostering a diverse, multi-racial environment imbued its operation with a unique sense of street-level savvy. Throughout the Kitchen's history, it has eschewed the conventional wisdom of researchers and white papers in favor of its first-hand experience with each new plague afflicting DC's impoverished class. Egger and his team became skilled at spotting each popular intoxicant, and differentiating one from the other. "At first it was alcohol, and that's easy, because you can smell it," Robert reports. "Heroin's different. Folks just nod off, even when they're in mid-sentence. And crack? That is some insidious shit. Never seen anything like it. It would make decent people steal, and some people just disappear." In a 1995 interview, Egger admitted his training program's early record was "checkered. [It's] a rough, rough business." At the time, Robert said DCCK had produced 100 graduates. Ninety-two, he said, had found jobs initially, but only 52 were still working. While some graduates simply were not ready for independence—a new paycheck was often a gateway to old habits—Egger named crack as the primary culprit. "It's an epidemic . . . It's the most destructive force I've ever seen."[31]

Crack did everything it could destroy Carolyn Parham. A DC native with tight braids and piercing eyes, Parham's personality is strong like steel—steel that has been melted down and

---

[31]   Goar, Carol, "His kitchen feeds dignity to D.C.'s hungry, homeless," *The Sunday Star* (Toronto, CA), June 18, 1995, A1.

hammered flat, time and time again. Before her 18th birthday, Parham was shuffled between five foster homes, two group homes, and even a boarding school in Erie, Pennsylvania. Her final stop in this painful odyssey was a Northeast DC group home, where she first started using drugs. "First it was weed, then booze, then crack. I was 19 when they put me out."

It did not take long for Carolyn to find an abusive relationship with a fellow user. She moved in with him. It quickly became a crack-ridden prison. "He'd drug me in the morning and lock me in the house," she remembers. Three years of drugs and brutal beatings caused her to lose vision in her right eye. Finally, at age 22, she had had enough, and climbed out a window. Wandering down Franklin Street, her severely swollen face and mouth attracted the attention of a passing cab driver, who sped her to DC General Hospital. "When it's an emergency, you decide to get help. But it doesn't take long for that emergency to pass, you know? So the cabbie said he was leaving to get me some McDonald's and cigarettes. I figured I could bail out of there before he got back," she admits. "Right then, the guy shows up and tells me to get back inside the hospital. I turned around and passed right out. When I came to, they told me I had a brain tumor, was seven weeks pregnant, and had to get help."

Her tumor was benign. It was her addiction that could prove lethal. Dutifully, Carolyn went to a first-stage detoxification center, and then onto Samaritan Inns, a drug recovery program serving homeless DC residents. She stayed clean for 18 months and gave birth to a daughter. Finding work and housing was hard, though, and Parham ended up returning to her abusive ex. "Too many women think they need a man," she says, shaking her head with a self-aware grimace. She relapsed, and found another, equally destructive love interest, whom she soon married. The next eight years were brutal. "I'd use for two, three months, and then get clean. But I couldn't stay that way. There were a lot of jobs, a lot of moving." In February 2001, Carolyn was using hard but managing to hold down a maintenance job at Walter Reed. She had saved up two weeks' worth of vacation time, which she took. A bender followed. "Over the course of those two weeks, I went from walking my kids all the way to school, to just short of the school yard, to an alley close by, so I wouldn't embarrass them with how messed up I looked."

Her younger daughter reached her breaking point. "Mom, I'm sick of holding my sister at recess when she's on the ground, crying!" she screamed in the alley near her school. Even today, a decade later, Carolyn wells up recounting the exchange. "I went into treatment that day and never looked back," she says.

Parham's road to recovery was an uphill one. "The welfare-to-work folks first sent me to the Culinary Job Training program. I wasn't interested a career, but the DC employment office would pay me seven dollars an hour while I was in training. But then, someone else at the office said my tumor meant that I couldn't stand long enough to go through the program." Nothing if not contrarian, Carolyn replied, "Please! If I could run around on streets getting high for weeks, I can handle standing in the kitchen." A CJT staffer named Tammy Williams "stood up and took personal responsibility for getting me through the program." Williams found a neurologist who would see Carolyn, and he signed off on her participation. That afternoon appointment represents the only time Parham missed during her 12 weeks enrolled in the Kitchen's training program—a truly remarkable feat, given what she encountered next.

Carolyn started class at DCCK in July 2001, "just five months clean." To her surprise, she enjoyed the program, even the invasive self-empowerment sessions taught by the growling Ron Swanson. "I love Ron, and always have," she says with a smile. In fact, for the next decade, the recovering addict and alcoholic former priest would meet most Friday evenings at a local buffet for crab legs. Despite being early in her recovery, Parham embraced Ron's class immediately. "Men come here trying to be tough after being incarcerated. Women come here having learned not trust people—but if you don't open up, you'll block your blessings. Ron breaks down those walls. And like he says, if everything in your life was great, you wouldn't be in the basement of this shelter trying to get a culinary license. So open up!" she chides. Carolyn excelled in the program. Marianne Ali put her outgoing student to work alongside a group of volunteers from the elite Georgetown Day School. "They could only come for 90 minutes, so they'd disrupt the normal flow. Marianne had me guide them through special, shorter projects." Things were looking up, until a stretch of rainy days in early September.

On September 11, the eyes of the world were fixed upon a smoldering gash in the New York skyline and a devastated swath of the Pentagon. Across the Potomac, Carolyn finished a long day of training and headed home. She made her way to the small basement apartment in a notorious drug den on Taylor Street she and her husband were renting for $325 a month. The place was destroyed, with several feet of standing water silently inflicting permanent damage. Her husband, still using crack, suggested they call FEMA. An assessor came out and gave them a voucher for a room at Motel 6 and a take-out dinner. The man said he would process their claim and send along a check for moving expenses. *"Bull,"* Carolyn figured, but she did appreciate the efforts of the Red Cross workers he summoned that night to extract her family's belongings and help move them into the motel.

That Friday, Carolyn found a check for $5,000 in her mail. Most people would be thrilled at that sort of efficient government support, but most people haven't battled crack addiction for their entire adult life. She crept into her daughters' room and "watched them sleep all night long. My husband came in, high. I wanted to get high so badly. But kept telling myself, if I cash this check and get high, my girls will go into foster care and I'll never see them again."

Remembering Swanson's lessons on personal responsibility, she made it through the night—barely—and in the morning headed to a local women's program that ran Narcotics Anonymous classes. She and a staffer walked over to a Wachovia branch and deposited the check, with the staffer serving as a co-signer. Without the co-signer, Carolyn could not withdraw the funds. A month later, FEMA sent another check. "It was like the world was playing with me." This time was slightly easier; she took her girls to lunch, and deposited the rest. "I figured I could cover three, four month's rent, finish the training program, and by then have a job that would pay our bills. I took my girls and left my husband. That's where our life started over."

Carolyn's commitment, gratitude, and outgoing, forceful personality—"I am an outspoken person," she says matter-of-factly—made her a natural fit at the Kitchen, but there were no culinary openings for her. Instead, Carolyn found a food service gig at Paul Public Charter School in Northeast DC. But Parham is a hard person to forget. When DCCK decided to create a position managing its volunteers, Carolyn was the obvious choice. In 2004, Parham began overseeing a massive volunteer operation, coordinating the scheduling, orientation, and safe direction of the more than 10,000 people who visited the Kitchen each year. Externally rough with a warm heart, she spent nearly a decade as the perfect stagehand for Robert's vaunted show. Carolyn played up the fear that strikes most volunteers after they feel their way down the dim shelter hallway toward the Kitchen. Barking orders, she made most groups shuffle uncomfortably in their folding chairs during orientation. Then she would tell her story, pulling the trigger of Egger's calculated epiphany with an authenticity that no polished fundraiser or besuited executive could hope to duplicate.

As effective as Parham was, of course, the Kitchen's best public performer would always be Robert Egger. After he had fired them up with an ambitious, optimistic vision for an inclusive, innovative future, Egger loved to tell audiences to get their heads out of the clouds. "Don't look to the stars," he would urge them. "Look for the gold at your feet." The Kitchen fished Carolyn Parham out of a drug den, plucked Marianne Ali from a dead-end job, and helped Ron Swanson find his life's purpose after retirement. Each of those people, in turn, searched for the glinting gold in the mud of DC's prisons, shelters, and streets. While most of the riches keen-eyed Kitchen staffers find are humans whose value has been hidden, sometimes they discover treasures of a worldlier sort.

Since 1990, DCCK has produced nearly 1,200 graduates, but only one true legend. Dorothy Bell, a short, slight black woman with a voice so high and sharp it's almost musical, completed the Kitchen's job training program in 1995. "I hit bottom in 1994," she says, "drinking and druggin'." Bell sought support at Clean and Sober Streets, a treatment program upstairs from DCCK. She had a little hospitality experience on her resume, and told her counselor she wanted to give the Kitchen's program a shot. She took to the no-nonsense teaching style of Susan Callahan. "I'd say 'I can't do this,' and she'd say 'Yes, you can.'" Callahan developed a quick admiration for her student, and upon graduation, Bell became the first DCCK graduate to land a culinary position at the Kitchen. After stints in Fresh Start and Contract Foods, she landed at the Kitchen's produce station, directing Kitchen volunteers as they turned donated fruits and vegetables into salads and more usable meal ingredients. At first, Bell recalls, "Sometimes, I didn't want to put my hands on those tomatoes because they were so messed up." In DCCK's early days, fresh produce donations were an absolute crap shoot, with most of what rolled in being total crap. Wilted, brown lettuce, mushy cantaloupes, and half-rotten tomatoes made up the bulk of Dorothy's inventory. From Bell's perspective, her job was simple: "cut the good from the bad," and teach volunteers to do the same.

As diverse as the Kitchen's volunteers could be, for 15 years, they nearly all shared one common experience: getting straightened out by the venerable Miss Dot, who became a foundational pillar of DC Central Kitchen's daily operation. *"Ooh Lord,"* she muses, looking back on the more than one-hundred thousand people she brought through her produce station. "I loved working with all of them, but some didn't know what they were doing, and wanted to put the good in with the bad." Her piercing voice stopped many volunteers frozen as they went to drop a moldy potato slice in the 'keep' bin, or recover a dropped carrot from the floor, or fiddle with their hairnet without washing their hands afterwards.

Sometimes, she relied on her regular volunteers to keep the first-timers in line. Her favorite regular was a lithe, blonde woman with a broad smile named Nancy. Nancy visited the basement kitchen twice a week for months on end, eventually inspiring Dorothy to designate her as her sous chef. For Miss Dot, Nancy was a very nice lady who was cheerful, agreeable, and could be trusted to successfully cut the good from the bad. As the Kitchen's executive staff soon realized, Nancy and her husband Robert were hugely successful investors who, in time, would permanently change the financial position of DC Central Kitchen because of Nancy's friendship with Dorothy Bell.

Money, power, and influence never mattered much to Miss Dot. She raves about her friend Nancy as her favorite volunteer of all time because of her persona, not her portfolio. And when President Clinton glided into the Kitchen after the sewage downpour of 1998, trailed by a cadre of cameramen and reporters, he sidled up next to Dorothy and began slicing into some green peppers. Responding to a press question, Clinton reached up to fix his presidential haircut, and then reached out to grab another pepper. Miss Dot would have none of it. She shrieked at him about the health violation, seized him by the arm, and pulled him over to the sink in the middle of the kitchen, demanding that he wash his hands. The President played along effortlessly. The Secret Service was less easy going about the altercation. The Kitchen, for its part, had the perfect anecdote to describe the point and the power of its job training program. "You've got a graduate of our program in charge of salad prep grabbing the President of the United States and scolding him for a food safety violation," says a tenured DCCK employee. "Now *that's* self-empowerment."

The pallets of produce that roll into DCCK are far fresher today than they were when Miss Dot earned her first paycheck from the organization. Her description of cutting the good from bad now applies less to DCCK's fruits and vegetables than it does to the work of Marianne Ali, Ron Swanson, and the rest of the Kitchen's culinary instructors. Where the average person might discard a head of lettuce with dying outer leaves, or a tomato with a deep bruise, or a man with bad attitude and worse rap sheet, the Kitchen carefully peels and slices away at those imperfections, looking for something valuable within.

DC Central Kitchen's impassioned hatred of waste in all its forms not only led to powerful program outcomes. Squeezing the most of every available resource stretched its budget when philanthropic funds were hard to find and inspired donors who felt confident that each dollar would be used to the greatest possible effect. The interaction of money and mission ultimately shaped the Kitchen's evolution, profoundly influencing strategic choices of where it would work, what programs it would pursue, and who it would dedicate itself to serving.

Chapter 5   Money Matters

Robert Egger's first foray into fundraising exposed him to the harsh realities of what money meant in the nonprofit sector. His opening salvo of grant proposals in 1988 was met with a volley of rejection letters—except for that one vital grant of $25,000 from the DC-based Abell Foundation. Looking back, he is not surprised his letter failed to break through the deluge of proposals that land in foundations' mailboxes each year. "A lot of nonprofits are like brain-eating zombies," he says. "Once they seize on the fact that there's money somewhere, they're out on the doorstep and you'll never be rid of them. And if they get money from you once, they're even more relentless."

Egger swore to never join the ranks of the fundraising undead. "I wanted to avoid being dependent on what I was beginning to see as the whims and flavor-of-the month funding policies of the foundation community . . . I wanted to be damn sure I was not a slave of the system I had entered. I wanted to redefine, recharge, and rededicate the sector—not spend most of my hours drafting grant proposal after grant proposal just to keep the operation afloat for another six months."[32] The annual grant calendar is a grueling one, with most foundation boards reviewing proposals in late spring and around the holidays. For

---

[32]   Egger, *Begging for Change*, 35.

nonprofits that become reliant on these funds, summer and late winter are painfully lean periods. Private foundations, moreover, can be fickle and opaque in their decision making—it is their money after all—and those internal actions can have profoundly detrimental effects on individual nonprofits' day-to-day financial health and ability to plan beyond their next grant. Too many nonprofits become proposal-writing hamsters, chasing grants on a wheel.

Ever the showman, Robert used his start-up funds to do something big and flashy: recovering and re-purposing the leftover food from George H.W. Bush's inauguration. That particular production turned out to be a huge hit, and Robert embraced a philosophy that would guide his fundraising from that day forward: *chase the mission and the money will follow.* It's not an uncommon sentiment. Most nonprofit leaders and professional fundraisers will agree in theory, in no small part because the inverse is so unseemly. In practice, though, most organizations are more reflexive. *Set a broad mission, see who will pay for various parts of it, and emphasize, shape, and fund those parts. If there's money left over, subsidize the less attractive activities or ditch them altogether.* It's pragmatic, but not particularly inspiring.

Running nightclubs, however, had taught Robert all about the importance of inspiring people's imaginations. And so, in its early years, the Kitchen wrote what grant proposals it had to while Egger was out front, drumming up press and publicity. Provoking heart- and mind-changing conversations was part of DC Central Kitchen's central purpose. Egger figured that the more people he could talk to, the better he could serve the mission and the more money would flow in as a result. "What's the fastest, smartest way to make change happen?" he asks, before answering his own query. "Be an example."

Exuding confidence and conviction, Egger captivated audiences. "Robert was absolutely committed to this idea, and donors responded," recalls Chapman Todd. At one point, at the behest of its board, the Kitchen hired a company that specialized in direct mail appeals to potential donors. The hired guns told Robert "to make a straight-out appeal to people's hearts." Their studies showed that more individuals would respond to statements about the sweeping nature of hunger in America, and how hard the Kitchen was trying to help. Robert figured his raw instincts could outdo the pricey professionals. He challenged them to send two letters, each to half of the Kitchen's mailing list. The company would write one, Egger, the other.

The consultants' letter started by saying, "I'm sure you're as upset as I am about the huge number of Americans that go hungry every day. But did you know that among those 36 million hungry people are *14 million children and millions of elderly people?*"

Egger's began with three bullets: "Empowerment. Recycling. Job Training. Let me tell you how we can use our Heads AND our Hearts to address these key social issues." Robert's raised more money.[33] The Kitchen elected to write its future appeals on its own.

While he showed a great aptitude for bringing money in, Robert also proved adept at keeping that money around as long as possible. He never bought anything new and never paid for something used when he could get an even older, more battered version for free. Kitchen equipment, computers, furniture, paper—nothing was purchased unless it was essential and time-sensitive. Robert demanded "maximum results with the minimum amount of resources."[34] Egger's stringent approach

---

[33] "One Man's Hunger to Change the Way Food Charities Operate," *The Chronicle of Philanthropy* (13: 3), November 16, 2000, 29-33.

[34] Egger, *Begging for Change*, 99.

to spending became something of a cultural institution at the Kitchen. "When I got here," says one Kitchen employee hired in the mid-2000s, "people were coming to me asking for permission to buy new pencils. And they would only ask once they'd used that pencil all the way down the nub."

In those tough, early years, Robert's fiscal conservatism served the institution well. As its programs and client base grew, however, uneven donation patterns began to hinder DCCK's daily work. "Making payroll took a lot of very careful checkbook-watching," reports Todd. "But we did secure a $100,000 line of credit from Signet Bank. When things got really tough, Robert would tell us to 'take a bath in that cool, refreshing Signet cash.'" Credit was no substitute for revenue, though, and Robert's daily chatting and cajoling could not fully support the expanding operation.

In 1994, DCCK recovered nearly 400,000 pounds of food and delivered just short of one million meals to more than 60 area agencies. With all the resources that operation demanded, the Culinary Job Training program had become hard to sustain. Now almost six years in, the Kitchen still did not have a full-time training chef. According to Todd, DCCK "had exhausted all the usual suspects in the foundation world just keeping the core food distribution side of things afloat at that point." Even if they did somehow secure a grant for a new position, that person would be vulnerable once that specific line of funding ran out. To avoid the pitfalls of the grant world, Robert and Chapman began searching for a steadier revenue stream.

In 1995, a District nonprofit and clearinghouse for nonprofit services, The Community Partnership for the Prevention of Homelessness (TCP), offered the Kitchen a chance at that steady income. Through the federal Department of Housing and Urban Development (HUD) and its McKinney-Vento Act funding, TCP was charged with assembling a 'continuum of care' for DC homeless residents. To obtain the funds, TCP had to herd DC's disparate nonprofits into a cohesive planning process. Despite their competing values, missions, priorities, and programs, most of the groups involved could agree on one thing: since federal funds would be distributed in accordance with the raw number of people each organization served, they should all try to serve more people. More was better.

Perhaps unsurprisingly, DC Central Kitchen disrupted even this one sliver of consensus. Yes, it was good for shelters and treatment centers to nudge their clients toward job training programs and other services that would help them become independent. But these front-line service providers were paid for each person they initially admitted and then pushed out into another, higher-threshold program like DCCK's, regardless of whether or not the client was prepared for that push. Robert reasoned that the shelters and drug rehab programs thus "had more of an incentive to refer as many people as possible rather than enforcing strict guidelines on who was physically and mentally ready for the Kitchen."[35] Egger and Todd hit the warpath, taking on not only the specific plans for distributing the funds in question, but the larger concept that bigger numbers equated to better, more meaningful results.

For years, the typical focus of HUD's grant-making had been transitional housing programs. Efforts to train and employ homeless citizens fell in a catch-all category of afterthoughts named "Supportive Services Only." The 'people-in' versus 'people-out' style of recordkeeping that worked for transitional programs did not suit the Kitchen, which feared it would be inundated with unprepared students. HUD and TCP expected the Kitchen to measure its success according to the number of people who entered the program compared to the number

---

[35]   Egger, *Begging for Change*, 57.

of people who ultimately got jobs. In that instance, says Todd, "numbers like 50 or 60 percent might look good or great to social service professionals who knew the real deal, but when all these other [housing] programs were showing their funders 95 percent success rates, we couldn't compete, and it would drive us crazy because we knew that those kinds of success rates were not fair comparisons."

DCCK tried to push its students hard early in the course so that uncommitted individuals would "self-select" themselves from the program and, pretty soon, the remaining students would comprise "a group that was going to be focused and, for the most part, stick with it and succeed." As far as Chapman and Robert were concerned, losing "half the class in the first week might be a good sign . . . but from a government contract perspective, it might seem like the program sucks." They agitated for a change in metrics, instead focusing on the level of success in finding employment among those who completed the program. "We went through some serious back-and-forth on the program operation, entrance criteria, rules, what programs we could accept trainees from, and the like," says Chapman. "We got some—but not all—of what we wanted." With a handful of limits and safeguards in place, DC Central Kitchen ultimately did settle down and manage to get its slice of that HUD money. It was enough to hire DCCK's first culinary instructor, Susan Callahan.

Thanks to these funds and Callahan's steadying presence, 1996 was the first year the Kitchen was able to run four full culinary course cycles. The grant entailed strict reporting requirements, which meant Susan, Chapman, and others had to begin conducting more consistent and detailed evaluations of the program. The professionalism that marked DCCK's food recovery operation from the outset finally began to reveal itself in its job training activities. Moreover, these funds were the first supplement to DC Central Kitchen's method of 'rock star fundraising'—where Robert would go on tour, put on a show, and trust the fans to open their wallets. It would take years to bring to fruition, but the Kitchen eventually embraced a more technical, balanced approach to cultivating diverse and sustainable revenue streams.

In the meantime, the organization remained focused on its short-term problem of paying a growing pile of bills. 1997 brought the Kitchen's first run-in with the unintended consequences of restricted funding. Years earlier, a local Presbyterian church with flagging membership had launched a homeless services program. The nonprofit they founded revitalized the institution, expanded its services, and eventually required a new building. Their valuable downtown Washington real estate attracted the attention of the International Monetary Fund, and the church swung a deal to relocate to a more affluent, residential segment of the District. Homeowners near the planned site responded angrily, fearing an influx of panhandling and crime. The fight spilled into the national media and required a Federal ruling in favor of the church's freedom to exercise the charitable dictates of their faith, regardless of the impact on property values.[36]

Unable to persuade a judge, local residents came up with another plan to serve their purposes. They convinced another small nonprofit to retrofit a Winnebago for food service and set it up a few blocks away, farther from the high-end homes, where it effectively pulled unwelcome clients from the neighborhood. Rooted in an uncharitable purpose, it proved to be a less than successful venture. The owners of 'The Winny' ultimately ran into financial difficulty and had to shut down. Egger, always in the market for used equipment, decided to investigate. He soon

---

[36] Interview with Keller, Craig, February 12, 2013; "Our History," Western Presbyterian Church, accessed March 4, 2013, http://www.westernchurch.net/index.php/who_we_are/history/.

won a self-described "coup" in landing The Winny along with some funds dedicated to running it.

While the vehicle came at no financial cost, it was far from free. Robert had to agree to keep The Winny in the same spot, perpetuating the unseemly goals of its previous owner. "The goal was to eventually get it somewhere else east of the [Anacostia] River, where there were no street-level services," says Egger. "Meanwhile, there were dozens of organizations feeding people at different times throughout the day in the same six block radius, just so they could have bragging rights to serving people within view of the White House." Making a distasteful short-term bargain to secure a longer-term vision, Egger saw to it that The Winny became the first mobile home of DCCK's street-level outreach program, First Helping.

First Helping had two fathers. Egger's experiences with the Grate Patrol had instilled in him a desire to do that type of good work, but better. He wanted to offer higher quality food, in line with rigorous sanitation standards. Handing out breakfast sandwiches could not be the focus, though. Instead, meal service would be the Trojan horse through which DCCK attracted homeless clients before planting the seeds of personal progress. Food would be followed with counseling, case management, and referrals. To balance those priorities, First Helping needed to be professionalized and business-like, rather than a rag-tag volunteer outfit. Getting his hands on The Winny was the first step in fulfilling Robert's vision.

As the program was getting started, Egger was tending bar at Chief Ike's Mambo Room on Tuesday nights to earn some extra operating cash. A young man named Craig Keller began turning up at the eclectically decorated Adams Morgan saloon—half tiki bar, half fraternity house basement—to prod Robert into giving him a job at DCCK. Initially, Keller had his eye on an open grant writing position, but carried a resume that listed graduate degrees from Harvard and MIT along with time spent living in the Community for Creative Non-Violence (CCNV) as a homelessness activist. Instead of handing him their grant portfolio, Robert and Chapman realized they had someone who could run The Winny and its associated program well. "Craig had a pretty clear vision of what he wanted to do, and he turned up at the right time to fit into an opportunity that DCCK had stumbled into," recalls Todd. "He was the right man for the job. It was a combination of us having to do this street feeding program . . . as a condition of us getting the money that we wanted and needed . . . One thing led to another and First Helping was born."

In the late Eighties, Keller had hoped to be an academic who performed social service work on the side. Eventually, he flipped that plan, and took a part-time, $10-an-hour job at DCCK. In addition to sharing Robert's commitment to serving food with a sense of dignity, Keller wanted "to build trust and respect through service." Clients began asking Keller for help navigating the social service system, looking for everything from metro tokens to mental health treatment, IDs to eyeglasses. Craig dedicated himself to having updated, comprehensive information on hand for them. He started providing meals in Northeast DC's Ivy City neighborhood at a series of city-owned trailers outfitted with bunk beds to house 24 people at a time. When the local drug treatment programs that he referred clients to were unresponsive, Keller drove clients to West Virginia or Baltimore for treatment—all while getting two or three miles per gallon in his lumbering Winnebago.

As First Helping's services grew, so did its community profile and need for funds. When the unseemly bargain around The Winny ran out after three years, Keller began bidding on contracts issued by DC's business improvement districts and The Community Partnership to perform outreach services in different neighborhoods, contracts Egger had generally tried to shy away from. Keller added staff and young AmeriCorps volunteers. First Helping ultimately moved into a new office downtown, and at its peak swelled to 19 staff members, some 40 percent of the Kitchen's total employee roster at the time. Robert started calling Keller "Craig, Inc."

Under Keller's leadership, First Helping began to pride itself in the technical quality of its social services and call for greater programmatic integration across DC's continuum of care. The Kitchen, meanwhile, was more interested in the power of food and tough love than clinical best practices. There was talk of spinning off First Helping as its own organization. "First Helping took many of its cues from the Kitchen," recalls Keller, "but in many ways it took on a life of its own." He knew that the relationship was complex, yet continued to see great value in DCCK's "absolutely amazing support," which included everything from free food and fundraising assistance to health insurance and accounting services.

Ultimately, the question resolved itself when First Helping lost anything resembling an ability to stand on its own. Keller elected to leave the program after a decade at its head. The leadership transition, combined with public sector belt-tightening and inside baseball, wreaked havoc on the outreach program's large but undiversified funding base. First Helping's handful of sizeable contracts began to expire, shrink, or end up in the hands of other organizations. The tight restrictions embedded in each contract meant that First Helping had little latitude in directing the location or scope of its services. Before long, the attrition of its contracts meant that the program's services were restricted to one small corner of the downtown 'Golden Triangle' neighborhood and the severely underserved communities east of the Anacostia River. The diminished position of First Helping pained Keller. Referring to the combined impact of his departure and the role of city officials in the contract mess, Keller argues that "the work that we should not be personality-based. It should be in systems that survive after people leave."

Keller is right, but relatively few organizations are able to build the robust systems, programs, and brands necessary to move beyond the power of individual personalities. Despite the gains First Helping and the Kitchen's job training program made in receiving structured funding from groups like The Community Partnership through the Nineties, DC Central Kitchen's overall fundraising still largely relied on Robert Egger's connections and charisma. And much of Egger's big, brash persona became associated with his militant take on financial management.

Egger was unafraid to draw sharp distinctions between his organization and other notable players in the nonprofit sector. Truly convinced that the nonprofit pie was only so big, he reacted with violent revulsion when other organizations or their leaders seemed to be more interested in 'getting theirs' than doing good. At any given time, Robert was known to have a mental list of those he deemed the leading and latest examples of self-interested hypocrites draining the sector of finite resources. A common culprit was the CEO of an area anti-hunger group that had an annual budget strikingly similar to DC Central Kitchen's. While Egger set his salary at just $55,000 in 1998, his counterpart earned $145,000 that same year. A decade later, that same executive's compensation had swelled upwards of $350,000.[37]

He also famously savaged controversial fundraiser Dan Pallotta in print—an uncommon public airing of grievances in a nonprofit world that is awfully proud of its ability to play

[37]   Rucker, Philip, "Chief's Pay Criticized as Charity Cuts Back," *The Washington Post*, July 17, 2008, accessed November 16, 2012, http://www.washingtonpost.com/wp-dyn/content/article/2008/07/16/AR2008071602658.html?/

nice. For a decade, Pallotta's TeamWorks organization ran and promoted hugely popular bike rides for charity, breaking new ground in grassroots fundraising and cause marketing. But when the public discovered that, on average, 45 cents of every dollar he raised went to 'overhead' administrative costs, not charitable causes, he faced a revolt. By comparison, most legitimate charities spend between 10 and 25 percent of their resources on overhead. His salary, some $394,500 annually, seemed to confirm suspicions that Pallotta was diverting undue resources from his stated cause.[38] By the time his DC AIDSRide rolled into town in 2002, Pallotta and his team managed to direct just $500,000 to local AIDS-related charities—of out $3,600,000 raised.[39] The company folded shortly thereafter.

Egger ripped Pallotta for having "strip-mined the causes of AIDS and breast cancer for his own gain" and left the nonprofits that relied on the money he raised to "contend with an angry and betrayed donor pool, a local community that's more wary of these types of charitable events, and operations that grew accustomed to the cash flow from these events." Pallotta fired back with a successful book, and since has developed a reputation as an industry "maverick," demanding fair pay for top talent in the nonprofit sector.[40] He argued that TeamWorks brought more money and more awareness to the causes it championed than any other promoter could have. Who cared what percentage went to charity as long as the absolute number of dollars reaching those organizations continued to grow?

For all of Egger's hardline rhetoric, much of his agitation entailed calling for a reasoned approach between two

---

38   Wilhelm, Ian, "A Maverick's Defense," *The Chronicle of Philanthropy*, December 11, 2008, accessed November 16, 2012, http://philanthropy.com/article/A-Mavericks-Defense/57518/.

39   Egger, *Begging for Change*, 93.

40   *Ibid.*

unacceptable extremes. While he targeted Pallotta for incurring excessive overhead costs, Robert also decried the widespread assumption that "if a high percentage of every donation goes to serving 'the cause,' the organization [must be] 'efficient' . . . 'efficient' doesn't translate into 'effective.'"[41] He railed against the unreliable nature of grant funding and its onerous reporting requirements while demanding that donors do their homework on the nonprofits they supported. By becoming more informed, Egger said, donors could ensure that only those agencies that demonstrated results survived. The rest, he figured, should be relegated to the forces of creative destruction. Supporters called him a visionary. Detractors labeled him a hypocrite.

Robert's most charged battle took place within the walls of his headquarters, between his basement kitchen and its upstairs neighbor, the Community for Creative Nonviolence (CCNV). With Mitch Snyder's passing, his partner in love and work, Carol Fennelly, had assumed leadership of the storied organization. For two decades, CCNV had premised its programming on the assumption that homeless people were just like anyone else; they just didn't have homes. "It wasn't true," says Egger. "It's not dehumanizing people to say that they're in deep, that they need serious help to get back on their feet." Within the thick walls of that shelter, CCNV attempted to live out an egalitarian ideal, where clients, staff, and directors all lived together—and individuals often fit into more than one of those categories. There was no formal case management structure and no timeline for moving people out of the shelter into real homes. While Snyder's charisma and vision had covered up many of these day-to-day deficiencies, later leaders were less successful in keeping up appearances.

After three years of Fennelly's tenure, her brusque management style and supposed opposition to change had

---

41   Egger, *Begging for Change*, 96.

alienated others within the organization. A *60 Minutes* exposé alleged "that some shelter employees were selling drugs and donated clothes."[42] While there was a clear need to improve the organization, Fennelly's race may also have been a factor. Fennelly and Snyder were both white; the profound majority of their clients and colleagues, black. The racial divisions DCCK had sidestepped wracked CCNV. The shelter's directors staged a coup, and appointed formerly homeless computer programmer and failed drug dealer Keith Mitchell to run the organization. A homeless man running a shelter—something that could really only happen at CCNV—attracted plenty of initial attention, much of it positive. Early on, Mitchell appeared to be a force for progress. He pledged to offer professional case management and limit shelter stays to one year. He pledged a more authentic and representative approach to leadership. "I'm not Mitch," he told *The Washington Post* at time of his ascension to the top job. "I'm not a saint. Let Carol be the last saint. We'll make mistakes. But we want to prove we can do this."[43]

From inauspicious beginnings, Mitchell began an audacious effort to expand his power and influence. Though he initially pledged to shy away from politics, in a matter of months Mitchell was campaigning for the office of DC's shadow representative. He was disqualified, however, because the hundreds of homeless residents who signed his ballot bid had listed their mailing address in lieu of a residential one.

Two years later, his store of public goodwill disappeared as quickly as it came. In the fall of 1996, an internal audit, conducted, in part, due to the urgings of a suspicious Egger and DC Central Kitchen, reached *The Washington Post*. CCNV

---

[42] Twomey, "The homeless are where her heart is."

[43] Sanchez, Rene, "A Leader of Homeless Who Walked the Walk; New Director Came to CCNV off Streets," *The Washington Post*, February 14, 1994, A1.

had previously received a $200,000 HUD grant to develop the case management system Mitchell promised to institute. The audit proved that Mitchell had wildly misused those funds. He claimed that, instead of providing case management, he had spent the grant money on immediate needs, like food—even though DC Central Kitchen had delivered CCNV's meals for free each day. Egger publicly refuted Mitchell's assertions, and the audit showed Mitchell had cashed $50,000 in personal checks he made out to himself. Moreover, federal funds had supported his legal expenses stemming from a DUI charge. He had also recently moved out of CCNV and into a townhouse, raising further suspicions. Mitchell was unrepentant, declaring his intention to become mayor. "This is my right of passage as a black leader," he defiantly told *The Post*.[44]

Unlike in Hollywood, where any publicity is good publicity, among nonprofits, anonymity always beats bad press. Image is everything, and any betrayal of trust provokes swift and sweeping backlash from donors, media outlets, and regulators. A nonprofit turning out to be ineffective is understandable, even expected, but one caught in the acts of embezzlement and self-enrichment faces a special fury. CCNV's transgressions were especially disappointing, given the organization's central role in passing the 1987 McKinney-Vento Act, which secured the HUD funds it later squandered. At the center of a press firestorm and federal investigation, Mitchell was charged with theft and making false statements. He pleaded guilty in March of 1997.[45]

Egger was incensed. "Our greatest currency in the nonprofit sector isn't money. It's trust," he argues. CCNV's shortcomings threatened to further discourage donors already let down by a

---

[44]   Harris, Hamil R. and Robert E. Pierre, "Internal Audit Sparked Federal Probe at D.C. Shelter," *The Washington Post*, November 4, 1996, B1.

[45]   Miller, Bill, "Ex-Shelter Director Pleads Guilty to Taking Funds," *The Washington Post*, March 6, 1998, B5.

series of scandals in local DC politics. "At some point, I was afraid funders would just up and say, 'screw DC, you're all corrupt' and it would hurt all the organizations doing good work here," he says. But while other organizations ran for cover, Robert saw an opportunity to change the face of homelessness in DC forever.

From the day DC Central Kitchen moved into the basement of the Federal City Shelter, its continued presence there has been uncertain. It has no lease, and instead operates according to a Memorandum of Understanding that guarantees only minimal notice from the District before the Kitchen can be removed for any reason. "This is a full city block in the heart of downtown, DC," says Egger. "The land is worth 20 or 30 million dollars to developers. The day will come when a cash-strapped city sells that land, and we needed to be prepared for that."

Egger proceeded to tug ears, twist elbows, and kiss asses all across the District, trying to win support for a radical new plan: "Sell the shelter and let a developer knock it to the ground. Buy land over near the convention center—a mixed neighborhood— and poll the residents about what type of retail locations they wanted but didn't have. Then build a full-service center with the first floor dedicated to retail. Upstairs, you'd have shelter facilities, social service agencies, and training programs that worked with the retail outlets to prepare people for good jobs. And of course you'd have a new kitchen that could help us meet the growing demand for our meals and job training program." In a letter to then-Mayor Anthony Williams, Egger envisioned a "job training and employment machine" that would generate enough excess revenue to "seed a partnership with Fannie Mae, the Housing Authority, local unions, construction companies and volunteer groups to renovate 100 [or more] units of delinquent housing." These units could provide a temporary, transitional independent living program, lasting between six and 12 months, "for those who have passed through the shelter system and who are now earning money." The independent living initiative would help recovering individuals sustain and consolidate their progress toward self-sufficiency in a way that required a minimal amount of taxpayer dollars. Egger told Williams his idea was "a public relations master stroke."[46]

He made some initial headway among District officials and potential partners who were sick of the chaotic corruption spilling out of the enormous shelter on Second Street. "But they lost their nerve," Robert seethes, recalling the episode. When the media coverage and public outraged fizzled, so did the city's willingness to embrace a sea change in its approach to homeless. Blaming "the ghost of Mitch Snyder," Egger asserts that it was easier to scold CCNV and muddle through with a decrepit building and ineffective programs than uproot entrenched organizations and take on the risks associated with trying something new. Keith Mitchell isn't the great villain in Egger's narrative, nor is the organization he led. The villain is the confluence of widespread cowardice, limited imagination, and petty self-interest that led the District's leaders to accept the unacceptable. Authority figures once again failed to follow through on Robert's vision.

Egger's super-shelter never happened. The Federal City Shelter still stands. For its part, CCNV rallied to meet its financial obligations, modernize its programs, and recover some of its standing in the community. Yet Robert's campaign against nonprofit corruption was far from over.

As memories of Keith Mitchell faded, a much bigger, more pervasive scandal was starting to smolder at the United Way of the National Capital Area, a prominent institution and, at the time, perhaps the single leading figure in the DC nonprofit

---

[46] Correspondence from Egger, Robert to Mayor Anthony Williams, August 18, 1999.

community. His public outrage over the Mitchell scandal helped establish Egger as an impassioned advocate for responsible financial management. He was brash and outspoken. Sometimes, in the eyes of many, he spoke too much. Even among those who disliked his irreverent tone, however, Egger had a reputation as an incorruptible fiscal pit bull, rigorous in his cost controls and vehemently opposed to self-professed do-gooders getting rich with other people's money.

The reputation of the local United Way chapter, meanwhile, was far less impressive. Oral Suer, who had headed the organization for almost 30 years, was caught using company credit cards and salary advances to illegally obtain nearly $2 million above and beyond his salary, already just shy of $200,000 annually.[47] He ultimately plead guilty to defrauding the organization of a half a million dollars—but not before his successor, Norman O. Taylor, could sign him to a sweetheart deal, including a $6,000 per month "consulting contract" and a $1 million pension.[48] Taylor's complicity meant that the era of abuse did not end with Suer. Under Taylor, posh executive compensation continued—he earned $225,000 annually—and more dishonest practices emerged.

Every nonprofit relies on the good faith of its contributors, as it takes their money and in turn pledges to use those dollars in the best possible ways, smartly advancing its stated mission. For the United Way, however, this foundation of faith takes on an even higher level of importance. Originally rooted in the Community Chest organizations of the early 20th century, United Way chapters act as monetary clearing houses, conducting massive fundraising campaigns that appeal to area employers

---

[47] Wolverton, Brad, "What Went Wrong?" *The Chronicle of Philanthropy*, September 4, 2003.

[48] Johnston, David Cay, "Grand Jury Is Investigating United Way in Washington," *The New York Times*, July 17, 2002.

and their workers. Donors give directly to the United Way, and the United Way pledges that it will pass those funds on to nonprofits that have been carefully vetted and shown to do good work on behalf of the community. When this model works, it produces remarkable efficiencies. Donors do not need to research individual groups. Charities can spend less time chasing down donations and instead receive steady, predictable income. And at their best, United Ways become central hubs for distributing financial resources, coordinating community-wide projects, and disseminating best practices.

The United Way of the National Capital Area (UWNCA) took that idealized model and shot it all to hell. Under Suer and then Taylor, that United Way chapter "counted as its own money that it had not helped raise, charged different donors different prices for its services and gave executives excessive perquisites."[49] Sometimes those different prices turned into outright price gouging. In certain cases, "62 percent of contributions that had not been earmarked for specific charities were used to cover administrative expenses."[50] The UWNCA had a uniquely strong position because of its Combined Federal Campaign (CFC), an effort that worked with government agencies to proactively solicit charitable gifts from federal workers. As the seat of American government, Washington, DC's CFC was and remains the nation's largest, making it big business for the United Way and a host of marketing groups seeking to help individual charities stand out from the rest of the CFC crowd. The tremendous influx of funds, some $90 million at its height, became a private piggy bank for UWNCA executives who assumed their stellar brand

---

49   Strom, Stephanie, "Washington United Way Names an Interim Chief," *The New York Times*, September 21, 2002.
50   Strom, "Washington United Way."

was above reproach and their detached, uninformed board of directors would never catch on, let alone call them out.[51]

In the fall 2002, however, other UWNCA staffers decided they had seen enough, and began publicly blowing the whistle on Taylor. After 19 months of internal agitation, the UWNCA's director of corporate fundraising campaigns issued a memorandum to the board outlining Taylor's abuses, which was later leaked to *The New York Times*.[52] Taylor went from embattled to unemployed.[53] The UWNCA desperately needed new leadership, a United Way outsider who still knew nonprofits, someone who could remain above the reproach of auditors and prying journalists while inspiring nervous donors to start giving again. They called Robert Egger.

Egger was surprised and flattered when a humbled pillar of the old guard asked for his help. "I'm a jerk," he freely admits. "But I'm a jerk who steps up." Despite his critiques of most every element of the nonprofit status quo, Egger had always appreciated the United Way. "Without its support," he says, "we never would have been able to expand the DC Central Kitchen's services to include a job training program or our for-profit catering division." When local groups began beating their chests and pointing out that they weren't "like the United Way" Egger came to the weakened organization's defense. He figured there was "no reason to kick it while it was down. If this organization went under, so too would many of the organizations that relied

---

51 Greenwell, Megan, "21 Regional Nonprofits Withdraw From United Way," *The Washington Post*, April 29, 2009.

52 Johnston, David Cay, "United Way Official Knew About Abuses, Memo Says," *The New York Times*, September 3, 2002.

53 Salmon, Jacqueline L. and Peter Whoriskey, "Audit Excoriates United Way Leadership," *The Washington Post*, June 25, 2004.

on its monthly checks."[54] He accepted the offer to climb aboard the United Way's sinking vessel and take its wheel.

From his first day at the United Way, everything Egger did was about money—both how he brought it in, and what he did with it. UWNCA was in the middle of its hallmark campaign, and giving was non-existent. When a *Washington Post* interviewer asked why people should bother to give to a group that had betrayed its trust, Egger eschewed the usual guilt trips in favor of a logical appeal. As the head of DCCK, "I needed to be able to function like a business. I needed to be able to plan and develop long-term strategies. When people give to [the United Way], their money is pooled and through that process of combining donations big and small, I was able to receive a monthly check from the United Way that I could count on. Please remember, while it's important to give, impact is what's really important. When an organization can plan and build, that's when you're going to get impact. Not when they have to rely on random donations."[55] And when so many donors' response had been to head to the sidelines, Egger urged them to head back into the fray. "What I'm after and what we want to build is a community-based United Way. This is what I tell people . . . it's your United Way. Jump in with both feet. Volunteer. Serve on the board. Make some noise. It's not about one interim Vice President or new board, although those are great steps."[56]

Despite his rhetorical acumen, Egger knew that his actions would be his best form of communication. Robert's first action as the UWNCA's new Executive Vice President was to set his annual salary at $85,000, a third of what Taylor had made. "It was a huge pay increase for me because I'd been making $55,000 a

54   Egger, *Begging for Change*, 54.
55   Levey, Bob, "Q&A with Bob Levy," *The Washington Post*, October 8, 2002.
56   Levey, "Q&A."

year at the Kitchen, but a lot of people were surprised, given the fact that the average annual salary for the head of a UW chapter is more than $200,000."[57] His new colleagues at the United Way, as well as several other DC nonprofit directors, urged him not to make a show of his salary and "take at least $150,000." If he would work for cheap, how would it make his higher-paid subordinates or the heads of other chapters look? Egger had been hired, however, with the expectation that he would trim at least 30 full-time employees from a bloated UWNCA payroll. He saw the compensation question as a case study for his theory about zero-sum nonprofit economics. "Agreeing to a salary of $85,000 rather than $150,000 or $220,000 would be the difference between keeping a couple of mid-level or front-line employees rather than firing them. Sure, I could have gotten a higher salary, but would that have been the right thing to do?"[58] Moreover, Egger knew that the majority of UWNCA campaign contributors were working and middle class, making less than $60,000 each year. "I think it's important," he told *The Post* at the time, "that these generous givers are able to relate and see that I'm in this for the right reasons."[59]

Among other reforms, Egger oversaw the installation of an entirely new board of directors, a 30 percent reduction in staff, and the implementation of "a flat 10 percent charge covering administrative and fundraising costs." It was bitter medicine, but it laid the essential groundwork for a rebuilding effort that would last a decade. The selection of Egger had been an uncharacteristically bold move for the stolid United Way, and it snapped several key community leaders into action. Upon seeing Robert's early results, the head of utility giant Pepco fired off a press release, saying "I actively support Robert Egger

---

[57]   Egger, *Begging for Change*, 54.

[58]   Egger, *Begging for Change*, 55.

[59]   Levey, "Q&A."

as interim executive director, and have great confidence in UWNCA's new board of directors. These factors—combined with the fiscal management reforms adopted at UWNCA—make me confident in our decision to commit our support."[60] Egger had a new stage, and he began directing a high-profile show of his principles.

Robert's departure necessitated some big changes back in the basement kitchen on Second Street. While he was contemplating the move to the United Way, Egger phoned DCCK General Manager Cynthia Rowland and took her to a Saturday morning breakfast. He explained that he was leaning towards accepting the position. "But the only way I can do this," he told Cynthia, "is if you take over DC Central Kitchen." Egger said he would return to DCCK after he had righted the United Way ship, but with no clear timetable. For the foreseeable future, someone else had to lead DCCK.

After four years at the Kitchen, Cynthia knew the organization inside and out. She understood its programs, its cash flow, and its mission. What the introverted Rowland hated and dreaded, however, were the public aspects of nonprofit leadership and fundraising in particular. "I was honored," she says, "but I am not a fundraiser. I don't like it." Though conflicted, Rowland's appetite for new challenges won out, leading her to say yes, conditionally. The board of directors would need to come through in a major way, and give her the support she needed to keep the press requests and donations flowing.

DC Central Kitchen had always been led by Robert Egger. Each nonprofit board is different, and while DCCK's had

---

[60] Dobkin, Robert, "Pepco Affirms United Way Funding, Endorses New Leadership," Pepco press release, December 16, 2002, accessed 16 November 2012, http://www.pepco.com/welcome/news/releases/archives/2002/article.aspx?cid=241/.

plenty of avid fans, its members had played a comparatively passive role in steering the organization. "When Robert left," remembers Rowland, "they had to get more involved and more engaged." At Cynthia's request, the board convened an emergency meeting a few days after Egger's departure. "They really stepped up," says Rowland, "I knew I had the whole board behind me."

Rowland's strongest backer was the board's chair, a boisterous, charismatic Spanish chef named José Andrés. First introduced to the Kitchen by his business partner and then-DCCK board member Rob Wilder, Andrés had already been active with national hunger-fighting nonprofit Share Our Strength. "Maybe it was because I was young," recalls José in his glimmering office in DC's revitalized Penn Quarter, "but I felt like Share Our Strength was not the right place for me. I was looking for somewhere to belong." He wanted to connect with something more local in a city he had lived in for years but still barely knew. At Wilder's suggestion, Andrés headed down to Second Street to volunteer at DCCK. "It was the first time ever in my life that I was in a room and I was the only white person," he remembers. Until that day, Andrés had believed "DC was a dangerous city. But after a few hours in that environment, I asked myself why society creates these stereotypes. We see things as strange only because we have never experienced them." The trap of the calculated epiphany was set. As José began to interact with the students and staff, Robert emerged and engaged the young chef in a fast-paced yet meandering conversation about poverty, service, and jobs. "Robert is quick to fire you up on topics like hunger and creating opportunity. And he's always 100 miles ahead . . . he planted a seed in me." Andrés' first trip to the Kitchen became a freeing experience. "I became an addict of the Kitchen," he says. The trap had been sprung.

Andrés' passion quickly led him to the DCCK board, and then to the position of chair—moves that mirrored his meteoric rise to the top of America's culinary scene, where he received his own PBS show, a James Beard award, and a lecturing gig at Harvard. "I was probably the most unprepared chair in the history of any nonprofit," he says with a laugh. Shortly into his tenure, Robert announced his plan to leave the Kitchen for the United Way. "It was shocking," remembers José. "But Robert said, 'The Kitchen is more than me. It's an idea bigger than of all of us.' Not all leaders can convince their followers of that. But he made me believe that." José had come to know Rowland well, calling her "a very good leader," and vowed to support her in any way he could.

The board gave Rowland license to hire the Kitchen's "first real Development Director." Through the Nineties, Egger had hired a string of narrowly trained grant writers. Because he was so good with an audience, Robert figured he really only needed someone who could handle the tedious cycle of proposal writing and reporting while he devoted his time to showmanship. In time, that division of labor "stretched him so thin," Rowland recalls, and when it was time for her to succeed him, those shoes were simply too big. She hired a well-rounded development professional who wrote the organization's first fundraising plan, preparing DCCK for a variety of grant deadlines and cash flow concerns.

Rowland certainly needed the help. As head of the local United Way chapter, Robert was barred from corresponding with her, a strict separation that forced DCCK to sink or swim without him. In some ways, Cynthia enjoyed running the show, and true to her character, she focused on achieving gradual, steady improvements in program outcomes. "Ultimately," however, "these roles weighed on me. I finally experienced some of that 'it's lonely at the top' syndrome."

When Robert did return to the Kitchen in 2004 after an eleven-month tenure that set the United Way on the path to restoring its credibility, he says he "knew I would have to be the one who adjusted, not the people who had grown and evolved while I was gone." Even so, Rowland was torn. "Staying in my current position did not make sense, but going back to our old roles didn't make sense either." She stayed on for a few months as Executive Director, while Robert assumed the title of President. "It was uncomfortable being the ED," she says, "but it felt uncomfortable to not be the ED either." Egger, sensing her frustration and fatigue, told her to take a month off to get her bearings back.

Several major figures in the DCCK's history—Cynthia Rowland, Chapman Todd, Susan Callahan, Ron Swanson, and Marianne Ali among them—speak in strikingly similar terms about the bipolar character of the Kitchen. *Exciting but exhausting. Challenging but fun. Energizing but tiring.* The specter of staff burnout was a constant presence in the alternately too hot or too cold basement kitchen. In other organizations, high levels of attrition among senior staff would seem to indict the leader who remained a constant fixture throughout. Each of these individuals, however, speaks effusively of Robert Egger, on and off the record.

For more than two decades, Egger's energy, enthusiasm, and irrepressible optimism inspired the people around him to elevate their work. Yet few could keep pace with him for long. Employment at DCCK is more a sprint than a marathon, and Egger told several employees over the years that their strides had slowed too much, that it was time for them to move on. Some staffers, including Ali and Swanson, just needed a break, and returned recharged. Rowland, however, resolved little during her time away. "I started to feel that I wasn't bringing my best to the Kitchen. And I was starting to feel an itch to replicate the work I'd done in my early days at the Kitchen for other groups as a consultant." She did not wait for her coach to call her to the sideline. In the summer of 2004, she asked Robert to begin the process of hiring her replacement.

Part II: Mike Curtin's Kitchen, 2004-2012

Chapter 6 Broke

Like Robert Egger, Northern Virginia native Michael F. Curtin, Jr. was a fixture in the local restaurant scene. And like Cynthia Rowland, he had a resume that was all business. A proud contrarian, Mike was a devout Catholic steeped in eastern religion and a privileged graduate of Williams College who flamed out of his pre-med major by flunking Math 107. He was a lifelong community service volunteer with a fiery, score-settling temperament that made him a successful, if undersized, rugby player. Light-haired with a ruddy complexion and closely-cropped goatee, Curtin's outward appearance is as Irish as the blood in his veins.

The son of a successful attorney bearing the same name, the younger Curtin attended Gonzaga College High School, a storied Jesuit institution in a tough part of DC, not far from the building DC Central Kitchen would one day call home. As part of their commitment to social justice, the Jesuits converted the basement of one pricey Gonzaga building into a charitable outfit that provided meals and comfort to homeless men frequenting the city blocks around the school. The Father McKenna Center, named for a prominent member of the Gonzaga faculty, attracted a line of men each morning that stretched past the campus's brick entrance on North Capitol Street. As a freshman,

Mike recalls deciding that "I didn't want to walk by them. I wanted to come to school early and help."

A few years later, after failing that college math class, Curtin was in need of a new undergraduate course of study. "Basically," he confesses, "I needed to find classes that didn't end in '-*ology*.'" Curtin soon became intrigued by Japanese culture and spent his post-college years in Osaka as part of a shaky, slow developing plan of someday returning to the US and "making a million dollars off of being 'the Japan guy,' whatever the hell that was."

In the late Eighties, he headed back to DC and caught on with a few flush Japanese corporate types who wanted to renovate a downtown hotel and happened to need an American-born Japan guy as a go-between. Curtin came to love the restaurant business and ultimately opened his own in an affluent District suburb, naming it The Broad Street Grill. Designed to be "the Cheers of Falls Church," the Grill became "a busy community gathering place." That community orientation meant that Curtin soon found himself inundated with requests from nearby nonprofits looking for help hosting events and raising money. Curtin decided he would pick two organizations and channel his impact. One group was called Hoop Dreams, the other DC Central Kitchen. A mutual friend seated on the Kitchen's board had introduced Curtin to Egger at a social function. Mike asked lots of questions about DCCK and, in Robert's recollection, "had this incredible energy for social justice." As the conversation percolated, it turned to a semi-notable public figure whom Curtin described, with impressive frankness, as "crazier than a shithouse rat." Both passionate, pragmatic, and profane, Robert and Mike developed a quick and easy rapport.

On the outside, Curtin's restaurant was a successful pillar of his hometown. But a business designed to run on tight margins could not withstand the loss of an early investor and a crippling cash flow problem. "Pay day was the worst day in the world for me," he remembers. *'How am I gonna pay these people?'* was the question that plagued his waking moments. Mike concealed his struggles from his wife and father, convinced that he would find some new way forward under his own power. "I was way too proud to admit that I was failing from a financial standpoint." In his darkest, lonely moments closing up the restaurant for the night, Curtin wondered if his family might be better off without him.

One Saturday morning, hopelessly in debt, he called his father for help. The elder Curtin guided him through the process of declaring for bankruptcy. "Here I was, this guy who had attended great schools, become a business owner—but I had to tell the world I was a failure. I had to accept that I was at the bottom and start digging out."

Curtin worked on a few consulting gigs, trying to run down a steady paycheck. As he and his wife Maureen worked to cobble together their household finances and provide for their three children, Mike discovered the open posting for Cynthia Rowland's replacement on a Friday afternoon. He fired off an application immediately and called the head of Hoop Dreams, a woman he knew was close with Robert. He explained his interest in the position. She hung up on him. Then, she picked up the receiver and called Egger. Robert rang Mike moments later, and they set up a meeting for the next morning. Egger walked away from that Saturday breakfast impressed. "I wasn't looking for a seasoned nonprofit professional. And beyond his general business sense, I really liked that Mike seemed like he had something to prove."

Maureen joined Mike for a walk-through of the facility on Second Street the following Monday. As they walked by the insulated Cambro cubes where DCCK's hot meals were stored as they awaited delivery, Mike noticed a white sheet of paper taped to one of the Cambros stacked at eye level. The box was destined for the Father McKenna Center. "The Kitchen pulled together all the threads of my life," Curtin declares, "Japan, my restaurant, the Jesuits." Perhaps more importantly, his long, draining decline to financial rock bottom infused him with a sense of humility and gratefulness that another man of his abilities and advantages might have lacked. "I feel a connection to the Kitchen [because] it was a chance to rebuild my life. Like our students, I came here broken, looking to become the person I wanted to be."

Once he started at DCCK full-time, Mike's mix of for-profit skills and nonprofit volunteer experience gave him a unique perspective on leading a direct service organization. "I came in wanting to do good, but knew that I couldn't do good for everyone. I wanted things that were tangible, real, and had measurable results, things that would create small little pockets of victory." The same way a good restaurateur keeps a keen eye on his food and labor costs, Curtin sought to maximize DCCK's achievements on the margins, where a nonprofit with a small operating budget could make a big difference.

Like Robert, Mike appreciated the value of a good show. An early mentor of Curtin's told him that a restaurant is 'living theater.' "If you think about the last time you had an amazing night out on your birthday, or your anniversary, you don't remember what you ordered," Mike explains. "You remember the experience. The food is almost the least important piece, because by the time you've even sat down, let alone tasted your meal, you've made six judgments about the place that will determine your memory of that night." Curtin knew that helping the Kitchen continue its ascent would not involve simply finding new ways to hand out more food. "I had to ask, what's going to make my show better, or different, than all the others?" Early on in his Kitchen tenure, Mike saw DCCK's greatest show: a graduation ceremony for its Culinary Job Training program. Each one brings tears to the eyes of most everyone in attendance, from tough ex-convicts wearing gleaming white jackets to skeptical corporate types seeing if the Kitchen is worth a donation. Halfway through the event, Curtin was already awed and leaned over to Egger.

"This is amazing," Mike whispered. Robert bobbed his eyebrows playfully and smiled.

"This shit never gets old," he replied.

While he quickly took to the Kitchen's theatrical style, Mike started with even less nonprofit fundraising experience than Cynthia Rowland. "Never having been a wealthy man myself, it was hard for me to understand how philanthropic people could be." Even today, "I'm not entirely comfortable asking people for money," he confesses, "but I've always been very comfortable talking about we do, the impact we have—and then the conversation reaches a natural point where we talk about the impact we can have together." Drawing on his deep reserves of Jesuit imagery, Curtin casts himself as more of a fundraising role player. "I feel like a priest on Easter. If you've got the material, you almost can't help but knock it out of the park."

While Mike took his cues from the love gospel of the Book of John, Robert often said that he preferred to take his from the Book of James—James Brown, that is. In fact, Robert's philosophy on fundraising was rooted in his nightclub-running past. As he wrote in 2004, his second career drumming up donations had a lot to do with his old gig handling drunk drummers and demanding fans. Both took "a modest dose of bullshit, a serious commitment to the bottom line, and dedication to putting on a good show day in and day out."[61] Rock and roll was in the Kitchen's DNA, and though Curtin would ultimately emerge as a nonprofit executive with legitimate fundraising chops, it was perhaps no coincidence that someone with a music industry

---

[61] Egger, *Begging for Change*, xvii.

background would step up to lead DCCK's development activities to new heights.

Brian MacNair grew up outside of New York City, learning how to talk fast and cut to the core of any conversation. He headed upstate for college, studying the music business and earning pocket money by serving up wings at BJ's, a Fredonia dive. Brian was working in the kitchen when BJ's defeated two hot sauce-slinging local legends, Duff's and the Anchor Bar, in a staged battle for the best buffalo wing. MacNair moved to Manhattan after graduation, working in the record industry for several years. He loved the music but hated the business. "It was too aggressive for me," he recalls. He took his sales acumen to Outward Bound, where he developed new skills in running fundraising galas, cultivating individual contributors, and managing donor databases. Special events were his passion, merging the thrill of putting on a great show with a sense of social meaning he never found in the music biz. But after a decade of New York nonprofit work, MacNair needed a new challenge. He thought back to those days in Duff's kitchen, decided to become a chef, and moved to Washington, DC for a job running hotel banquets.

Brian liked cooking, but missed having a real mission. He started scoping out volunteer opportunities, and eventually found DC Central Kitchen in 2003. Once a week, he headed to Second Street from his home in Alexandria, Virginia, tied a bandana around his head, and helped prepare the Kitchen's meals. "On my first day in the kitchen, I noticed a tall, middle aged man smiling at me from the other end of the prep table," Brian remembers. "I smiled back and said hi. Turned out he just wanted to talk. He told me he had been in prison for 15 years, decided to turn his life around, and got out and did all the right things. But no one would hire him. After a year, he was out on the street, and told his parole officer he was heading back to prison, where at least he'd have three square meals. The P.O. said, 'Before you do that, why don't you go check out DC Central Kitchen.' So he came down here, but was pretty down on himself, saying 'no one would give me a job.' One of the Kitchen supervisors told him, 'You did 15 years? I did ten. Guy over there did 20. Now put on an apron and start chopping.'"

"As it turns out," Brian says, smiling, "that man was in the last week of the culinary training program and already had a job lined up on Monday. I was hooked." MacNair became a regular presence at the Kitchen, and eventually DCCK's staff got wind of the volunteer chef with a fundraising background and rock and roll soul. MacNair hesitated for a few months, but their pestering eventually convinced him that the Kitchen was the perfect place to blend his passions. He joined the organization in August 2003.

Broad-chested with a 6'2" frame, MacNair is physically imposing, but his ready smile constantly cuts through his black beard. His large hands swallow most others' when he shakes them, and his mother's Italian blood gave him a swarthy complexion that lets him blend in with nearly any ethnic group like a cultural chameleon. Valuable as that versatility would prove to be at a diverse organization like DCCK, that dark skin and thick facial hair nearly put him on a federal watch list when proposing to his flight attendant girlfriend. After boarding a flight she was working, he, with the blessing of her co-workers, snatched the intercom with the intention of making a public proposal. A bearded brown man making sudden moves on a plane after 9/11, however, thoroughly terrified his fellow passengers. They relaxed, somewhat, when she said yes.

Before MacNair, the Kitchen's fundraising and communication efforts had been regularly undermined by staff turnover. With each replacement, relationships with funders were cut off, records lost, momentum broken. A lack of personnel continuity contributed to shortcomings in messaging clarity. It was readily evident that the Kitchen was doing many things, but few people, inside or outside of the organization, understood why it was doing *those* things. As powerful as Egger's voice and vision were, the rest of the organization had not developed the ability to replicate them in other formats, like newsletters, press releases, or grant proposals. Brian's background, as well his blunt style and relentless editing mantra of "less text," made him an adept and essential proxy for Robert's rhetoric. He took the helm of the Kitchen's Development Department upon the prior director's departure in 2004. MacNair quickly ran off a list of glaring needs, and spent the next nine years shepherding DC Central Kitchen toward financial sustainability.

First, he had to figure out how DCCK was piecing together its existing budget. Several area foundations were making consistent gifts, but the Kitchen had no set plan for what to ask them for, or when. Lots of checks came in thanks to Robert's relentless pitching, but there were no records of which gifts were from new sources, and which came from old friends. "Relationships are the key to successful fundraising," says MacNair, and knowing who was contributing and why was central to cultivating those connections. "We had some 15,000 names across different systems and records, but there was no information, no history attached." Without data on his past and present donors, he was flying blind. In response, Brian developed the Kitchen's first grant calendar, structuring its proposal and report submission processes. He then hired a new development associate to help him assemble a working database of donors, a grueling process that would take years.

MacNair also drew on his previous careers to add a critical tool to the Kitchen's fundraising strategy: a signature event featuring the city's best chefs. While Robert regularly raised money by giving talks at planned gatherings, actually holding events was not the organization's forte. In the late Nineties, Robert ran a small but popular 'Kitchen Kabaret' atop the Kennedy Center that featured guests like Larry King and Paul Prudhomme—and raised less than $50,000 annually. The Kabaret gave way to a football-focused event run in conjunction with the World Bank. MacNair attended the second iteration of that fundraiser just six weeks after joining DCCK. "I knew we needed a big event, but this was not it. Football didn't mesh with DC Central Kitchen, and having [professional] cheerleaders there was just weird. Our female donors shot them nasty looks all night." José Andrés, Chair of DCCK's board of directors at the time, concurred. Once an NFL team had agreed to help the Kitchen run its major fundraiser, Andrés and the board figured they had found their headline event. But after the concept flopped twice in consecutive years, they agreed it was time to move on. Yet it was not readily clear what else the Kitchen could do. DC's culinary scene was heating up, which brought more great chefs and restaurants into partnerships with the Kitchen, but it also meant other organizations were hosting food-centric galas, saturating donor demand. "We needed something new and exciting. There was already some kind of tasting event every single week," remembers MacNair.

And so the new employee turned to the Kitchen's increasingly prominent Chair. MacNair headed to Andrés' hot Spanish restaurant, *Jaleo*, on Seventh Street, just south of the National Portrait Gallery. Always festive, the restaurant was unveiling a slew of tomato-related specials celebrating the *Tomatina*. Each year, a town in the east of Spain named Bunol hosts this pulpy mess of party in which 40,000 revelers pelt each other with 100 tons of fresh tomatoes. Brian laid out his dilemma. José waved at a poster for the *Tomatina* and laughed. "We can host a food fight!" he suggested playfully. Brian quickly chuckled, then stopped. "We *can* have one—but the fight is between chefs on stage."

At the time, *Iron Chef* was on its way to becoming the king of cable food shows and already a major cultural touchstone in several countries. With DC attracting more and more big-name chefs—and younger aspirants hoping to join their famed ranks—the Kitchen could leverage its existing relationships with the restaurant industry in a new way. The on-stage chef battle could showcase the skills of four local chefs and declare a winner. Other restaurants could provide samples on the side to the guests, whom Brian figured would include both traditional donors who liked attending nonprofit galas, as well as the new 'foodies,' a growing subculture of people obsessed with all things culinary. MacNair and Andrés became fast friends, and began fleshing out an event that shared Brian's rocker attitude and Andrés' ebullient spirit.

The first Capital Bite Night: The Ultimate Food Fight debuted in the fall of 2004 in the glimmering atrium of The Galleria at Lafayette Centre. Thanks to DCCK's reputation and José's connections, MacNair secured a series of culinary stars, including Roberto Donna, Jeffrey Buben, Ris LaCoste, and, according to the industry insiders at the James Beard Foundation, the best chef in New York City, Marcus Samuelsson. The PA announcer for the local pro football team, Mark Kessler, brought his memorable growl to his role as Master of Ceremonies. The notable names helped cover for a series of difficulties behind the scenes. "It was a nightmare to pull off that first year. We ended up begging people to come and ended up with a crowd of maybe 200," remembers MacNair.

Loading in 17 restaurants and setting a stage up for the battle was no easy task for MacNair and the five coworkers he had on hand to help. "We had no idea how many staff we needed," he admits. Curtin, in just his third week at DCCK and still foolish enough to wear a full suit and starched collared shirt to work, was soon snarled in duct tape, improvising electrical set-ups for the dozens of hotplates the event demanded. At the end of night, MacNair and Marianne Ali were left alone to handle the daunting cleanup effort. It took hours.

First-time fundraising events are rarely profitable and best treated as learning experiences. Capital Bite Night: The Ultimate Food Fight had its flaws, but in all, this pilot attempt cost the Kitchen just over $100,000 and brought in a profit of more than $50,000. MacNair vowed to improve in 2005, and his first move was to apply his favorite invocation: *less text*. Rebranding their invention as Capital Food Fight, MacNair and Andrés reached out to Xavier DeShayes, Executive Chef of the Ronald Reagan Building and a regular face at the Kitchen, where he taught guest lessons to its culinary trainees.

At some 3.9 million square feet, the Reagan Building is the second largest federal edifice behind the Pentagon. As the workplace for 7,000 federal employees, including many serving the Environmental Protection Agency, it is also a curious tribute for a president who railed against 'big government' and prized deregulation.[62] Its posthumous political irony aside, the Reagan Building's size and resources made it an ideal partner for the Kitchen and its young event. That Xavier arranged for DCCK to have the space for next to nothing helped as well. "Xavier and the Reagan Building were the ideal partners, the real event experts," Brian reports. "Staging, electricity, security—all those little, but important things you don't know about when you're just getting started. They taught us the key technical pieces that

---

[62] O'Keefe, Ed, "Reagan Building hums along with little mention of president's 100th birthday," *The Washington Post*, February 4, 2011, accessed November 13, 2012, http://www.washingtonpost.com/wp-dyn/content/article/2011/02/03/AR2011020303779.html/.

helped make the event a success." That year, revenue jumped another 50 percent, to more than $200,000.

Capital Food Fight's growth was important, but nowhere near sufficient to meet the Kitchen's increasing financial obligations. Demand for the Kitchen's meals and job training services were both up, and the organization's annual budget had grown to nearly $2.5 million. It was time for another MacNair mantra: "*Think big, act big, and ask big.*"

For nonprofit fundraisers, the dynamic between shaping budgets and structuring funding requests, or 'asks,' is more than complex. It is a constant struggle, and one with no clear answers. Since its inception, the Kitchen had prided itself on keeping its costs as low as possible, while maximizing the impact of those minimal assets. Funders, however, tend to give smaller sums to smaller organizations. For donors who care about what their dollars actually do, limited budgets suggest limited impact. For other contributors—those looking for recognition and social validation rather than philanthropic meaning—small, relatively obscure groups may offer insufficient bang for their self-serving buck. What appears to be a conservative, prudent approach to strategic budgeting can, in practice, undermine an organization's financial wellbeing.

In many ways, then, bigger is better. By setting ambitious fundraising goals in their operating budgets, nonprofits communicate greater capacity to their funders and can, by that token, request larger sums. This 'stretch' strategy comes with significant risks. First, groups must attain those goals, or come reasonably close, lest they be exposed as frivolous do-gooders with lofty dreams, rather than carefully regulated, clear-eyed strategists. Second, as these larger requests produce increased income, organizations must work quickly to expand the scope and impact of their programs accordingly. And third, they must expand fast enough to show a powerful return on these additional funder investments while simultaneously hedging against the possibility that any newfound funding could disappear a year later. The hamster wheel giveth, the hamster wheel taketh away.

Despite its inherent uncertainty, MacNair believed this path offered the greatest promise for DCCK. "Robert had always thought big, but our budget and fundraising made us seem insignificant," he says. Egger's swagger had to be more widely diffused. "We were a kickass organization that was fundamentally different from those church-basement-type operations," Brian attests. "So we made a conscious effort to stop showing up at every little charity fair with a tri-fold display. The Kitchen couldn't afford to be seen swimming in that pond anymore. We wanted people to recognize that we were a big fish." To help feed that fish, MacNair fathered a new method colloquially referred to around the Kitchen as MacNair Math. By the end of any planning meeting or fundraising pitch, Brian would inflate the numbers in front of him at least to the nearest $10,000, and often add an extra zero here and there.

If DCCK was going to move from chasing $5,000 and $10,000 foundation checks to $50,000 and $100,000 ones, however, it needed to add some professional substance to its punk rock style. "Robert had all these ideas that came out in his talks and later in his book, but not much of that came through in our fundraising and communications," says Brian. "We had to do a better job of telling our story, and doing it in a humanized way." In the first two years of his tenure, Brian had increased the number of direct mail appeals—in essence, letters to individuals that ask for monetary contributions—and shifted their focus. In the few years prior to MacNair's arrival, these letters had included winding descriptions of programs and their budget needs, straying from the 'heads and hearts' approach of DCCK's founder. *Less text.* MacNair decided to focus on Kitchen clients or staff members, and often those who were both, providing a short, punchy narrative proclaiming the difference DCCK made in their life alongside a compelling photo. Anecdotal feedback on these changes was fabulous, but through the end of 2005, individual giving remained flat.

With old media ineffective, it was time to turn to some new ones. The 1990s Internet boom came and went, and the Kitchen missed most of it. A hard-coded HTML site emerged in 1998, but even its designer, a young, jack-of-all-trades assistant to Chapman Todd named Tim Forbes, describes it as having "a god awful design aesthetic." Even email was uncommon at the organization until the year 2000. At the very least, DC Central Kitchen was uniquely well-suited to survive the faux-crisis of Y2K. By 2005, however, these technological deficiencies were glaring. That year, MacNair began pushing out new web content through dccentralkitchen.org on a consistent basis. Those articles became the backbone for a new online newsletter. The rise of online communication allowed the Kitchen to contact its followers more often, more cheaply, and less desperately. "We wanted to include people in the bigger DC Central Kitchen story without constantly hounding them for money. We shared more and asked less."

In time, MacNair's methods would reap big dividends. In 2004 and 2005, however, they were just enough for the Kitchen to scrape by. These scrapes were especially close ones, thanks in large part to the cyclical, seasonal structure of nonprofit fundraising. Like many organizations, the Kitchen's fiscal year was the same as the calendar year, January through December. As is the case for most nonprofits, but especially those operating in the hunger space, a disproportionate amount of DCCK's charitable donations—more than 40 percent—would not show up until December. And 80 or 90 percent of that sum came in during the last two weeks. The combination of compelling influences at this time—holiday guilt, schmaltzy sentimentality, year-end foundation board meetings, tax benefits, and the like—provided a perfect storm of much-needed income, while effectively serving to depress giving the other 48 weeks of the year. MacNair and the rest of the organization were forced to play a harrowing waiting game, hoping for a buzzer-beating influx of funds before the calendar turned. They narrowly survived in 2005, and 2006 was shaping up to be even harder.

Despite their name, nonprofits are obsessed with money. Whatever the nature of their programs, each organization must navigate an uncertain swamp of complex financial considerations, from setting fundraising goals to tracking expenses to obtaining crucial lines of credit. And unlike for-profit businesses, whose only bottom line is financial in nature, nonprofits must carefully calibrate their activities to simultaneously serve their mission while securing their fiscal position. Managing a nonprofit's finances is a hell of a job. Few people, even those within the sector, have any interest in taking on these tasks. Fewer still are actually qualified to perform them.

In its first decade of activities, DC Central Kitchen had muddled through financially, employing a string of bookkeepers and outside accounting consultants to help DCCK leaders keep some semblance of order. Cynthia Rowland was the first to professionalize the Kitchen's financial practices. "When I came on board, we were in difficult financial times," she recalls, "and we needed solid data for decision making." Rowland's core skills were financial in nature, and her six years with DCCK were largely consumed with laying a sound fiscal foundation for future growth. When Rowland departed, Egger and Curtin decided to hire a senior financial manager to complement Curtin's operations-focused position. The woman they ultimately found to serve as the Kitchen's Controller, Glenda Cognevich, became the essential third piece of a leadership team including Curtin and Brian MacNair that would drive the Kitchen's rapid growth and professionalization in the years to come. "If I had to list the five best things that ever happened to DC Central Kitchen," states Egger, "Glenda Cognevich is absolutely on that list."

Individually, each of the three embodied a critical component of what Robert Egger had brought to the Kitchen by himself for so long. Cognevich shared his fiscal conservatism, MacNair, his style, and Curtin, his fire. Being the guy who raised the money, directed those dollars, and set DCCK's vision pulled Robert in many competing directions. Sometimes, it was difficult for colleagues to predict which 'hat' he would have on at any given time. When would the financial watchdog trump the ambitious, risk-taking visionary, or vice versa? For the Kitchen to continue to grow in ways that stayed true to its roots, Egger had to replicate his best qualities without conferring his responsibilities onto a single replacement. As the founder transition process went on, he installed a trio of leaders that could counterbalance one another as the organization moved forward. Instead of Egger wrestling with himself, the Kitchen now had three strong personalities who would hold heated meetings and fire repeated volleys of late-night emails. Taking a seat at the table with two alpha males like Curtin and MacNair would intimidate most new hires. Not Cognevich.

As is true for many nonprofit financial leaders, Glenda came to the field "by sheer coincidence." The systems-oriented Southerner with a bob of curly blonde hair was, like so many other DCCK staffers, a recovering restaurateur. After studying hospitality management in her native New Orleans, Cognevich spent the better part of a decade working for a major hotel chain. After the Soviet Union's demise, she served as a Peace Corps Volunteer in Uzbekistan, where, in a telling summation of the new world order, she taught capitalist principles through pizza-making to puzzled former members of the proletariat.

Her work in Tashkent eventually led her to enter the nonprofit sector, and the Russian speaker with a slight southern drawl began a second career in international development and conflict resolution. Glenda's business background made her the most numerate of her colleagues, and she was conscripted to the work of QuickBooks. She added an MBA from The George Washington University, and was poised for a comfortable career as a corner office CFO. And then Hurricane Katrina swallowed her beloved New Orleans.

Katrina shook Cognevich to her core and reopened old wounds. Thirty-six years earlier, Hurricane Camille had destroyed her family's house. "I questioned my international focus when there was so much work to be done here at home," she recalls. It was time for a career change. "If I couldn't find a good job in New Orleans, I could at least do something in my adopted community." She had met Robert in 2000, and now reached back out to her friend, thinking her mix of financial know-how and hospitality experience would suit her and the Kitchen equally well. In April of 2006, Cognevich came aboard, and quickly began fixing a severely unfavorable income-to-expense ratio.

That spring, the Kitchen's finances were fucked. Despite MacNair's early progress in winning foundation grants and the promise of Capital Food Fight, the organization had almost nothing in the way of net assets—the essential reserves that the for-profit sector calls equity. Like so many of its clients, DCCK was living hand-to-mouth. While the demand for the 3,500 meals it served up each day was steady and growing, its income was wildly inconsistent. As struggling households must do, DCCK had to be careful about what bills to pay when, which purchases to delay, and which creditors to call back later. According to

Robert, "Glenda masterfully handled our debt, and that's a skill set very few nonprofits possess."

While Curtin, MacNair, and Egger had some sense of the organization's tenuous position, no one knew how deep the problems ran until Cognevich plunged down the rabbit hole of old records. After just a few weeks on the job, she had to present some most unwelcome news to her new boss. Riding together to the SYSCO Food Show in Baltimore where DCCK was slated to pick up more than 40,000 pounds of leftovers, Cognevich turned to Curtin and declared, in her usual frank fashion, "We aren't going to make payroll this week."

The Kitchen needed a large and rapid infusion of cash, something no established foundation or District agency could provide. In Curtin's rolodex, there were only two hitters heavy enough to make that type of contribution—and they were married to each other. The next day, Curtin dialed Nancy Torray, the volunteer who had struck up a friendship with Miss Dot and ultimately joined DCCK's board. After exchanging pleasantries, Curtin held out his hat.

"We're in a bit of a tight spot. If you were thinking of giving us a gift at some point this year, we would really appreciate having it now, rather than at the end of this year." Nancy, on the golf course with her husband, handed him her cellular phone.

"What do you need?" asked Robert Torray.

"If we had $100,000, we'd be fine."

"OK. If this was a bridge loan, could you repay it?" Curtin answered yes, without pause.

The Torrays' check arrived before the end of the day.

Glenda Cognevich had added crucial detail to DCCK's understanding of its financial position, but the general picture was not news to Curtin and Egger. They knew they were running chronic deficits, and they knew why. Each day, the Kitchen was serving thousands of meals to District-owned shelters. While some foundations were on board to support the meal program, the city and its primary conduit for funding social service programs, The Community Partnership for the Prevention of Homelessness (TCP), paid nothing. When the District had faced severe financial hardship in previous years, the Kitchen willingly provided meals to its shelters for free. But by 2005, DC was flush with funds, a beneficiary of the housing bubble, booming federal spending, and rapid gentrification. The Kitchen, meanwhile, was undertaking heroic measures just to make payroll. In September of that year, *The Washington Post* ran a piece warning of "lean times" at DC Central Kitchen, and the normally cocky Robert Egger readily admitted his organization was "struggling."[63]

In response, DCCK began a series of conversations with some of DC's many deputy mayors. The Kitchen needed money. The District, meanwhile, wanted better meals with more meat and fresh produce, a desire Curtin understood. "We had just had a two week run where we served red beans and rice every day. I told our chef, Gary Bullock, if you come into my office one more time and tell me we're doing red beans and rice again, I'm gonna spit. He shrugged and said, 'It's all we got.'" So Curtin offered the city a deal: "If you pay us half of what each meal costs us, we'll commit to raising more money and improving our meals."

Curtin's offer circulated throughout the city's maze of agencies and departments. He met with minor official after minor official throughout that fall and winter. Finally, an answer came. Through The Community Partnership, DC would allow DCCK and other area food providers to submit bids for a shelter meals contract. After 17 years of receiving free food service,

---

[63]   Levine, Susan, "A Growing Hunger for Help," *The Washington Post*, September 15, 2005, accessed December 15, 2012, http://www.washingtonpost.com/wp-dyn/content/article/2005/09/14/AR2005091400922.html/.

DC was finally willing to pay for its meals, but there was no guarantee the Kitchen would be the one paid. Worse yet, the specifics of the contract bidding process gave an extra 12 points to organizations designated as Certified Business Enterprises, *for*-profit entities headquartered within DC. As a nonprofit, DCCK entered the bidding process at a significant disadvantage.

Curtin was displeased. The Kitchen, however, dutifully assembled its bid and submitted its materials in December 2005. The District pledged to select a winner by April 15. That date, just days after the Torrays' critical contribution, came and went with no word from the city. On April 25, TCP emailed all of its bidders, telling them no decision would be available until May 15. Egger phoned Curtin.

"This is bullshit. Let's go on strike," fumed Robert. It was a radical move for DCCK, which had never, since its first day in 1989, missed a day of meal deliveries. Generally speaking, direct service organizations are notoriously non-confrontational, especially when it comes to dealing with government funders. "Too many people in this sector are terrified to speak out," says Egger, "because they're worried they won't get their next grant." Two decades earlier, the provocative Mitch Snyder rose to national prominence because he possessed more political courage and public relations savvy than the rest of his contemporaries put together. In the years after his death, risk aversion reigned.

But an equally pissed off Mike Curtin liked Egger's incendiary idea, and they began to sketch out a plan. They would publicly suspend meal deliveries to the District's shelters—but if those residents were going to go hungry, so would Egger and Curtin. "This wasn't a Mitch Snyder display of theatrics," says Robert. "It was about solidarity." For good measure, they worked out some creative behind-the-scenes partnerships to provide extra meals to organizations not run by the DC government, and arranged for them to discretely drop those additional dishes at the shelters. In practice, the only people in a DC shelter that would not be fed were the two executives in CCNV's basement.

While Egger's day-to-day role at the Kitchen had begun to wane as Curtin came into his own, Robert's outsized personality and superhuman energy made him the organization's best weapon when it came to street fights in the public square. The pair announced their fast on May 1 and scheduled a rowdy press conference later that week. As word spread, fellow nonprofits called Mike to share their excitement and pride at what the Kitchen was standing up for and what it was standing up to. Sensing the power of a unified statement, he encouraged them to join him in front of the cameras at the press conference. Each organization politely declined, fearing fallout in its own relationship with the District.

While other nonprofits wanted no part in DCCK's agitation, the press could not get enough. Television and print outlets swarmed to the story, aiding the Kitchen's efforts to shame the District into action. Initially, The Community Partnership demurred, saying the strike had taken "everyone by surprise. It took us seven months to get the contract from the District. If you compare us to others, we're just about on the mark."[64] But the ongoing delays fit a larger narrative of a DC bureaucracy that was at best bumbling and inefficient, at worst self-serving and corrupt. It was TCP's policy not to share information pertaining to bids currently under review. The policy was meant to maintain a level playing field between bidders, but the resulting opacity made the organization seem out of touch and, to some, even inhumane. After the initial public shock at a community organization refusing to provide meals over something as crude

---

[64] Killian, Erin, "DC Central Kitchen founder protests city with hunger strike," *Washington Business Journal*, May 5, 2006, accessed December 20, 2012, http://www.bizjournals.com/washington/stories/2006/05/01/daily48.html?page=all/.

as money, the Kitchen dominated the debate in the week that followed.

Time was on DCCK's side, if its leaders could hold up. Curtin and Egger were receiving more attention than at any time before, but they had less and less strength with which to summon their 'A-games' for each interview. The day after their press conference, both men seemed depleted. "I think they used up all their testosterone in front of the cameras," figured one DCCK staffer. Mike said those days brought a strange alternation of "desolation and consolation. I felt alone, but never more connected with our mission. There was a sense of hopelessness, but also a belief that there was a reason for it." Egger may have lost some of his vigor, but maintained his sense of humor. "I sway between moments of complete euphoria and having a Big Mac attack," said Egger to a reporter as the fast dragged on. "It's Day Five and it's Cinco de Mayo. I want a fucking burrito and margarita."[65] His sense of purpose did not diminish, either. Despite 17 years of fighting hunger full-time, Robert had never known hunger himself. After losing 11 pounds off his already lean frame in just over a week, he vowed an even more passionate commitment to eradicating it from his city. Curtin also saw an opportunity to send a message to his own staff. "A lot of our staff had been in those shelters, so we wanted to use this opportunity to show respect to them as well. These men and women did good work, and deserved to have that work paid for."

On May 9, the city relented. The fast lasted eight days, winning the Kitchen its first major fee-for-service contract and stabilizing its finances before the Torrays' bridge loan ran out. Five months later, Mike asked Glenda to begin the process of paying back the couple's loan in $10,000 installments. The first check went out in October, and Curtin planned to hand the second payment to the Torrays personally at Capital Food Fight.

---

[65] Killian, "DC Central Kitchen founder."

Curtin slipped the check into his blazer pocket and headed to the Ronald Reagan Building. He smiled as he handed it over. Robert Torray was stunned.

"I was thinking about doing something else for you," he said, "and now I'm sure of it." He handed the check back to Curtin, forgiving the remaining $90,000 on the loan, and pledged another $900,000 to DCCK. The funds were to serve as rainy day reserves, finally giving Glenda the net assets she so needed. Torray pledged to manage the sum and help it grow through stable, long-term investments. A year later, he added another million to DCCK's 'Torray Fund.' "He didn't give us that money just because he liked us," remembers Curtin. "We had been good stewards, and done what we had said we would do."

After the crisis of that spring, MacNair's diligence began to pay off. He and his team revamped their grant proposal language and strategy, finally finding a way to replicate Robert's passion within the conventions and limitations of that rather technical form of writing. They went to existing supporters and asked for larger sums. They tracked down lapsed funders and rekindled those relationships. They made big, bold requests of new prospective partners. Several huge contributions rolled in that summer. Altria, the amalgamation of Phillip Morris and Kraft Foods, made its final gift to the Kitchen, after several years of support, in the amount of $100,000. Bank of America took notice of DCCK, providing a two-year, $200,000 grant and selecting the Kitchen for its Neighborhood Excellence Award. Along with the cash came admittance for MacNair and Curtin to special leadership summits, vaulting them to new levels of prominence within the nonprofit sector.

This hot streak continued through the rest of the year. The Kitchen tapped a host of new foundation prospects with unprecedented success. Online giving by individual donors spiked, and, contrary to Brian's concerns, did not cannibalize the more traditional revenue streams of personal checks and United Way designations. Capital Food Fight jumped another $100,000 in earnings, thanks in large part to José Andrés convincing his friend, author and TV star Anthony Bourdain, to co-host the event with him. Together, they infused the event with charisma and testosterone, blending good looks and culinary mastery with a healthy serving of dick jokes. That year's 700 guests loved them, and the profane pair cemented the Food Fight brand for years to come. Brian's big asks afforded the Kitchen the resources to start 'acting big.'

To measure up to these large new contributions and that 'stretch' budget, program staff raced forward. Among the programmatic gains of 2006 were some significant strides for the Kitchen's Culinary Job Training program. That year, CJT produced 62 graduates, an increase of 21 people over the previous year. The key was improved student retention, largely attributable to a new internship component. While the Kitchen had dispatched a few students as interns occasionally in years past, 2006 saw the program commit to connecting each student with a one-week internship before graduation. Generally, internships are supposed to lead to jobs, but that was not the Kitchen's goal.

The internship concept emerged, in fact, because Mike Curtin and program director Marianne Ali had discovered a surprising trend relating to when trainees quit the program. Many students dropped out in the first two weeks, which was predictable. However, a second wave of trainees kept quitting in Week 10 or 11, just before graduation. "It didn't make any sense," Ali says. "They were so close!" It turned out that for many students, the Kitchen was the first place that had ever welcomed them. They finally felt safe, valued, at home. When graduation drew near, the prospect of leaving that comfort zone terrified them, and they withdrew. The internship component, then, was meant to offer Kitchen trainees a controlled immersion in the world of work, making it clear that after a week, they could 'come home' to Second Street.

To work, this plan required willing collaborators to host a rough batch of students with limited training. When talking to prospective hosts, Curtin says he and Ali "made it a no pressure situation. Most job training programs try to turn internship sites into employment locations. We said, 'Don't hire them. Focus on being an internship site, and we promise not to hassle you about taking them on full-time.' It worked like a charm." Partnering with the Washington Convention Center, Eurest Dining Services, and the Hotel Association of Washington, DC, the Kitchen found stable host sites that pledged to give students an array of immersion experiences over the course of five days. "If we put our interns in restaurants, I knew what would happen. If someone told me as an owner or GM that I had free labor for a week, I'd treat them like it: 'Go in the corner and chop carrots. I'll see you in five days,'" Curtin claims. "So we worked with big institutions and hotels, where they had a pastry station, a grill, and so on, and made them pledge to rotate our students through each of them." The internship program represented the type of systematic improvements Curtin had been brought on to identify and implement.

Egger, for his part, was still out there thinking big. His budding friendship with Mohammad Yunus, founder of the Grameen Bank and visionary pioneer of microenterprise, inspired Robert with a series of new causes. As Robert wrote in an early 2007 letter to donors, he would spend the next year pushing the Kitchen in "two different directions—both up AND down." He planned to "take it up" by bringing meaningful microenterprise from the Indus River valley to the banks of the Potomac, helping the Kitchen's culinary graduates launch street cart businesses that served food prepared by Fresh Start Catering. Meanwhile, the Kitchen was to "drill down by investing in [its] staff."[66] After years of wrenching the most it could from every dime, the Kitchen made a commitment to pay living, competitive wages and provide full benefits to all full-time staff. In the years to follow, social enterprise and staff compensation would change DC Central Kitchen dramatically. How the Kitchen made its money and how it spent it would come to matter as much as the meals it served and the people it trained.

---

[66] DC Central Kitchen, 2006 Annual Report, March 2007.

Chapter 7 Stella

Looking back, Michael Curtin jokingly refers to his period as a restaurant owner as his "first experience running a nonprofit." His business background gave him a fundamentally different viewpoint as he began to settle into the frenetic environment of DCCK. If Egger was the purist, a nonprofit sector 'lifer' with two decades of political battle scars fighting for ideals, Curtin was more pragmatic, diplomatic, and systems-oriented. He merged his managerial sensibilities, however, with what Egger calls "that Jesuit fire"—a fierce underlying commitment to social justice and a life lived for others; a commitment that will be judged someday, in some unearthly realm. Despite their differences, both leaders shared a passion for the Kitchen's core programs, preference for casual clothes, and predilection for profanity— strategically used, of course. They worked in adjacent broom closets that had been converted into offices, Egger turning outward to chase the Kitchen's larger mission, Curtin looking inward to improve the day-to-day performance of its programs.

It did not take long for Curtin to pull off a cultural coup that would permanently reverberate through DCCK's daily work. In October 2004, the Kitchen was bracing for its busiest season, both in terms of food donations and media coverage. As most hunger organizations learn at some point in their first year of operations, donors tend to assume that Thanksgiving and Christmas are the times when food is most needed. This, of course, is crap. The holidays are when people are the most sentimental, the most bloated with rich dinners and decadent desserts, and the most surrounded by strewn wrapping paper and unnecessary gifts. 'Tis the season for feeling guilty. Hunger is a year-round crisis that stubbornly refuses to contain itself to convenient periods for company food drives. But everyone, from charities to corporations to commentators on the nightly news, plays along. It is, after all, good for business.

And so, every November, a local news outlet could be counted on to send some cub reporter down to Second Street. The Kitchen called this 'the cupboards are bare' story. Unfailingly, a line would form outside DCCK's truck bay, with well-meaning citizens clutching frozen turkeys. The Kitchen's needs obviously went beyond that particular form of poultry, but with protein donations so hard to find, it was in no position to turn the birds away. The real trouble started when they had to store all those turkeys.

Founded upon a virulent opposition to waste in all its forms, the Kitchen tried to squeeze every last cent of value out of the tools and equipment it had. In Robert's first proposal for the Kitchen in 1988, he cited "the high failure rate of restaurants" as reason to expect that "equipment [would be] available throughout the year . . . and, quite possibly, for free." "Things were different then," says Egger. "Before the economic boom of Nineties, turnover in the restaurant business was constant. It wasn't that we were just cheap. You could get quality stuff donated, and it was plentiful." From its earliest days, DCCK had set itself up as the eager bottom feeder of the culinary world.

In 2004, this commitment was embodied by its rickety freezer, which was cobbled together from two separate units and run on several second-hand compressors. Without a steady stream of belly-up businesses passing along spare parts, the thing ultimately had more in common with the Frankenstein monster than an average Frigidaire. It failed constantly, and generally struggled to maintain freezing temperatures. Whenever it went down during the winter months, the Kitchen's spare supply of Thanksgiving turkey spoiled. This pattern had repeated itself for years.

Curtin figured this waste was entirely avoidable. "If we need a new freezer," he wondered, "why don't we buy one?" The question was simple, the answer less so. Since its founding, DCCK had never bought a brand-new piece of kitchen equipment. To some in the organization, buying new and carrying the cost of depreciation seemed like a form of failure, an admission that they lacked the necessary creativity to do more with less.

The business owner in Curtin countered this line of thinking. "Isn't it more wasteful to let all these turkeys spoil when an up-front investment can prevent that? Don't we owe a responsibility to our food donors?" he asked. Mike cornered and cajoled people throughout the organization, working to win them over to his side. He coupled his position with a new proposal: "I said, 'Let's do an online campaign, specifically to get this freezer,' which we had never done before." Through October and early November, the surprisingly effective web appeal pulled in thousands of dollars, which accompanied a timely grant from a local foundation, the Philip L. Graham Fund. Curtin ordered the new freezer, which arrived the Friday before Thanksgiving. The kitchen staff affectionately named it Stella.

With all the work that had gone into securing Stella, Curtin realized, "We hadn't done the 'cupboards are bare' story!" He got on the phone to a friendly network, which was all too happy to send someone down for a feel-good Thanksgiving piece. As they had so many times before, scores of neighbors lined up across the parking lot, ready to hand over their frozen turkeys and other Thanksgiving fixings. Among them was a father with two children, all three clutching brown paper bags full of groceries. The man introduced himself and his sons to Curtin, who was greeting the crowd of donors. He asked for a quick tour of the Kitchen and Mike was happy to oblige. As they looped around the prep tables and shining steel kettles, the father asked his boys to explain why they had visited DCCK that evening.

"We were fighting," said one sheepishly, "and started throwing food at each other." The other boy sighed and looked at his shoes.

"And Dad said we should use our allowances to buy this food and give it to people who didn't have any, so we wouldn't waste it anymore." The father nodded, thanked Curtin, and headed off into the cold November night, his hands on the shoulders of chastened sons.

"The amazing thing for me, and why I remember that conversation to this day," says Curtin, "is the way the Kitchen can mean so many important things to so many people, the way we can offer them what they need. He was able to teach his boys something that night about family and community, when all I was focused on was those turkeys and that freezer."

That freezer proved critical in its own way. Yes, the turkeys came, stayed cold, and provided thousands of main courses over several months. More importantly, however, the Kitchen began its transformation from an operation focused on the recovery and reuse of the old and unwanted to one that was willing to make key investments in its capacity to change lives. Curtin views these types of investments as a sign of respect for his staff and the effort they put forth each day. "What we're doing is already hard. We don't need to make it harder with blunt knives and broken ovens," he asserts. "We have to be stewards of our money. So investing in capacity is a good choice when it empowers staff to do their jobs, and do them better."

Subpar equipment was not the only factor limiting the Kitchen's overall effectiveness. When Mike Curtin arrived in 2004, he discovered an organization marked by silos and segmentation. DCCK's inability to efficiently share resources and information across program areas was largely a function of perhaps its best quality: its entrepreneurial eagerness to say 'yes' to new opportunities and challenges. After 15 years of continuous operations, the Kitchen had increased its daily meal production for area shelters and nonprofits, expanded and formalized its job training program, added a street outreach service, and experimented with a variety of social enterprises. "We were always nimble," remembers one senior staffer, "Robert, and later Mike, wanted us to be prepared to take on any new emergency."

The flip side of DCCK's responsiveness, however, was that it would quickly tack a new project onto its organizational core, put someone in charge of running it, and move on to the next crisis. Once a project moved beyond the pilot phase, it tended to float along steadily or gradually wither. Only under Cynthia Rowland had the Kitchen really begun to demonstrate the sort of careful, sustained management capacity necessary to push programs toward higher levels of performance. While each major program of DCCK tied into Robert Egger's original vision—especially the interaction of food recycling, meal production, and job training—in practice, these programs sometimes appeared as disparate and cobbled-together as that old, beat-up freezer.

One major division split DCCK's busy kitchen in half. The Kitchen's central meal production program for the city's shelters did not share its basic equipment—knives, carts, and the like—with its Fresh Start Catering arm. Fresh Start, meanwhile, did not plan its purchases in conjunction with the revenue-generating Contract Foods operation, missing out on bulk purchasing discounts. "We had double staff, and double, even triple ordering," remembers Curtin.

As the two social enterprise initiatives, Fresh Start and Contract Foods, had emerged in the last decade, they had always been seen internally as separate from the nonprofit side of the Kitchen. The primary distinction at play, and one DCCK staff actively promoted at the time, was that while the shelter meal initiative relied on donated food and volunteer labor, the social enterprises paid for their products and people. "There was a fear," says Curtin, "of the DC Central Kitchen name stigmatizing the food we sold through catering and contracts." The Executive Chef of Fresh Start at the time, Jerald Thomas, went so far as to erect an actual barrier between the two departments' storage areas. He hung a partition of chicken wire that ran through the pantry room, and jerry-rigged a door out of three rolling bread racks bound together by more sharp wire. "It didn't work as well as I'd hoped," he says with a belly laugh. "Once we'd open that door in the morning, folks would leave it open 'cause they were so afraid of getting cut on that damn chicken wire."

Much like its meals, DCCK's programs were also segmented. First Helping, the street outreach effort, would direct homeless men and women to shelters and recovery programs, but almost never guide them into the Culinary Job Training program. While enrolled in CJT, men and women with serious histories of struggle would benefit from the intensive self-empowerment coaching of Ron Swanson and Marianne Ali. But the culinary graduates who found work in one of DCCK's programs received no social support, as if those deep-seated demons could be exorcized in 12 weeks. While some of these struggles were institutional in nature, others were more personal. "People were afraid to borrow a cart from across the kitchen because that damn cart *belonged* to someone," remembers an astounded Curtin.

Over the next two years, Curtin went about the difficult business of breaking down many of these internal barriers. He organized more planning meetings. He rolled catering and Contract Foods together under the Fresh Start banner. A new position, the Partnership Program Manager, focused on facilitating working relationships with all the other agencies the Kitchen dealt with across its many programs, recalling the spirit of Chapman Todd. Curtin worked to squash the personality-driven turf issues by constantly reminding individual staff of their relationship to DCCK's larger mission. He made progress, but the overriding culture of risk-taking at DC Central Kitchen meant he was playing whack-a-mole with the additional silos created by new programs, priorities, and positions. "There are goods and bads to our entrepreneurial, fast approach. If you move quickly, I believe, you'll produce so many things that 'the bads' fall off and 'the goods' rise to the top . . . Our first instinct as an organization is to say yes, and that's something I would never change."

One thing DCCK said yes to in 2007 was Robert Egger's vision for bringing microenterprise to the United States. Energized by his interactions with Nobel Peace Prize winner Mohammad Yunus and inspired by 'the power of small purchases' in the social movements led by Mahatma Ghandi, Martin Luther King, Jr. and Cesar Chavez, Egger wanted to chart a new direction for DC Central Kitchen. And it was going to start on the streets.

Any visitor ambling past the tourist attractions of Washington, DC will soon spot an unsightly yellow food cart pushing candy, soda, hot dogs, and polish sausages disingenuously passed off as 'authentic DC half-smokes.' In the 1990s, there were thousands of near-identical carts across the District, offering the same stale selection of low-grade food products. The permitting process was a mess. Carts had to be no more than seven feet long and four-and-a-half feet wide, making real food preparation almost impossible. Each night, proprietors were required to park their carts in one of three private depots, where oligopolistic owners would strong-arm vendors into "under-the-table deals in which they [had to] buy ice, propane tanks, towing services and food or face higher rents or even the threat of eviction."[67] By the middle of the next decade, public sector mismanagement and private sector manipulation had unwittingly conspired to drive the number of licensed carts down to just 600. The street food scene had become "an embarrassment," said Curtin to *The Washington Post.*[68]

Where Curtin saw an embarrassment, Egger saw an opportunity. He devised and championed a new social enterprise program called Capital Carts. The Kitchen's glimmering stainless steel carts would sell high-quality food prepared by Fresh Start Catering. DCCK culinary graduates would lease the carts, purchase and serve the food from Fresh Start, and become entrepreneurs while leveraging the brand and back-end services of DC Central Kitchen. The timing seemed to be just right as the DC government declared itself fed up with the current cart community and pledged to rejuvenate it. The District opened up a small downtown demonstration zone where DCCK and another new for-profit cart would be allowed to operate free of some District restrictions. Initially, DCCK decided to hire one of its graduates to run the cart, with the idea that she would eventually generate enough business to lease the cart from the organization and purchase the food Fresh Start made each day for her to sell.

The program got some great early press, but the economics of the Capital Cart—Curtin and company stopped at one— never worked out. Hauling the cart to and from the depot each morning and night was a struggle. "It cost us more than $500 to

---

67   Carman, Tim, "New Street Food Options in Washington, DC," *The Washington Post*, October 1, 2008.

68   Carman, "New Street Food Options."

keep it on the street each day," remembers Curtin. "That's a lot of cups of soup."

While sales volumes lagged, the Capital Cart's financial problems were compounded by Egger's other big push: investing in Kitchen staff though decent salaries and good benefits. The shift toward organization-wide living wages had been in progress for some time. "When I came up in nightclubs," says Robert, "there was no such thing as overtime and really no such thing as a 40-hour week, but when our drivers began taking on night shifts and extra delivery runs, some began to hear from their families that they were being taken advantage of. That was never the intention, but addressing those concerns set us on the path to fair and just compensation for everyone." By the time the Capital Carts program rolled around, Egger wanted cart operators to have access to the Kitchen's generous benefit package, through which the Kitchen paid 100 percent of health insurance costs for each of its employees. The desire was principled, but did not prove very practical. Extending this coverage would make each operator "a member of DCCK's staff, and each cart a DCCK program," says Curtin. "For decades, DC food carts worked, barely, for individual entrepreneurs," he continues, "but for a company to make the cart model work, you'd have to do 50 of them."

When the Kitchen's single cart floundered, Curtin says, "We had to accept failure." Egger's vision for microenterprise had been based on Yunus' model, which thrived in a loosely regulated environment with extremely low labor costs. It simply did not translate to the red-tape-ridden streets of DC and to an organization that wanted to pay its people well enough so they could live somewhere besides those streets. In 2009, DCCK began leasing the cart to Zola, a popular DC dinner spot owned by long-time Kitchen ally Dan Mesches, who was willing to take a hit to bail out his friends. DCCK received a flat monthly sum for the rights to the cart, while Zola kept the sales. The deal stopped the Kitchen's financial bleeding, but the overall venture was no more viable. Curtin soon told his friend that Zola would be better off without the money-losing line item, and gave him an honorable, amicable out. By 2010, the District's drive to revitalize street food through new carts was totally dead. Sick of local government dithering, other impatient entrepreneurs had begun operating out of small trucks, and the concept spread virally. Suddenly, restaurants across DC began hustling to keep up with the trendy, low-cost revolution launched by the city's food trucks. The Kitchen had been onto something, but mistimed its leap.

Capital Carts represented a difficult period in Egger's and Curtin's relationship with one another. The original visionary was convinced it would work, but the man charged with safeguarding and expanding that vision simply could not make it so. While another founder might have been tempted to reassert his power after a disagreement with his *de facto* successor, Egger did not. Instead, he continued his gradual embrace of new projects outside the Kitchen. "To Robert's enormous credit, his way of letting go let all of us build the confidence we needed," says Mike. In the middle of the Cart program's spiral towards failure, Egger formally relinquished the position of Chief Executive Officer to Curtin.

Curtin says that Robert "never sat me down and said 'Someday, you'll be in charge,'" but the two men had "built a foundation of trust and conversation" that carried them through the large and small challenges posed by founder transition process. "He will always be Robert Egger, the founder, the visionary behind DC Central Kitchen, and I am entirely comfortable with that," says Curtin. "My job is to take Robert's vision and grow it into the future. Not to make us bigger, necessarily, but more impactful.

I want people to keep saying 'Man, those guys are kicking so much ass,' and the challenge is finding new ass to kick."

At a programmatic level, the change was less dramatic than some may have expected, as both men were equally committed to providing fair wages and full benefits for Kitchen employees. Egger, the fiscal pit bull, had come around on the issues of staff salaries and high-quality health insurance because he embraced it as an issue of justice for his organization's graduates. Curtin agreed, believing that adequate compensation showed a critical level of respect for the work his employees did, especially those punching in and out of hourly shifts in that basement kitchen. While embracing these concepts philosophically raised little objection, living up to them financially would continue to place heavy demands upon DC Central Kitchen.

To steal a phrase from Ice-T, social enterprise ain't easy. In the past decade, many of America's most successful businesses have generally placed their greatest emphasis on reducing labor costs, increasing worker productivity, and enhancing market share— sometimes to the exclusion of maintaining the quality of their product. Offering a good product at a competitive price while paying good wages to people who would otherwise struggle to find work, then, sounds nearly impossible to some, if not totally insipid. Making enough money is difficult enough when it's your *only* goal. If meeting one bottom line is tough, managing a 'multiple bottom-line' of making money, helping people, and protecting the environment borders on the impossible.

The Kitchen learned that the coolest concepts—ones loaded with 'synergies' and 'virtuous circles'—can still go bankrupt in the harsh, gladiatorial arena of dollars and cents. Capital Carts bottomed out, and it was not the Kitchen's first failure. In the mid- and late-Nineties, DCCK ran a sizable bakery that consumed half of its kitchen space. Early on, Fresh Start's oversized pastries had won some positive reviews, including one from then-Mayor

Anthony Williams, who especially liked those "big-ass muffins."
It was not long before a bakery in Delaware approached the
Kitchen about a wholesale deal for 'Mayor Williams' Big Ass
Muffins.' For years, DCCK trucked its massive muffins north
across state lines. At the time, however, the Kitchen lacked the
business acumen and spare resources to grow and diversify its
bakery business. When the outfit in Delaware went under, the
DC Central Kitchen Bakery bottomed out too.

The Kitchen was further hamstrung by a unique double
standard between for-profit and nonprofit entities. Businesses
are supposed to take risks with their money, investing in new
products, developing new systems, breaking into new markets,
and so on. But nonprofits must be careful stewards, avoiding
risk and loss at all costs. Thus, while social enterprise activities,
by their nature, tend to be more costly and less lucrative for
the nonprofits launching them than profit-focused ventures,
they also have less room for error. In effect, donors seem to
say to nonprofits, *"Earn more of your own money, without losing
any of what I've already given you, while remaining focused
on your mission."* Few organizations pull off this challenging
triangulation.

Going forward, the Kitchen's social enterprises needed to
haul in more income more consistently. For a decade, consumers
had chosen to purchase products from DCCK because of the
people it employed: struggling women and men who would
be essentially unemployable outside the Kitchen's walls. Curtin
figured that the sort of larger, steadier food service contracts the
Kitchen needed to raise money and provide steady employment
had to be distinguished by more than who served the food.
The food being served had to be special, too. Like any other
entrepreneur, Mike needed to find an angle. As it turned out, he
did not need to look very far.

In 2004, Robert described thoughts on the intersection of hunger and obesity in tellingly brief terms. "Am I worried about fat homeless people? No."[69] Egger was ahead of his time in even nodding toward the systemic effects of obesity on American productivity, but the daily efforts of DC Central Kitchen had focused largely on putting otherwise wasted food to work, whether it was red delicious apples or delivery pizza. The causes of food justice, healthy food access, stronger local food systems, and superior school-based nutrition programs were all on the periphery of the US nonprofit sector, and far removed from the front lines of homelessness and acute hunger that DCCK had called home for 15 years.

In its early years, the Kitchen invested a great deal in encouraging people to rethink their positions about food waste. "If we can recycle aluminum," asked one old Kitchen poster, "what's so hard about broccoli?" DCCK did fight to improve the quality of its donations, but these struggles generally involved pushing back against people passing off items that were rotten or damn close to it, belying a sense of disrespect for the Kitchen and people it served.[70] With the Kitchen being so picky about the short-term safety of its ingredients, it could not afford to turn away donations that, while hardly healthy, ultimately complied with food sanitation standards. At one point, DCCK was serving upwards of 10,000 pounds of donated pizza annually. For years,

---

69   Egger, *Begging for Change*, 160.

70   To the organization's credit, it has never been associated with any instance of food-borne illness. Sometimes, though, the Kitchen's reputation for using leftover items would drive it to take its food safety practices, and the public image of those practices, to an extreme. Whenever staged photos of staff or volunteers popped up in the press that omitted unsightly but necessary gloves and hairnets, Egger would soon storm through the facility, demanding answers.

the breakfast sandwiches served by the Kitchen's First Helping street outreach program were largely recovered from gas station convenience stores. And dessert was a non-negotiable item for many clients. Referencing the shelter facilities upstairs from DCCK headquarters, one long-time employee declares, "Riots. There would be riots if we didn't bring up the leftover cakes we get." The active and former drug users served by the Kitchen are notorious for consuming more sugar than an unattended seven-year-old on Halloween. In the pragmatic logic of DCCK staff, any large amount of sugar beats any small amount of heroin.

There were costs to this approach, however, both physical and financial in nature. While private gyms and prissy farmers' markets became trendy hangouts for the well-to-do in America, obesity increasingly became a poor person's affliction. According to a 2010 District survey, in Wards 7 and 8 where DCCK's services were concentrated, fully 40 percent of all residents were not just overweight, but clinically obese.[71] White flight and pervasive poverty created perverted food systems in DC's low-income communities. Without grocery stores nearby, many residents of these communities came to rely on corner stores, fast food chains, and shabby storefronts known as carry-outs for their nutrition. Thanks in part to school budget cuts and the elimination of home economics classes, cooking knowledge waned. Business owners became convinced there was no demand for healthier options. Some corner stores even began to balk at carrying diet soda. In time, the Kitchen began to see that not all nutrition was

---

[71]   Garner, Tracy, Daniella Trombatore, and Uzma Raza, "Obesity in the District of Columbia," Government of the District of Columbia, Department of Health, Center for Policy, Planning, and Evaluation, January 2010, 18, accessed February 5, 2013, http://newsroom.dc.gov/show.aspx?agency=doh&section=2&release=19808&year=2010&month=5&file=file.aspx%2frelease%2f19808%2fFINAL%2520Obesity%25202009%2520Report.pdf/.

created equal. According to one former First Helping staffer, clients who consumed the donuts and sugary coffee at their breakfast station were more likely to see their energy and mood crash later in the day, sometimes leading to belligerent and destructive altercations with the social service workers charged with helping them get back on their feet.

But as late as 2007, the growing national movement for fresh, local, even organic food had yet to permeate DC Central Kitchen's grand strategy. Much of the rhetoric surrounding these causes was high-handed and detached. "We didn't want to get in the business of bringing arugula to the 'hood," recalls one employee. The food justice movement consisted more of advocacy workers than direct-service organizations, and, from the vantage point of DCCK's basement kitchen, its prescriptions seemed as remote as the largely privileged, suburban, and white voices calling for them. The Kitchen figured it had bigger problems than fat homeless people. The world, it seemed, was coming apart.

2008, and the financial crisis it brought, proved to be among the most critical years of the Kitchen's history.[72] Whenever the country's prized engines of economic growth and job creation—for-profit enterprises—stumble, philanthropic giving suffers. For many donors, doing good is a luxury good. This problem goes deeper than the budgetary hell it wreaks on a financially dependent nonprofit sector. Whenever the for-profit sector crashes, nonprofits are supposed to be the airbags, providing food, shelter, and clothing, not to mention health care, education, and innovative policy responses. And they are expected to offer all these things at discount rates. The times

---

[72] Other significant years included 1997, when the Kitchen launched its first social enterprise, and 1990 when it began its job training program and hired Chapman Todd.

when nonprofits are needed most are the times when the vast majority of these hand-to-mouth institutions are compelled to do the least.

Two years after backing away from the precipice, the Kitchen's finances were fucked again. The generous gift of cash reserves contributed by Robert and Nancy Torray took an unavoidably big hit in the market's upheaval, losing a significant portion of its value. Private foundations, the Kitchen's most critical financial lifeline, saw their assets diminish as well, and most chose to either freeze or scale back their giving. Other nonprofits were caught in the same trap of having more work to do and fewer resources to do it with, making an already competitive fundraising environment downright Hobbesian. DCCK's hallmark initiative, the Culinary Job Training program, was primed for a fall. With experienced, educated workers flooding the nation's growing pool of unemployed job hunters, how were people struggling with homelessness and addiction supposed to compete? Any resulting drop in DCCK's performance metrics was sure to scare off funders who expected steady year-to-year improvement and tied their contributions to such gains.

The Kitchen had to cut costs somewhere. Laying off staff, many of them graduates of the job training program, would cripple the organization's effectiveness and simultaneously turn out a slew of hard-to-employ men and women with little appeal to other firms. Moving to a cheaper facility was not an option, as they were already allowed to operate in the basement of the Federal City Shelter for free. The decision-making triumvirate of Mike Curtin, Brian MacNair, and Glenda Cognevich dug into DCCK's books, looking for the next largest category of expenses. It was food.

At first glance, the idea of an organization founded on leftover food shelling out upwards of $800,000 per year on meal ingredients is jarring. Though the organization had grown from preparing several hundred meals each day to several thousand, its general procurement practices had not matured accordingly. Donations were impossible to predict and generally, once they arrived, were time-sensitive. Not only did the Kitchen have limited storage capacity, but many goods were provided at or near their expiration date. Since donations were unlikely to be shelf-stable, purchased food items had to be, as they waited their turn for an appropriate, complementary gift of surplus goods.

Fruits and vegetables presented the biggest problem. The United States throws out 40 percent of its farm products, and produce comprises half of that waste.[73] Food sellers, be they wholesale or retail, tend to hold on to fresh produce for as long as it is shelf-stable, which is not long. As a result, many donations of fruits and vegetables are on the verge of rotting or well past it. Nationwide, few food banks and pantries have the infrastructure to recover, store, and redistribute fresh produce. This lack of capacity contributes to their reliance on canned and boxed goods, instead of bright, leafy ones. DCCK, meanwhile, faced a different challenge. Because fresh produce donations were scattered and often small, the Kitchen focused on recovering other items, especially proteins, and bought its fruits and vegetables in primarily canned and processed forms. To manage their costs, Kitchen staff ordered these items from massive foodservice wholesalers, who tended to rely on foreign suppliers. In sum, it was cheaper and smarter to order canned apple slices with added corn syrup from Chile than fresh ones from the nearby Shenandoah Valley. Or so they thought.

Curtin decided to push back against this thinking. A serendipitous conversation with a Virginia Department of Agriculture staffer named Dave Robishaw directed Curtin's

---

[73] Gunders, Dan, "Wasted: How America Is Losing Up to 40 Percent of Its Food from Farm to Fork to Landfill," National Resources Defense Council, August 2012, 5, accessed February 5, 2013, http://www.nrdc.org/food/files/wasted-food-IP.pdf/.

attention to a new farmer's cooperative in Harrisonburg, Virginia. About two hours west of Washington, DC, the Shenandoah Valley Produce Auction (SVPA), had assembled a slew of small, local, and primarily Mennonite growers looking for a new, more stable source of revenue. A recent string of bad luck, from falling milk prices to an Avian Flu outbreak, had hit the Shenandoah hard. Urban consumers in the gentrifying neighborhoods of DC and Baltimore were showing more and more interest in farmers' markets, but these institutions are often bad business for small farmers. They drive long distances to move relatively small quantities of their products, and since they deal with retail consumers, every apple, potato, or pear must meet a series of arbitrary aesthetic standards relating to size, shape, and color. Pumpkins, understandably, do not know what they are supposed to look like, but those that turn out a shade too green or a little too oblong are often left in the field to rot. The retail-driven farmers' market model makes for thin margins and tremendous waste.

Lacking sound retail options, this group of Shenandoah farmers founded the SVPA to auction off bulk quantities of their produce to anyone who would pay for it. Two weeks after their first exchange, Curtin and Robishaw headed out to Harrisonburg to see the operation in person. Surrounded by fields, the auction consisted of a neatly kept dirt lot and, in the center, a lengthy concrete slab 100 yards long and some 25 yards wide. A thin roof stood atop the slab on metal posts, leaving the structure open on all sides. Curtin tried to track down the Auction's director, a Mr. Showalter. The search proved surprisingly difficult, since, due to a quirk of long-time residents having many children, nearly all of whom stayed in the same small community, it seemed like every third person was a soft-spoken, straw-hatted Mennonite named Showalter.

The produce Curtin found was beautiful, even when it was too imperfect for high-end retail. The Mennonite farmers took special pride in what they grew and harvested. They were careful craftsmen, no different from a master carpenter or artisan potter. The auction model offered these goods at surprisingly low rates, partially because the participating farms were so close to each other that they operated under all the same conditions. When one surprising stretch of weather, for example, caused everyone's cantaloupes to ripen the same week, each farmer had to move their melons in one day at the auction, sending prices into a free-fall. Prices were also low, however, because the Shenandoah farmers had not found a way to profitably move their goods into the DC wholesale market. They needed a buyer—a big one—with the trucks, refrigeration units, and processing capacity to purchase these fruits and vegetables in bulk and get them to urban consumers. Curtin figured his industrial kitchen serving several thousand meals a day with a built-in catering company seemed like a decent fit.

Drawing on a plan he had first sketched out on a cocktail napkin after the 2007 Capital Food Fight, Curtin pitched Showalter and his members on a deal. The Kitchen would come out each week and purchase their best stuff, called 'firsts,' at these competitive rates. The farmers would also bring their 'seconds'—items that were too blemished or misshapen to sell to retail consumers. Since these goods were going to be plowed under as seed at a loss anyway, the Kitchen would pay the SVPA members a reduced price to take those seconds off their hands. And if they had anything they felt like donating, the Kitchen would throw that in the truck, too. The SVPA was, to say the least, skeptical. "These city folks from a nonprofit are going to drive all the way out here every week and spend all this money?" paraphrases Curtin.

Sure enough, a DC Central Kitchen box truck rolled into that dirt lot a week later, and each week after that. The firsts were immaculate and the Kitchen primarily reserved them for the programs that required the use of purchased food, like Fresh Start Catering. The real business was in the seconds. Pallets of sweet potatoes the size of footballs rolled into the shelter basement. That Shenandoah Franken-fruit may have spooked the average Safeway shopper, but by the time DCCK's staff and volunteers were done peeling, slicing, and dicing it, any second became indistinguishable from a first. The Kitchen began recovering so much fresh produce that it had to add an evening volunteer shift, where groups gathered from 5 to 8 p.m. to peel and process these items by hand. In 2009 alone, 4,000 people volunteered their evenings to help the Kitchen handle all its incoming fresh fruits and vegetables. The early results of its partnership with the SVPA inspired the organization to reach out to dozens of other local growers, replicating its unique purchasing and recovery model. At the end of the growing season, some of the SVPA's Mennonite farmers trekked into the big city to volunteer at that evening shift themselves. The elusive Mr. Showalter pulled Curtin aside. "You have no idea how this partnership has changed our community," said the grateful farmer. "Now *that* is sustainable agriculture," says Curtin in retrospect.

Thanks to this sudden infusion of fresh produce, the nutritional and aesthetic qualities of DCCK's meals improved and the public perception of the Kitchen's meal service operation began to change. "They said, 'Oh, you aren't just serving shelter gruel anymore,'" says one DCCK staffer. DC Central Kitchen's well-publicized shift to fresh, healthy, high-quality food—part reality, part promotion—precipitated the dramatic and critical expansion of its social enterprise activities. The basement kitchen was about to become more of a business than ever before. "It's just that our product was empowerment," says Curtin.

Chapter 8 Crops and Convicts

Thanks to its burgeoning partnerships with local farms, DC Central Kitchen's meals were fresher, healthier, and higher in quality than ever before. The Kitchen's new nutritious, local bent gave Curtin the angle he needed to press its social enterprise activities forward. In years past, DCCK's mission had been the strongest selling point for its various revenue-generating activities, while product quality and customer service sometimes lagged behind. Thanks to the influx of local produce and continued staff professionalization, the items being sold became as compelling as the organization selling it. Curtin finally had a worthy product. In 2008, he went looking for buyers.

Almost a decade earlier, DC Central Kitchen had tried its hand at serving school food. The Kitchen cobbled together a good faith effort through its Contract Foods social enterprise arm, but it lacked the capacity to do the job well. However, the traditional model of school-based food service—one that relies largely on plunking frozen starches into a deep fryer—attracted growing amounts of negative attention in the mid- to late-2000s, and some institutions started clamoring for something better. At DC's Washington Jesuit Academy, a small private school infused with a social justice mission, President Bill Whitaker and his CFO, Brian Ray, were among those who thought it was time for a change. Whitaker, Ray, and Curtin had known each other for years as members of DC's 'Jesuit Mafia,' a collection of prominent local Catholics steeped in the Jesuit commitment to social justice, and many of them tied, in one way or another, to Gonzaga College High School. Curtin had attended Gonzaga and Whitaker worked there for a decade before taking the helm of WJA.

Washington Jesuit Academy tries to prevent the cycle of poverty from afflicting new generations, putting middle school boys with low incomes and high records of achievement through a strenuous academic program that equips them for top high schools and, in time, colleges and jobs. With DC Central Kitchen beginning to emphasize the role of cheap, unhealthy food in driving diet-related disease and perpetuating poverty, a partnership with WJA appeared to be a natural fit. "There was this mission compatibility that we loved," says Ray. "It wasn't going to be the cheapest bid, but we thought it could be the right bid."

In June of 2008, Whitaker, Ray, and Curtin sat down at the Dubliner, a famous, poorly lit Irish pub just off of Capitol Hill with bi-partisan appeal and really good cheeseburgers. Whitaker wanted "the whole deal," Curtin recalls, "fresh produce, scratch-cooked meals, even a salad bar." Moving from freezers and fat fryers to fresh produce and fair wages would cost WJA $220,000 for the year, a 30 percent increase that averaged out to $3.50 per lunch.[74] As a private school, WJA had the resources and programmatic latitude to shoulder the increased costs of providing three free, healthy meals to each student each day. The most important component of the partnership, however, was neither scratch-cooked meals nor extra scratch for the

---

[74]   Bruske, Ed, "What a D.C. private school can teach us about school lunches," *Grist.org*, April 6, 2010, accessed November 24, 2012, http://grist.org/article/committed-to-better-school-food-dinner/.

Kitchen. "I wanted them to hire our graduates to do the food service," says Curtin. Ray agrees, saying "the hiring piece was what won us over, but we knew it would take a lot of work to make that happen."

The WJA board of directors was less enthusiastic. "I understood the reticence," says Curtin. "They had to make sure their kids were safe and secure, and here we were actively training ex-offenders. But we knew our intake systems worked, and making money off this deal wasn't the most important thing. It was creating jobs for our students." Ray recalls the negotiations as similarly challenging. "The contracting process was difficult. We had to hammer out some important lines, but we all really wanted to make this work." Curtin kept prodding, and just two weeks before the start of school, cut a deal that would further restrict the types of offenses that graduates working in WJA could have on their records. Those with any type of violent conviction were barred, leaving plenty of men and women who had been found guilty of basic drug possession charges and the like.

In time, the contract with WJA would give Howard Thomas a second chance. Wiry, athletic, and well over six feet tall, the charismatic Thomas now constantly flashes his broad, bright smile. His future didn't always look as bright. Returning home to DC after running afoul of the law, Howard says his biggest focus was "just looking to stay out of trouble." He became reacquainted with an old friend named Curtis, who shared a similar background but seemed to have done well since the two last spoke. "He looked good," says Thomas. "I asked him what he was doing, and he said was in school at DC Central Kitchen." Howard thought little of the referral at the time.

A few weeks later, when walking through his neighborhood on a warm, early spring morning, Howard spotted a white van parked on the corner with a small contingent of youthful,

Caucasian volunteers serving breakfast. "Usually, when white people showed up in my neighborhood, they were either looking to buy drugs or sell something. But that was the day I learned you should never judge where you get your help from." The van was DC Central Kitchen's First Helping street outreach unit. Howard grabbed some coffee and struck up a conversation. The outreach team told Howard about the Kitchen's job training program and helped him navigate the admission requirements, securing everything from a tuberculosis test to a police clearance.

There were few other places that openly embraced unemployed ex-offenders, and fewer still with any luck finding those people jobs. Howard ventured down to Second Street and applied for the Culinary Job Training program, but kept his expectations low. In April of 2009, Marianne Ali offered him a spot in the Kitchen's 75th class. As it turned out, he proved to be an excellent student, nailing his weekly skills tests and food handler's licensing exam. He quickly found a job at a local steakhouse, but when DCCK secured the WJA contract, Ali called Howard, thinking he offered the right mix of culinary talent, compassion, and first-hand knowledge of how tough the real world could be. "I went from destroying lives," he told an interviewer in 2010, "to changing lives."[75]

Quietly, Curtin had hoped that putting grown men with lengthy rap sheets and rough histories alongside aspiring young boys would, in practice, turn out to be far less dangerous than it sounded. "They were from a lot of the same communities," he says. "We figured that they would find some common ground and our staff could serve as examples of, not only what they could overcome, but the types of mistakes they could avoid." Without being asked by any of his superiors, Howard began getting to know some of the boys in his lunch line each day, and

---

[75]   Swantek, Josie, "Bringing School Food Home," Run Riot Films, 2010, accessed April 15, 2013, http://vimeo.com/16663471/.

pushing back on the common refrains of "Gross!" "That's nasty!" and "What is *that*?" with a little sly salesmanship. "I've got to sell it to them," he says. "I chop up the things they say they won't eat so fine that they don't know what's in it." Then, when the boys circle back for seconds, they discover they are asking for more kale or onions or yogurt. Howard deploys a Trojan horse doused in Tzatziki sauce.

One day during the 2009-2010 school year, Mike Curtin's desk line lit up with a surprise call from Principal Whitaker. "I need to talk to you about Howard," he began. Curtin's heart sank. Whitaker explained that he had been walking through the WJA lunchroom and spotted a half-dozen parents streaming into the adjacent kitchen. For an educational administrator, the unexpected appearance of parents at school usually spells trouble—it's easier to be outraged than engaged. Whitaker poked his head in warily. Howard had independently recruited some of his boys' parents to come in for a cooking class, preparing cheap, easy, and healthy turkey chili. The grand experiment was working.

A former boxer with a rangy frame, Howard quickly commanded the boys' respect and made the high-minded ideals of the food justice movement seem practical, even cool. "He's an absolute rock star," says Brian Ray. "He knows who he is, he isn't afraid of where he's from, and he loves what he does every day. A lot of our boys don't see that at home, so it's important they get it here." In time, some WJA students began asking follow-up questions about how to identify and prepare food that would help them become bigger, stronger athletes. Now their conversations go further. "Howard knows every one of our students by their first name," Ray attests. "There are so many days when he'll step out from the line after he's done serving and he'll be surrounded by 10 or 12 boys. And he's giving them advice. It's not about sports. It's *'don't screw this up,'* and he's reaching them on a whole new level."

Howard makes a point to shoot hoops with the boys after lunch on Friday afternoons, with free flowing conversations between free throws. He drives home the same message, week after week: "Stay in school, get your education. That other stuff, like being cool, meeting girls, it'll come on its own time." The talk works. One student who had shared Howard's lanky reach and skills on the hardtop said he was tempted by the idea of attending a public high school peppered with attractive members of the opposite sex. Howard urged him to pick the elite all-male academy that was recruiting him and focus on his grades and his game. A year later, the boy came back to say hello to his former mentors. Howard was out that afternoon, but he later found a note with his name on it: "Thanks for the talk."

The WJA equation of fresh, local ingredients, scratch-cooked meals, and fairly compensated cooks taking pride in their work took some time to balance itself. Initially, the boys complained about their new menus. Some parents sent their kids to school with paper bags of bologna and junk food. Whitaker and WJA would have none of it. While WJA staffers stamped out parental resistance, DCCK's chefs changed up their approach. "We had to get away from being *too* different. You can't do salmon with mango chutney every day. You have to work in healthy versions of tacos and pizza, too," says Ray. "We learned you don't have to serve something *frou-frou* to get at the healthy piece."

WJA and DCCK shared an independent streak, and it served them well in the early days of their new partnership. When WJA considered accepting District reimbursements for the meals it served students each summer, visiting officials told them the salad bar had to go. "They said because it wasn't pre-portioned, it didn't meet their nutrition standards," says Ray. The caloric restrictions of the public sector, intended to promote healthy eating, would have had the opposite effect at WJA. "Our boys are growing, so when they want more food, we push them toward the salad bar. And because we know that many of their families can't always afford to eat on the weekends, we let them take leftovers if they need them. Yeah, maybe we left some money on the table," Ray admits, "but I can live with that."

As the equation at WJA came into balance, it quickly attracted attention. DC's growing 'foodie' subculture, powered initially by a wave of new restaurants and later by the food truck revolution, had spawned a host of popular blogs and websites. The foodies loved the DCCK-WJA partnership, and visuals of excited schoolboys noshing on colorful food alongside Howard Thomas and his then-supervisor, chef and social media maven Alison Sosna, ricocheted across the Internet. While Jamie Oliver was turning healthy school food into a trendy cause nationwide, DC Central Kitchen's search for a sustainable social enterprise operation had placed it at the forefront of a bourgeoning movement. "I want this in every school," said DC Public Schools' food czar as he stood in the WJA lunchroom in 2009.

While that official's vision may have seemed especially ambitious at the time, Curtin was already beginning to think big. The truckloads of fresh food his staff was wheeling into the Kitchen each day had stretched the organization to the limits of its physical capability. With Stella packed to capacity, the Kitchen had begun renting freezer space across the city to store all the produce it was processing, packing, and vacuum sealing each day. Thanks to the new evening volunteer shift, DCCK was running at full-tilt from 6 a.m. to 9 p.m., and it was still struggling to keep up with the constant deliveries of local produce. "We needed a commissary," says Curtin, "a space that would allow us to consolidate all this back-end production. This second facility would allow us to more effectively use all these farm products, better manage our school food labor costs, and streamline our ordering and menu development."

A bigger, badder, more purposeful facility had been on the minds of Kitchen leadership for years. When Egger's push for a super-shelter floundered in the treacherous political waters of Washington, DC, he began campaigning for a super-kitchen. This shared space would aggregate fresh and donated food, blend nonprofit service with social enterprise, and efficiently serve all of the District's shelters, schools, jails, and Meals on Wheels-style entities. Egger envisioned a massive processing and freezing operation that would make quality nutrition a financially viable proposition for everyone involved. "It was another of my big, wacky ideas that needed someone to drill into it and make it practicable," says Robert. The Kitchen's imagined commissary grew out of that original sweeping concept, offering an intermediate step that would meet DCCK's near-term needs while testing the individual components of the super-kitchen in a circumscribed real world laboratory. Curtin and his Chief Development Officer Brian MacNair fanned out across the city, looking for an empty kitchen that would offer a relatively quick, cost-effective expansion.

In an ideal world, DCCK would have had the on-hand capital and financial security to expand in a measured, incremental fashion. Instead, while Curtin and MacNair were looking for a moderately-sized second space and CFO Glenda Cognevich had embarked on a two-year stint working overseas, leaving a stop-gap financial official in her stead, DC Public Schools (DCPS) decided to radically overhaul its approach to feeding students. Spurred by the DC Healthy Schools Act, passed in May 2010 at the behest of its champion, Councilwoman Mary Cheh, DCPS began soliciting bids for a healthy school food pilot program. Egger and Curtin were intrigued by the prospect of moving its operation at WJA to a grander stage.

Curtin tapped his Director of Revenue Generating Programs, Gregg Malsbary, asking him to assemble a proposal in response the District's daunting request for proposals (RFP). A trained chef, Malsbary had specialized in developing and running large culinary operations before joining DCCK in 2009. He first discovered the Kitchen while working as the Executive Chef of the massive Washington Convention Center, where he partnered with Marianne Ali to provide one of the first standing internship sites for Kitchen trainees. With slicked-back hair and a taste for sharp blazers, Malsbary is proficient in several languages of strange lands, with special fluency in American corporate-speak. He is an ardent believer in the importance of structure and process. DCCK's culture, which prized agility and improvisation over planning and detail, challenged him professionally and personally.

Much of Gregg's first year at DCCK was spent overhauling Fresh Start's catering operation, often by hand. Almost immediately, Malsbary recalls, "I had to take off the suit and get into chef's whites." Along with creating new menus and brand guidelines, he cultivated a new base of corporate clients, "ones that would give us consistent weekday business—breakfast, lunch, and maybe a reception on Thursday evening." Catering business picked up over the next few months, and in summer of 2010, Fresh Start received serious offers from an area theater and university to provide ongoing services. Malsbary's processes had finally gotten the social enterprise operation primed for gradual, sustained growth. Then the school food RFP dropped.

Gregg and the Kitchen's administrative staff scrambled to put together a plan for serving healthy, scratch-cooked meals at as many as 14 DC public schools each day. "I thought we could take what we were doing at WJA and just multiply it over a larger number of schools," says Curtin. They managed to push out the proposal on time, and a few weeks later, DCPS invited a series of bidders in for a round of tastings. DCCK was among them. "Suddenly, we had to create nutritious menus that would allow us to both feed in volume and set ourselves apart from the competition," remembers Malsbary, who turned to his Fresh Start menus for inspiration.

After the tastings, the District went silent. The decision deadline of early August came and went. The Kitchen began to assume DCPS had selected another provider and failed to notify them. MacNair recalls feeling a little relieved. Malsbary went to Curtin with the two offers from the theater and university. The theater had opened a gorgeous new facility and selected four approved caterers, three of them popular outfits led by esteemed chefs. The fourth was Fresh Start. The university, meanwhile, was eager to lose the contractor currently running its on-campus café and loved the local connection with a plucky nonprofit. "We hadn't heard from DCPS, and school started in two weeks," says Gregg. "I said we should move forward on the prospects we had." Curtin agreed. Malsbary signed contracts with both institutions, pleased that his preferred approach of measured, steady progress was beginning to pay dividends. The day after Gregg finalized a deal with the campus café, DCPS called. The Kitchen had been awarded a five-year contract to serve seven schools.

In its quarter-century of existence, DC Central Kitchen has pulled off one miraculous feat of food-related derring-do after another. Nothing pushed the Kitchen closer to its breaking point than the early days of the DCPS contract, initially valued at nearly $2 million annually. DCCK had 10 business days to figure out school food before 2,000 children lined up in lunchrooms across the city expecting to be fed. In a small-world twist, two of those children belonged to Chapman Todd, who was thrilled to hear about his former employer taking this courageous step forward but unsure of how it would perform. "This was a hugely visible program," says Malsbary, and there was no safety net awaiting the Kitchen if it fell flat on its face. "We had to staff up, get uniforms, find trucks, create menus, secure vending contracts, increase our purchases from existing providers, and even outsource those purchases to larger firms when our current contacts couldn't meet our needs," he says.

Equipment was a leading concern. "Everything we found in those kitchens was dilapidated, unkempt to the point of being unusable, or broken outright," Malsbary reports. The previous provider had really only needed three tools: freezers in which to keep processed, frozen goods, and steamers and fat fryers to heat them. The Kitchen held ceremonies to march the battered fryers out and decommission them. The freezers that survived were converted to refrigeration units. The shift to providing better meals required more than just better ingredients, says Gregg, because "to do local, scratch-cooked food, you need ovens, speed racks, extensive refrigerators, tongs, spatulas—real culinary tools."

Finding people to use these tools proved even more daunting. On August 1, 2010, the Kitchen had 70 employees. By September 1, it would have 118. Getting enough people with the right skills in the right places at the right times would have been hard enough as it was, but the Kitchen ran head-first into another barrier. The District had stringent regulations regarding who could work in its schools. Most new graduates of the Kitchen's job training program, even those that would have been permitted to work at WJA, failed the rigorous DCPS background check. Marianne Ali reached into the program's community of alumni and even instructors, scrounging up all of the folks with clean records she could. Long-time staples of DCCK's kitchen operation, including Chef Gary Bullock and even the revered Miss Dorothy Bell were conscripted into public schools service. Even then, Malsbary had to work through a local temp agency to secure enough qualified culinary staffers by the first day of school. "It was a lot of that scary six-letter word—*change*—all at once, and the Kitchen hadn't seen that much change in a very long time," he recalls.

Actually preparing 2,000 daily lunches in line with stringent Federal and District guidelines was going to be extremely difficult as it was. But after DCCK verbally and publicly agreed to take on the school food contract, the District proposed a series of amendments. In addition to healthy, scratch-cooked lunches, DCPS wanted breakfast served in classrooms and a supper program, efforts that required significant labor and supply costs. The Kitchen, accustomed to doing more with less, readily agreed. The complexity of DCCK's meal operation compounded dramatically. The payment it would receive for this work did not. Curtin's original plan of multiplying the WJA operation a few times over imploded. "I could not have been more wrong," he admits.

The extra requirements contributed to massive cost overruns in the early months of the contract. The Kitchen's food costs were too high. Fresh Start Catering's inspired menus needed more translation to the realities of school food service than Malsbary and his team expected. The creative flair Howard Thomas and Alison Sosna showed at WJA was ill-suited to the procrustean standards of the USDA and DC's Healthy Schools Act. DCCK was on the hook to provide a fruit, a vegetable, a whole grain, a protein, and a miniature carton of reduced fat milk. No more, no less. Serving hummus wraps and field corn summer succotash looked great on foodie blogs, but made little sense to the District's contracting professionals or the Kitchen's bookkeepers. These early menus also contributed to high labor costs. Seemingly small decisions, like cubing cantaloupe instead of simply slicing it, demanded more intensive culinary work and, in the aggregate, created a need for additional staff.

DCCK had figured that a single staffer could serve the food while operating the point-of-sale (POS) system at each school. While this double-duty method had worked in other school districts, the commitment to scratch-cooking demanded too much effort in the kitchen and required another full-time person to run the cash register. DC Central Kitchen was new to the big time school food biz, and it showed.

Once the meals were served, the Kitchen faced another challenge: kids had to eat them. Some schools pay their food providers an essentially flat rate based on the number of meals prepared each day. This system applied at Washington Jesuit Academy, ensuring a steady level of income for the Kitchen. DCPS, however, would only pay DCCK for each meal students actually took. Student participation in the school meal program, then, was absolutely critical. The more children who ate the lunch served at school, as opposed to bringing one from home or noshing on vending machine treats, the more money the Kitchen received. The switch to healthier options, in those early days, did little to inspire robust participation rates. At the Kitchen's largest school food site, lunch participation plummeted almost immediately, from 80 to 62 percent.

The tumult around the DCPS contract sent shockwaves throughout DCCK. The vision, dubbed "bringing school food home" by Egger, was compelling and clean: a value-driven local organization serving healthy, local food and paying DC residents a decent wage. The implementation turned out to be much more complex. MacNair began hounding funders, seeking to offset the contract's losses with contributions from donors who saw the social value of the Kitchen's efforts. Malsbary hired a number of experienced school food professionals, including a few chefs and a registered dietitian, who hustled to bring the organization up to speed. Curtin rushed to allay nervous stakeholders while squeezing his staff to improve their performance, and fast.

One key to that improvement was settling on a new, second kitchen facility. Curtin and MacNair found a space on Evarts Street NE, just north of the congested Route 50, a key access point to the District littered with cheap motels and fast food joints. A 6,000 square foot kitchen had been vacated by a bankrupt catering company and the building's owner was looking for a new tenant. At first glance, it fit the bill of a building Egger could approve of, an existing space that just needed a little TLC— perhaps $50,000 in cosmetic work and new equipment, but no more than $100,000. Curtin had his commissary. He signed the lease in October and his staff began preparations to move in.

For Fresh Start Catering, the move could not come soon enough. Tucked away in a corner of the Second Street kitchen, the catering staff was dealing with a growing list of crises. The two contracts the Kitchen had signed just before the DCPS firestorm struck were still in effect. Gregg pleaded with the university to delay its start date, but administrators had already gone about branding 'A Fresh Start' to its campus foodservice. "Forget about getting equipment into these places, I didn't have the manpower," remembers Malsbary. Fortunately, more of the Kitchen's graduates with checkered records could work on those ventures, and, somehow, Fresh Start managed to piece together a functioning operation on time and somewhere near budget.

The first day of school came and went, and while it was by no means perfect, every child in line was fed a quality meal. The press and larger community responded with strong shows of support for the Kitchen. All that good buzz aside, however, DC Central Kitchen's boldest foray into the realm of social enterprise presented a steep and costly learning curve. Through the end of 2010, the financial losses were tremendous, and it took MacNair's aggressive fundraising around the new facility expansion to keep the books in line. Malsbary turned his attention to overhauling that facility, and discovered a series of unpleasant surprises. The building's electrical and drainage systems "were a complete cluster," totally incapable of handling the large-scale production Curtin and his team had envisioned taking place there. "From there, it very easily turned into a half-a-million-dollar overhaul," says Malsbary.

In the spring of 2011, Glenda Cognevich returned to the Kitchen from her stint overseas. No one would have blamed her if she had stayed away. The costs of new building project were spiraling upwards, payroll had ballooned, and the DCPS contract was still losing money each month, although those deficits were shrinking. Before she had time to rethink her decision, Cognevich took a deep breath and dove into the labyrinthine accounting and requisitioning procedures of the District, hoping to reduce the painful lag time between DCPS payments. Curtin and MacNair made her job somewhat easier by soliciting big checks from funders, ones that reflected the Kitchen's big financial needs. To their credit, a diverse group of donors stepped up their giving, eager to support an organization that was trying so hard to support itself. Those were challenging days, but DCCK pressed forward, undaunted.

The cramped conditions at Second Street had turned the organization into a pressure cooker of hard-edged personalities and serious financial concerns. The Kitchen's leaders had plenty on their plates, and each was eager for a respite from new projects. Councilwoman Mary Cheh's ongoing fight for healthier food, however, presented an opportunity that even an exhausted DC Central Kitchen felt compelled to seize. In 2010, the influential food policy advocates at DC Hunger Solutions released a widely read report entitled "When Healthy Food is out of Reach." The group urged District officials to leverage public funds in attracting new food retail outlets to underserved DC neighborhoods, ones that would offer healthy, fresh items. Wielding the report, Cheh led the charge for the Food, Environment, and Economic Development (FEED) DC Act. Much of the legislation focused on providing incentives to large retail chains for opening full-service grocery stores in DC's 'food deserts,' especially those in Wards 7 and 8. While those long-term projects were under way, the FEED DC Act also provided resources to identify and improve existing conduits for fostering healthy food access, including DC's much maligned corner stores.

Widely derided as purveyors of 'liquor and lotto,' the corner stores in DC's poor neighborhoods generally live up to their lousy collective reputation. Part of their image problem is justifiably related to their inventory. Beyond the alcohol, tobacco, and lottery tickets they sell, which exact disproportionate financial and physical tolls upon low-income households, their food offerings are almost exclusively cheap, heavily processed items like candy, chips, and soda. DC corner stores are largely cash-based businesses with minimal reserves. When they stock an item, it needs to sell quickly or remain shelf-stable until it does. Pre-packaged food items make the most short-term business sense, especially for stores primarily frequented by customers on the go looking for easy-to-eat snacks.

District corner stores have a complex, contentious relationship with their communities that goes beyond their place at the epicenter of unhealthy eating. Most are owned by new Americans, predominantly immigrant families from South Korea and Ethiopia. From Marcus Garvey to Malcolm X, the proliferation of black-owned businesses has long been a deeply important issue for many African-American leaders. In the traditionally black neighborhoods of the District, especially east of the Anacostia River, the success of immigrant entrepreneurs appears to many a triumph for outsiders in a zero-sum contest against local residents. The electorally invincible Marion Barry, now the

Ward 8 Councilman, publicly voiced the private sentiments of many constituents when he told a local news outlet in 2012 that "We got to do something about these Asians coming in and opening up businesses and dirty shops . . . They ought to go. I'm going to say that right now. But we need African-American businesspeople to be able to take their places, too."[76]

For many corner store owners, the antipathy is mutual. Bulletproof glass dividers are common, not only shielding cashiers from customers, but preventing customers from even touching merchandise before they pay for it. While Barry was blaming store owners for infecting his ward with low-grade conditions and disrespecting his almost totally black voter base, those owners tended to feel that any improvements they made would be quickly rendered meaningless by vandalism, crime, and general consumer disregard. In practice, each side's perceptions served to reinforce the others'. If Cheh and her allies were betting on corner stores to become champions of public health and community development, they were picking a pretty sickly horse.

Despite their long odds, the bet made by Cheh and company turned out be significant. The District charged its Department of Small and Local Business Development (DSLBD) with implementing a brand-new Healthy Retail Food Program, where a nonprofit organization would be given $300,000 to get a minimum of 20 stores in low-income neighborhoods to stock and sell healthy food items, all within six months. The nonprofit designation was significant. DC, like many other municipalities, had met repeatedly with for-profit wholesalers and distributors to try and figure out the problem of healthy food access without

---

[76]   "Barry Comment Critical of Asian Business Owners," *NBC 4*, April 5, 2012, accessed January 2, 2013, http://www.nbcwashington.com/ blogs/first-read-dmv/Barry-Comment-Seems-Critical-of-Asian-Business-Owners-146185485.html/.

spending a great deal of public sector money. But produce distributors operate on extremely thin margins, between three and five percent per sale. In order to make any money, they have to focus on bigger customers and keep their delivery routes tight. Working with small retailers in poor communities breaks both of these cardinal rules. Successful distributors require minimum purchases, and no DC corner store can afford 650 apples, let alone fit them on their shelves and move them before they spoil. The stores that offered a few fruits and vegetables did so sporadically, when the owner could run to the sprawling Florida Avenue cash-and-carry, where the produce was expensive by wholesale standards and usually overripe. Once on the shelf of a corner store, cash-and-carry produce tended to be overpriced and spoil quickly. Good food was bad business for everyone involved—wholesalers, owners, and customers alike.

DSLBD needed a community organization that was willing to take on a business model that had been roundly rejected by actual businesses. Thanks to the growing popularity of food access issues, DC had no shortage of nonprofits, many of them quite new, interested in supporting the initiative. DC Hunger Solutions had run a small-scale healthy corner store program a few years earlier, making some inroads with business owners and generating some useful insights for future replication. The money, however, had run out before the organization figured out the biggest problem for any successful corner store venture: distribution. DC Hunger Solutions and several other groups were strong in their ability to advocate for new programs, promote community awareness, and teach people how to eat healthier. Or, as some DC Central Kitchen staff refers to it, 'the soft stuff.' The ability to do 'the hard stuff'—tasks that require rumbling trucks, whirring processing equipment, and straining human muscles—was less common among the DC nonprofits fighting for healthy food access. Thanks to recent investments the

Kitchen had made to support its produce recovery operation and school food program, DCCK did have plenty of 'hard stuff' capability, making it the clear front-runner for DSLBD's grant.

A winded DC Central Kitchen summoned its strength for another sprint. DSLBD first solicited applications for Healthy Retail Food Program funding in April, with the intention of selecting a winner in early May and launching the six-month pilot initiative that summer. When DCCK decision makers gathered to assemble their application, Mike Curtin and Brian MacNair quickly became the program's chief advocates. Curtin had discussed a corner store program in the abstract several times in the preceding year and, while he would have ideally been able to wait another year before embarking on a new venture, he also knew that large District start-up grants that suited DCCK priorities were rare. "I was nervous about pulling it off the drawing board that soon," Curtin admits, "but it was one of those opportunities that was too good to resist. We didn't know if we'd have another chance like that, so it was full steam ahead." Programmatically, MacNair knew that healthy eating was a hot topic for funders. More pragmatically, he also figured that $300,000 would go a long way towards helping him meet his large and growing fundraising goal for the ongoing construction across town on Evarts Street, which had ground to a full stop while Malsbary waited on a series of permit approvals from the District.

Cognevich was less enthused, leery of another go-round with District accountants in the midst of her school food struggles. "The real difficulty in my position," she states, "is that sometimes I have to say no to the innovators. Now, I've never just said no, even when I wanted to, but sometimes it's my responsibility to help them realize something isn't a good idea, or that it isn't the right time to act on a good idea." MacNair and his fundraising team swore up and down that they would structure the proposal so DCCK would cover all its costs, pay a good chunk of the new building's rent, and avoid any of the expensive oversights that had plagued the DCPS contract for the past year. Curtin wanted to press forward. Cognevich, having waved all the red flags she could, reluctantly gave them a green light.

Together with their staffers, Curtin and MacNair agreed on a target number of 30 corner stores in Wards 5, 7, and 8 and a plan to serve them. They would use their new second kitchen to prepare deliveries of fresh produce and healthy snacks, which would be stocked in small but appealing refrigerators and shelving units provided for free to store owners. DCCK would dispatch its registered dietitian and other qualified staffers to conduct community outreach and nutrition education sessions, stimulating consumer demand. The cash they did not spend on refrigerators and shelves would go largely to purchases of local produce and the continued employment of several graduates of the Kitchen's job training program who would process produce, prepare snacks, and make deliveries. MacNair added a new name for the program: Healthy Corners.

DCCK could not pass up DSLBD's money. And DSLBD knew the Kitchen was the only potential grantee that could keep up with its aggressive timeline. By early May, the Kitchen received word that it had won the grant, beginning an arduous period of contractual negotiations. Forced together by the FEED DC Act, the two organizations could not have been more different in their cultures, procedures, or values. Like most bureaucracies, DSLBD was wary of new projects, and this particular grant program was well outside its traditional expertise. Department staff tried to shoehorn much of the Healthy Retail Food Program into initiatives it already had in place, including storefront beautification projects, energy efficiency audits, and store owner training programs in account management and marketing. DCCK, accustomed to innovation and sometimes brash about the strength of its capabilities and 'street cred,' pushed back hard. The Kitchen wanted to focus on the program's food distribution component, its own area of strength and experience, and balked at repurposing funds toward outside consultants and the activities most familiar and dear to DSLBD.

That spring also witnessed the breaking scandal involving DC Councilman Harry Thomas, Jr. His theft of District funds through a pet nonprofit further poisoned the atmosphere surrounding negotiations.[77] DSLBD felt the need to be more cautious and authoritative than ever, lest any dollars disappear and the department find itself caught in the crosshairs of a spooked and defensive city council. DCCK, pointing to its sterling reputation for financial management, resented DSLBD's tone and bristled at its attempts to impose additional forms of fiscal oversight. The Kitchen figured its new public sector partner needed the legitimacy of DCCK's brand. The sudden scrutiny seemed hypocritical and belittling. The two groups proceeded to fight, line by line, through the contract and final budget. At one point, Curtin let loose some of his 'Jesuit fire' in *The Washington Post*, making it known that "DCCK almost decided to launch Healthy Corners without the city and its $300,000 grant," before hinting that an agreement was in the works.[78]

While these contentious negotiations dragged on through the record-setting summer temperatures of 2011, DCCK staff ventured out into DC's toughest neighborhoods to drum up

---

[77] Craig, Tim and Mike Dibonis, "Ex-D.C. Council member Harry Thomas Jr. gets 3-year sentence," *The Washington Post*, May 3, 2012, accessed October 17, 2013, http://www.washingtonpost.com/local/dc-politics/harry-thomas-former-dc-council-member-is-sentenced-to-more-than-three-years-in-prison/2012/05/03/gIQA7X7KzT_story.html/.

[78] Carman, Tim, "DCCK to deliver produce to D.C. food deserts," *The Washington Post*, August 17, 2012, accessed November 6, 2012, http://www.washingtonpost.com/blogs/all-we-can-eat/post/dcck-to-deliver-produce-to-dc-food-deserts/2011/08/17/gIQAZsczLJ_blog.html/.

store owner interest. The Kitchen elected to offer Healthy Corners' products, which included hand fruits, familiar vegetables, and prepared snacks like granola and trail mix, for free at the outset of the program. For store owners operating on thin margins in communities that were growing poorer by the day, experimenting with new products presented a considerable risk. DCCK figured that giving away free product, signage, and infrastructure would ease the fears of skittish storeowners while encouraging them to participate in the training sessions and consultant-led assessments stipulated by DSLBD.

The Kitchen's reputation and history proved also to be mixed blessings in the early days of Healthy Corners. DCCK's association with leftover, unwanted food made some storeowners leery. If the food was free to them, they assumed it came free to the Kitchen as well. The staffers and interns charged with signing up stores had to convince skittish retailers that as with any DCCK social enterprise, the food the Kitchen sold was food it actually purchased. After six weeks of chatting up cashiers, the Kitchen had assembled the dozen or so participants it needed to begin rolling out the program, and it began deliveries in early September 2011, a date influenced by the contract agreement, which did not occur until late August. Continued outreach recruited more stores, and positive feedback from several owners, especially those in the Korean grocer community, attracted a growing number of requests to participate in Healthy Corners.

By year's end, fully 30 stores were receiving weekly or bi-weekly deliveries of fresh and healthy food. The Kitchen's relationship with DSLBD improved as the program grew, and so did the level of store owner commitment. Curtin and his team were nervous as the January 2012 deadline for store owners to begin paying full price for their deliveries approached. Until then, they had received Healthy Corners' products for free or at steep discounts. As it turned out, when the owners had more skin in the game, they worked harder to call attention to their Healthy Corners displays, converse with customers, and plug new products. In fact, as Kitchen staff began digging into the data produced by Healthy Corners, they found that store owner commitment was the single most important indicator of success. It was even more critical than customer foot traffic, store size, or the presence of bulletproof partitions. Even in the stores where protective barriers separated customers from cashiers, when owners came out from behind that glass and interacted with customers, they saw significant gains in healthy food sales, no matter how high the rates of obesity or poverty were in their surrounding community. "The food desert issue has been blue ribbon paneled and white papered to death," says Curtin. "Everyone says getting healthy food into corner stores is a critical step, but that policy conclusion was never merged with the practical response of actually delivering that food to those stores until we did it."

Healthy Corners' early success drew on the capacity of the newly completed facility on Evarts Street, which opened its doors in August 2011. Curtin had originally planned to call it DC Central Commissary, but Egger was inspired by the building's potential as a place of experimentation and creativity. In a particularly dull DCCK board meeting, Robert slipped Curtin a folded-over scrap of paper. It read "Nutrition Lab." Curtin was sold, immediately renaming his new building. The additional space allowed DCCK to move much of its school food preparation out of tiny school kitchens and into a consolidated space where it could enforce standardization and quality control while finally establishing economies of scale. In its first year of operations, the Nutrition Lab created a dozen more jobs for the Kitchen's culinary graduates and allowed the organization to increase its recovery of donated fresh produce by 67 percent.

Malsbary stayed long enough to see the renovations through, but left quickly thereafter. For all the hurdles he faced completing that build-out process, "we ended up doing it. And it was doing everything it was meant to do," he says. The foundation for success laid, Malsbary was followed by savvy school food veteran Andrew Finke. Malsbary would look at a task, see a dozen or so sub-tasks, and develop nuanced plans to achieve each of them. Conditioned by years of managing contracts with school districts, Finke was more linear, charging from point A to point B and happily disregarding points C and D unless someone stipulated, in writing, that they were his problem. The two men did share a demand for high standards, an expectation that remained consistent despite the leadership transition. Their combined efforts paid off. In 2011, the Kitchen generated more money through social enterprise, some 56 percent of its total budget, than it did through charitable donations. Curtin and Finke continued to streamline the school food operation while renegotiating their per-meal reimbursement rate with the city. Steadily, the program crept from the red toward the black.

As Healthy Corners completed its sixth month of activities in March 2012, DC Central Kitchen prepared to wrap up its relationship with DSLBD. After submitting its final report to the city, the two entities parted amicably. After all the complex and sometime heated negotiations, Healthy Corners, according to Curtin, "turned out to be a model public-private partnership." The District stepped up with the necessary resources to entice a qualified private entity to provide a critical new service. Then, after a sufficient pilot period, public funds dried up. The Kitchen, in turn, used its early results to secure private resources from a number of foundations and corporate supporters to sustain and expand the program going forward. Within a year, Healthy

Corners would win a number of significant awards and see steady, month-to-month sales growth in its participating stores. At the same time, a brand-new organic market that opened in Ward 8 with the help of the FEED Act and $900,000 in public funds went under after just two years of operations. The failure was attributed due to a lack of customer interest and local suspicions that it was a covert anchor for future gentrification.[79] The sickly horse of DC's corner stores had triumphed.

With Healthy Corners becoming a permanent fixture of the Kitchen's programming, the organization now had a full menu of programs focused on health and nutrition in addition to those targeting hunger and poverty. Beyond its work with dozens of corner stores, the Kitchen would soon increase its healthy school food program to nine DC Public Schools on top of its continued work at Washington Jesuit Academy. Its long-standing Healthy Returns initiative, which delivered nutritious snacks and meals to summer camps and after-school programs, scaled up operations and doubled the number of children it served between 2009 and 2012. Together, these different programs constituted an integrated response to childhood hunger and limited healthy food access that no direct service organization had attempted before.

DC Central Kitchen's path-breaking approach to fostering healthy eating among low-income children involved two key thrusts. The first was a firm commitment to providing high-quality meals, no matter how much kids complained. When

---

[79]   Yates, Clinton, "Yes Organic Market needs more than a name change," *The Washington Post (The Root DC)*, December 14, 2012, accessed December 18, 2012, http://www.washingtonpost. com/blogs/therootdc/post/yes-organic-market-needs-more-than-a-name-change/2012/12/14/4acbc230-45e6-11e2-8e70-e1993528222d_blog.html/.

changing USDA regulations capped the calorie counts of school lunches in the fall of 2012, the din around school food reform reached new decibel levels. Across America, other efforts to overhaul school food met with stiff resistance from students, cash-strapped administrators, and even some small-government politicians, who condemned these "misguided" projects of the "nanny state."[80] In response, Curtin published a stern op-ed in *The Huffington Post* that urged advocates of healthier options to avoid imperious tones that alienated parents and other stakeholders, instead of rallying them to the cause. However, he had little patience for those who figured fatty food was an inalienable right. "Sometimes," Curtin wrote, "kids complain. And sometimes, grown-ups have to be grown-ups. And being a grown-up means, in part, taking unpopular positions because they're in the best interest of the young people in your care. The pundits and politicians who think that denying daily access to nachos and cinnamon buns constitutes a violation of human freedom are wrong; and if this generation is the first in U.S. history that fails to outlive their parents, they'll be dead wrong."[81]

When it came to kids and their diets, Curtin and the Kitchen unabashedly embraced a form of paternalism, albeit one that urged parents and teachers to join them in taking a tough stand on the side of health, rather than treating those adults like children as well. The proof was in the low-fat yogurt. The middle school that saw lunch participation drop to 62 percent

---

[80] Kasperowicz, Pete, "GOP bill would repeal Agriculture Dept. calorie caps on school lunches," *The Hill*, September 17, 2012, accessed November 25, 2012, http://thehill.com/blogs/floor-action/house/249849-rep-king-pushes-to-repeal-usdas-calorie-cap-at-school-lunch/.

[81] Curtin, Jr., Michael F., "We are hungry too: the fuss about healthy school food," *The Huffington Post*, October 17, 2012, accessed 25 November 2012, http://www.huffingtonpost.com/mike-curtin/healthy-school-lunch_b_1971520.html/.

when DCCK took over in 2010 had totally turned around by 2012, when participation shot up to 92 percent, exceeding pre-Kitchen levels. That fall, the physical capability of the Nutrition Lab and the Kitchen's increased institutional understanding of just how to "bring school food home" allowed DCCK to secure its first profits from the DCPS contract.

The second element of the Kitchen's unique strategy entailed a 'wraparound' effort to provide healthy options in school, after school, during school vacations, and at the corner stores children visited on their way to and from school. Other communities experimenting with superior school food provided plenty of anecdotal tales of students tossing out their lunches, only to run to vending machines and corner stores after school, looking for their sugar, salt, and fat fixes. The DC Central Kitchen model, meanwhile, tried to reinforce the healthy behaviors its staff was fighting for each day in DC's cafeterias by providing nutritious choices nearly everywhere children went.

As a nonprofit providing healthy school meals on a large scale and distributing nutritious snacks and fresh produce to corner stores located in food deserts, the Kitchen was truly in uncharted territory. To capture its multi-pronged response to childhood hunger and obesity, DCCK needed a name for its umbrella of nutrition-promoting programs. MacNair and his fundraising team settled on Healthy Futures. They stopped asking donors to 'give' and instead encouraged them to 'invest.' As bad as the Great Recession had been for so many people, DCCK began telling its stakeholders how much worse things could get if future generations were riddled with diet-related disease, unable to focus in school, and raised by chronically unemployed parents. An organization that had always prided itself in rapidly responding to crises was positioning itself to prevent them.

The Kitchen's new emphasis on the future was in some sense curious, because in the preceding few years, it had also become increasingly concerned with its trainees' pasts. "When Mike came on board," Marianne Ali remembers, "his biggest focus was the Culinary Job Training program and improving its ability to retain students." At Curtin's urging, Ali began digging into the results of the program she helmed. Thanks in large part to Clinton-era welfare reforms, the average size of each incoming class had ballooned above 30 students, and some cohorts numbered greater than 40. By the time graduation rolled around, however, most classes were down to 10 or 12 members. In response, Ali and her team took a number of steps aimed at helping students overcome the challenges they faced while in the program, but graduation rates still lagged below 50 percent. In 2008, however, "we realized the problem wasn't really with what happened during those 12 weeks. It was what happened before them. We had to overhaul our intake procedures," she says.

As the Kitchen examined the differences between the students who succeeded in the program versus those who failed, one common denominator seemed to emerge. "Surprisingly, it was the ex-offenders who turned out to be our best students and best graduates," reports MacNair. Former convicts had always been part of the Kitchen's client base, but only indirectly. Many individuals who are homeless, disabled, or mentally ill eventually end up in prison. When they get out, they still have the needs that contributed to their desperation in the first place. Others end up impoverished after their release from prison due to a variety of factors, including widespread reluctance among employers to hire applicants with criminal records. For both subsets, the Kitchen was one of the few area organizations that would welcome them into a no-cost vocational training program. However, DCCK had never explicitly sought out ex-offenders, and doing so presented a significant risk. Former criminals evoke little sympathy among donors and make prospective employers nervous. Even for DC Central Kitchen, this was edgy.

Why were ex-offenders more likely to complete CJT and succeed in the job market? For some, 'the system' worked. They used their time in prison to reevaluate their lives and commit to a new path. Then, they productively used their time at the Kitchen to prepare themselves for their next step forward. One graduate named William came to DCCK in 2010 after 17 years of incarceration. "After prison and spending some time in a half-way house, my whole plan was to make myself more marketable," he told an interviewer in 2012. "I thought I would be fine when I got out of prison, but [employers] were concerned about the amount of time I had been incarcerated and how I'd adjust."[82] Humbled in prison, and humbled again upon his release, he seized on everything the Kitchen had to offer him—which ultimately included a full-time job.

For most of DCCK's successful students, however, the explanation is more practical. Ex-offenders are supposed to return to society with a re-entry plan, one that accounts for basic needs like housing and provides ongoing case management. Unlike other individuals referred by a nonprofit or public agency serving a specific client population such as female drug users or homeless men, ex-offenders tended to arrive at DCCK enrolled in a whole menu of active services. With their core needs accounted for, DCCK could provide the capstone pieces of self-empowerment, vocational training, and job placement. The Kitchen's renewed emphasis on its intake process was not meant to help it cherry-pick easier cases. "We're still serving people that are squarely within the population we've always cared about,"

---

[82] Day, Paul, "Staff Profiles: William Ferrell, Culinary Job Training Class 81 Graduate," *dccentralkitchen.org*, March 20, 2012, accessed October 21, 2013, http://www.dccentralkitchen.org/staff-profiles-william-ferrell-culinary-job-training-class-81-graduate/.

says Curtin. "We just know a lot more about what the indicators are for a given individual to succeed in the program, and we're doing more to prepare those individuals for that success."

With the results of Marianne's data mining in hand, Curtin and MacNair had to find a way to sell the idea of repositioning their most prized program toward a demographic few felt pity for. For years, Egger had pleaded for donors to worry not just about what was good, but what was smart. Faced with the greatest public relations challenge of his tenure, Curtin reached into his predecessor's rhetorical arsenal and began telling anyone who would listen that "helping ex-offenders find work isn't just the good or right thing to do but the smart thing as well." Serving men and women who had hurt others was bound to strike some as unseemly. If the Kitchen couldn't convince everyone of the moral underpinnings of its position, it resolved itself to win the battle of simple mathematics.

In America, incarceration has become a major money loser for taxpayers. In the past two decades, the US crime rate has fallen nearly 40 percent.[83] And yet, the country's rate of incarceration is up 240 percent since 1980.[84] In 2008, when the Great Recession took hold, state and local governments were spending $75 billion to incarcerate their citizens each year.[85] There are many factors driving this costly, counterintuitive trend. Some are political. Being tough on crime has traditionally been bi-partisan in its popularity. Others are profit-related. Thanks to

---

[83] Teichner, Martha, "The Cost of a Nation of Incarceration," *CBS News*, April 22, 2012, accessed December 28, 2012, http://www.cbsnews. com/8301-3445_162-57418495/the-cost-of-a-nation-of-incarceration/.

[84] Schmitt, John, Kris Warner, and Sarika Gupta, "The high budgetary cost of incarceration," *Center for Economic and Policy Research*, June 2010, accessed December 28, 2012, http://www.cepr.net/ documents/publications/incarceration-2010-06.pdf/.

[85] Schmitt, et al, "The high budgetary cost."

shrewd lobbying and contracting practices, privately-owned prisons now hold 1,600 percent more Americans than they did in 1990. The two largest US private prison firms now earn a combined total of more than $3 billion annually.[86] The economic downturn of 2008, however, severely weakened state and local government budgets, and elected officials began scrambling for cost-cutting ideas. Prison expenses, along with nearly every other form of public good Americans had come to expect since the days of Franklin Delano Roosevelt, were suddenly negotiable. Some voices advocated for reduced sentences and early release programs. Others, like the Kitchen, suggested helping people who had already paid one debt to society avoid incurring any more.

With violent crime in a steady decline for nearly a generation, two of the largest contributing factors to America's growing incarceration rate are drug-related convictions and painfully high probabilities of recidivism. The two factors feed one another. Since the declaration of the War on Drugs in 1971, the number of Americans imprisoned for drugs has increased more than tenfold, from 40,000 to upwards of half a million.[87] Upon their release, most ex-offenders struggle to find work, regardless of the severity of their original crime. In DC, half of all ex-offenders are unemployed, and those who attended job training or GED

---

[86] Shapiro, David, "Banking on Bondage: Private Prisons and Mass Incarceration," November 2, 2011, accessed December 28, 2012, http://www.aclu.org/files/assets/bankingonbondage_20111102.pdf/.

[87] Teichner, Martha, "The Cost of a Nation of Incarceration," *CBS News*, April 22, 2012, accessed December 28, 2012, http://www.cbsnews.com/8301-3445_162-57418495/the-cost-of-a-nation-of-incarceration/.

programs in prison are no more likely to find employment.[88] Without steady work, ex-offenders are overwhelmingly likely to relapse, re-offend, and return to prison. The most recent figures available from the Department of Justice indicate that fully two-thirds of ex-offenders are re-incarcerated within three years.[89] Perhaps some, even many of these individuals are irredeemable. But with each incarcerated American costing taxpayers an average of $32,000 per year, spending less than one-third of that on the Kitchen's efforts to help someone who truly wanted to get back on his feet and back to work seemed like a smart investment. Curtin and company decided to drive home a potentially unpopular point: once released, most ex-offenders deserved a second chance at a decent job.

While MacNair and his team went about crunching the numbers necessary to support the Kitchen's new focus on ex-offenders, Curtin began using a powerful personal account to justify the strategic shift. Whenever the Kitchen's commitment to training formerly incarcerated citizens raised eyebrows among funders, colleagues, or District officials, Curtin told the story of Dawain Arrington.

When they speak in public together, Curtin and Arrington make a curious pairing. Curtin's modest size and fair complexion are accentuated when he stands next to Arrington, a tall, sinewy black man built like a NFL pass rusher. His imposing build, first forged in prison, is offset by an engaging smile. Dawain's early years seem like a strange, painful cross between *Les Misérables*

---

[88]   "Unlocking Employment Opportunity for Previously Incarcerated Persons in the District of Columbia," *Center for Court Excellence*, 2011, accessed December 28, 2012, http://www.courtexcellence.org/uploads/publications/CCE_Reentry.pdf/.

[89]   "Reentry trends in the U.S.," *Bureau of Justice Statistics, Department of Justice*, November 26, 2012, accessed December 29, 2012, http://bjs.ojp.usdoj.gov/content/reentry/recidivism.cfm/.

and *The Wire*. His parents were users. Left to fend for his siblings at the age of 12, Arrington stole food from a grocery store. He was immediately caught, convicted, and locked up. At 13, he was incarcerated again, this time for selling drugs. "I despised drugs. I saw what it did to my family," he says, but the money was too tempting. He sold drugs to feed a more capital-intensive business in illegal guns. Once a year, for the better part of a decade, he would re-offend and return to prison. If he survived to adulthood, an adolescent Dawain figured, that life would be lived out in jail. The severity of his charges continued to escalate, and he was paroled again in 2005, at the age of 32.[90]

"Some people waste their time in prison, but I didn't want to," says Arrington. He got his GED, acquired some trade skills, and began earning credits toward his Associate's Degree. Arrington had always been whip-smart, but growing up, his impatience outpaced and derailed his evident talent. He wanted more, faster. It made sitting in class hard. It made crime tempting.

When other employers refused to take on someone with such a long criminal record, he enrolled in the Kitchen's job training program in February 2005. Four weeks in, his impatience flared again. "My problem is that I'm never satisfied," Arrington admits. Two of his instructors, Tammy Williams and Chef Gary Bullock, "saw something in me I didn't see." They urged Dawain to stick with the program and arranged for him to get some part-time catering work so he could earn a little extra cash before graduation. As soon as he completed the training program, he landed a job in the Kitchen's Contract Foods division. Arrington spent three years generating revenue for DCCK, and when Curtin merged Contract Foods and Fresh Start Catering, Dawain earned a promotion to supervisor. His impatience found a better forum. "I brought that street sense to the workplace. The drive that can

---

[90]   Merica, Dan, "Growing up in prison, coping with freedom," *American Observer*, (17: 2) October 19, 2010.

take you from a corner boy to selling [kilos] can help you when you use it right." When a position in the main kitchen opened up, he leapt at the opportunity. "My favorite moments are when volunteers come in each morning, and whenever a new class starts in the training program," he says, beaming. "That's my excitement. That's what keeps bringing me back."

Dawain makes a point to reach out to each new class of culinary trainees. "The students haven't changed all that much since I've been here. They're all caught up in some kind of temptation." Lots of new students complain that they need money *now*, that they cannot wait until the end of the program to earn a paycheck. Arrington tries to straighten them out. Any money that comes that fast, that easy, comes with consequences—ones he knows better than most. "The program works!" he says, "But it only works when folks buy into it. You have to have the will to change your situation. If your problem is prison, the streets, whatever, we have people who can work with those problems sincerely."

Nearly destroyed by his impatience, Arrington is now focused on the long game. Even for all his early mistakes, he says, "I never had a child when I was young because I knew I couldn't provide for one." Dawain now has a young daughter, and he is passionately committed to her future. "I'm raising a *queen*," he says, his voice shaking but solid in its resolve. While he spent his formative years in prison, Arrington's child will be educated in a very different institution. He has been putting away money in a college fund since her birth.

The Kitchen did not fix Dawain Arrington. It offered a supportive space where a young man could walk out a new path he set for himself. As Curtin testified in a Federal hearing on ex-offender hiring in 2011, Arrington's success along that path offers proof of "what a job can do. As a community, we've spent close to a million dollars keeping Dawain locked up. Don't get me wrong—he did some bad things and deserved to be locked up. The chances are very good that if had not come to the Kitchen and not gotten a job, he would be costing us all money today. Instead he is putting money into our economy, helping others while he's doing that and, perhaps most importantly, changing the expectations of the next generation and those to follow— saving us all millions along the way."[91]

To help provide more paths for people like Dawain, Marianne Ali began revamping her program over the course of 2008. She ended the practice of taking just about anyone who wanted to enroll in CJT, setting a cap of 25 students per class. Applicants with histories of substance abuse had once only needed to be clean for 30 days. Marianne extended that minimum to 90, and eventually 120, days. By going all-in with ex-offenders, she had to definitively specify which prior offenses were permissible. No one with histories of sexual violence or crimes against children was welcome. She and Curtin figured more up-front restrictions might create a little addition by subtraction. "We wanted to create a culture of completion," says Curtin, "and by trying to establish that completing the program was the rule, not the exception, we thought more students would stick together and encourage each other to graduate."

Marianne agreed. "We used to bring in lots of people and have a tough policy for booting them. Instead, we started with a smaller number and began evaluating people through the process and reminding them of their progress . . . This fostered a deeper level of commitment from our staff, who all bought

---

[91]   Curtin Jr., Michael F., "Meeting of July 26, 2011—EEOC to Examine Arrest and Conviction Records as a Hiring Barrier: Written Testimony of Michael F. Curtin, Jr., President and CEO, D.C. Central Kitchen", *U.S. Equal Employment Opportunity Commission (EEOC)*, July 26, 2011, accessed December 5, 2012, http://www.eeoc.gov/eeoc/ meetings/7-26-11/curtin.cfm/.

into this, and we started having long conversations how about to keep individual students," she remembers. Because DCCK was truly the kitchen of last resort, failing there sent a message to its students that they could not succeed anywhere else. Ali and her team began working to make sure each admitted student had a fighting chance to be successful. For those who were not yet ready for the program, her staff sought to line up the services—stable housing, medical assistance, and the like—that those individuals needed to prepare to enter the next class. In time, Ali even added a special support group for ex-offenders that met weekly, a notable reversal for the woman who once dismissed the idea of CJT as a social service program.

The reorientation toward ex-offenders produced dramatic results. In 2007, before that shift in emphasis, DC Central Kitchen produced 52 graduates and achieved a graduation rate of just 62 percent. Sixty-one percent of that year's students had been incarcerated. The following year, when Marianne and her team began shifting their intake practices, class size shrank and the percentage of ex-offenders increased five percent; program retention improved to 76 percent. In 2009, when 84 percent of incoming students had criminal records, 81 trainees successfully completed the program with a graduation rate of 84 percent. 2010 was similar, as 92 students, 80 percent of whom were ex-offenders, graduated, reflecting an 87 percent completion rate.

Producing graduates was one thing. Finding them jobs, another. In the middle of the worst job market in generations, DC Central Kitchen had decided to focus its efforts on putting some of society's least employable people back to work. Beginning in 2008, the organization revved up its job placement activities, establishing a full-time position devoted to maintaining employer relationships, placing DCCK interns, and teaching the basic computer skills necessary for students to handle online job applications, since many had missed the Internet revolution while incarcerated. With DC's food scene on the rise, a fair amount of employment opportunities emerged for each new crop of graduates, and the Kitchen carried a significant amount of cachet in the city's culinary circles. There simply were not enough openings, however, for scores of ex-offenders to all find steady, full-time work. The Kitchen had to become a bigger, better job creator.

Since its inception, DCCK had pledged its desire to one day put itself out of business, shortening the District of Columbia's line of hungry people by the way it fed it. The Great Recession changed that calculus. "Our clients and our community needed us to create jobs, first and foremost," says Curtin. The big push for social enterprise, from WJA to DCPS and Healthy Corners, was never just about making money. "If we could just break even with any of these operations, but create steady jobs for our graduates," says MacNair, "we considered that a win." Desperate times demanded that the Kitchen find creative ways to *stay* in business, serving more food in more ways to more people.

The explosion of DC Central Kitchen's social enterprises dramatically improved its ability to bring fresher, healthier food to low-income DC residents. But Curtin and his team took special pride in being job creators in a time when that label had taken on a cynically political connotation. "We're proud of what we've achieved, bringing healthy food to schoolchildren and corner stores," says Curtin, "but at the same time, it's a little embarrassing for our county that a nonprofit in the basement of a shabby shelter has become the national leader in these fields when bigger, better resourced entities have not."

Signing the school food contracts, expanding its produce recovery operation, and opening the Nutrition Lab allowed the Kitchen to create 70 new jobs in just two years, doubling its total staff size. More than half of these positions were filled by Kitchen graduates, each of whom started at a minimum of

$12.50 per hour, with full health and dental benefits, a $25,000 life insurance policy, and two weeks of paid vacation. While these commitments gave the Kitchen a new level of credibility when urging other culinary industry employers to do better by their personnel, this moral high ground came at great cost. Some staffers wondered aloud if the growth was too much, too fast. At times, the Kitchen's commitment to employing its graduates pushed the organization's finances, and Cognevich's nerves, to the breaking point. It seemed that no matter how many donations MacNair's department brought in or new contracts the Kitchen signed, its cash flow was constantly lagging behind the salary and benefit payments it owed the men and women on payroll. While each of the Kitchen's revenue-generating enterprises had managed to break even or better by December of 2012, in line with the three-year turnaround typically associated with for-profit businesses, its year-end position offered little respite to Cognevich as she hustled to pay bills during the lean months of spring and summer. Curtin, while sensitive to his CFO's struggles, never wavered. "If we had overanalyzed the choice to move on school food when we did, we might never have done it, but now it's an essential part of what we do," he argues.

Between 2008 and 2012, the Kitchen produced 370 graduates, who in turn maintained a 90 percent job placement rate. A tenth of those men and women came to work at DCCK. The rest found jobs at convention centers, hotels, nonprofits, schools, and restaurants, a lineup of employers that, not coincidentally, mirrors the Kitchen's array of community allies. The shift to ex-offenders produced another critical statistic. While two-thirds of ex-offenders nationwide end up back in prison, the recidivism rate among Kitchen graduates in that four year span was less than two percent.[92]

Keeping these men and women in kitchens instead of prisons created a windfall for the District of Columbia. Marianne Ali and her staff calculated that just one entering class of culinary students in 2012 had cost DC $6.9 million in incarceration, post-release supervision, supportive housing, and rehabilitation costs in before their first day at DCCK. By training and placing each year's cohort of ex-offenders, DCCK swaps out nearly $2 million in annual prison expenses for more than $200,000 in new payroll taxes. With program expenses of less than $10,000 per student, every dollar spent on the Kitchen's job training program returns upwards of $3.50 to Washington, DC each year.

Before he ever incorporated DC Central Kitchen, Robert Egger dedicated himself to radically revamping the nonprofit sector—what it did, how it did it, and why it those things in those ways. The Kitchen's successes under Curtin's leadership represented major steps toward fulfilling Egger's original, expansive vision. When America was desperate for jobs, sick of being sick, and hungry for hope, DC Central Kitchen's programs were achieving spectacular results, hitting nearly every one of the country's leading crises and cool causes. Its efforts were not just based on best practices. They *became* the best practices. DCCK's rise to national prominence accelerated dramatically in the years following the Great Recession, earning prominent acclaim in elite publications like *The New York Times* and *The Atlantic*. That upward trajectory, however, had been established from the Kitchen's first days. Robert was always looking for a bigger, better stage, one that would allow his organization and

---

92   Department of Justice, Bureau of Justice Statistics, "Recidivism of Prisoners Released in 1994," Langan, Patrick A., and David J. Levin, NCJ 193427 Washington, DC 2002, accessed October 29, 2013, http://www.bjs.gov/content/pub/pdf/rpr94.pdf/

his chosen sector to change more lives and fix serious problems. That search would lead Egger and the Kitchen on a national, even global, series of adventures that shaped and in many ways defined their shared legacy.

Chapter 9 Ripples

Throughout the Nineties, Robert Egger used to answer his home phone, "The happiest man in America speaking." He may have been that happy, but he was never satisfied. "Robert is a visionary," says long-time colleague and confidant Cynthia Rowland. "Whatever the complete opposite of complacent is, that's him. He always looked at what we were doing and wanted to see it become bigger, better, and more beautiful."

For Egger, the Kitchen quickly became a practical platform for larger ideas. While he certainly cared about the day-to-day work of preparing meals and training individual students, Egger always tried to use those small successes to prove broader points about how nonprofits should use their available resources, solicit donations, pursue partnerships, and play politics. "I had created something everyone loved. But you can never be satisfied because our goal was to draw people into this larger conversation about hunger, poverty, and opportunity," he says. Anyone who has ever met Robert will attest to his ability to talk. The Kitchen's programs, whether they were led on a daily basis by Chapman Todd, Cynthia Rowland, or Mike Curtin, helped show Egger's audiences that he could back up that big talk with real action, too.

Before the Kitchen was two years old, Robert was already looking to take his show on the road. In 1989, he told the Associated Press that his efficient distribution operation was "the Federal Express of Washington food."[93] He had the industry right, but turned out to be a little off on the particular company. The United Parcel Service (UPS) took notice of the new nonprofit and approached Robert, looking to make an innovative investment in hunger solutions. "Who knew how to grow and manage a distribution program better than UPS?" muses Egger. The company made a significant financial investment in DCCK and encouraged Robert to look at replicating his program across the country. He did not need too hard of a nudge in that direction.

Working with other groups interested in fighting food waste, Robert helped lead a national conversation about best practices. With a big check from UPS, the handful of nonprofits in that vein founded a new network that would develop practical manuals, share strategies, and start new programs where none existed. Robert gave the association a name: Food Chain.

Egger began traveling the country, freely sharing the Kitchen's model and know-how with anyone who asked. He firmly believed in an open source philosophy, a commitment rooted in his early experiences trying, and failing, to sell the concepts behind DC Central Kitchen to the established anti-hunger organizations of Washington, DC. In his view, those entities turned out to be parochial and selfish when it came to sharing resources or embracing new ideas, to the detriment of their clients and greater cause. Many of the people and groups he encountered in his travels were considerably more open to his advice, but every community, it seemed, had its own entrenched interests. When visiting one Midwestern town that had shown interest in a central kitchen of its own, "a person from the local

---

[93]   "Thanks to Egger, homeless dine well," The Associated Press, July 7, 1989.

hunger movement told us, in a defensive tone, 'We don't want you stealing our hungry people.'"[94] No hungry people, no guilt-tripping fundraising appeals. No guilt-trips, no grants. No grants, no more local hunger-fighting organization. "Too many people out there want to wrap their arms around hungry and homeless folks, to 'protect them' and 'keep them safe,'" argues Egger. "I *hate* that shit. When you protect people instead of empowering them, you just end up with a steady reserve of dependent clients that you rely on to keep the money flowing. It's totally perverse."

With the support of UPS and later on, the Philip Morris Companies, Food Chain started nearly 60 'community kitchens' across the United States. Every program turned out to be a little different in practice, but each employed the general model of using donated food and volunteers to churn out prepared meals for hungry and at-risk citizens. Some even launched job training programs, which varied in their effectiveness.

Not joining that movement was DCCK's leading organizational peer, friend, and rival. Across the country, in Seattle, Washington, a chef named David Lee started a business called Common Meals in 1988. For years, he operated out of church basements, trying to provide decent, dignified food to agencies serving homeless and hungry clients. In 1992, Common Meals renamed itself FareStart and became a nonprofit organization. By then, FareStart had begun a culinary training program of its own for homeless and at-risk adults, using its social enterprise activities as in-house training opportunities for those students. Over the years, FareStart's trajectory of growth and progress mirrored the Kitchen's. The two nonprofits have competed for funding while comparing notes on their programs. Of the hundred or so community kitchens that now exist across the United States, DCCK and FareStart stand out as the two leaders, jockeying for top position. If community kitchens were the Justice League,

---

94   Egger, *Begging for Change*, 46.

FareStart would be Superman, with its brightly-colored brand standards and all-American mission statement. DC Central Kitchen, by that token, is Batman, down to the black logo, bad attitude, and cave-like headquarters.

In the early Nineties, a young *USA Today* staffer named David Carleton read about Robert's work and quickly became one of Egger's protégés. "The dude was an inspiration to me," says Carleton. "He turned on a light bulb. Robert was and is the inspiration for what I've done since." Before long, Carleton abandoned his corporate career path and moved across the country to take a leadership position at FareStart.

David calls Robert his "Obi-wan," but the two found ample room for vigorous disagreement over the course of their friendship. Sometimes they argued about the comparative positions of their two organizations in larger anti-hunger movement. Other times, they haggled over the philosophical nuances of social enterprise. And while Robert became the leading voice for Food Chain, David decided the organization was unsustainable.

"The community kitchens didn't see themselves as social enterprises," says Carleton. From his perspective, too many of Food Chain's members separated their job training activities from their meal production. He figured that putting trainees to work preparing meals for hungry clients was both the programmatic core of a successful kitchen and its best hope for financial sustainability. "The merging of those activities is the sweet spot," he says. But the community kitchens of Food Chain were leery of depending too heavily upon the free labor of unpaid trainees and preferred to leave their major activities in the hands of paid staff and volunteers. Once DCCK began receiving some District subsidies, for example, its meal production relied far more heavily on paid graduates of its training program, reducing the day-to-day involvement of its students in such efforts. The city expected a consistent level of quality in exchange for its payments, and new trainees often struggled to live up to the professional standards the Kitchen needed to meet. For outsiders, the distinction may seem inconsequential. Within the kitchen movement, however, this element of inside baseball was enough to fracture these groups in two and keep FareStart and organizations like it on the sidelines of Food Chain's fight for recognition and resources. Superman decided to sit that battle out.

Thanks to its continued expansion through the end of the 1990s, Food Chain did manage to attract attention from donors, partners, and even competitors. Its growth potential was limited, however, because it seemed to be on the wrong side of another increasingly prominent divide in the field of hunger relief. On one side were those groups that dealt with prepared food, including Food Chain's members and entities like FareStart. On the other side were those who recovered and distributed packaged, generally non-perishable items: food banks and the front-line food pantries that relied on them.

The latter side was older, larger, and far better resourced. Because of US agriculture policy and the large agri-businesses that it fostered, packaged, non-perishable items were seemingly always available on a tremendous scale. Without the concerns of spoilage and time-sensitivity, food banks began to build and leverage massive warehouses and supply systems. The types of firms handing over these processed, shelf-stable items always had more in-kind contributions to spare than those trying to pass off prepared foods before they expired. Unlike DC Central Kitchen, food banks also tended to count the value of all this donated food in their budgets, inflating their overall size and diminishing the total percentage of dollars spent on things like administrative overhead and staff salaries. For the many donors who used those metrics to determine their giving, food banks became compelling recipients.

Beyond the issues of supplies and accounting practices, the food banks had another structural advantage over the fledgling kitchen network: programming, or, more accurately, a lack of it. Community kitchens, especially those inspired by Robert Egger, often tried to add educational and empowerment services for those clients. Those services require money, and usually in significant quantities. Food banks, by comparison, tended to be much less ambitious in their supplemental programming, sticking to the straightforward business of parceling out groceries in ever greater quantities. Without built-in empowerment programs, food banks were even better positioned to keep their overhead and staff costs relatively low. One leading food bank plainly stated in a year-end donor appeal that "although we may not be able to take [this client] off of furlough from her job, she knows that she can count on us to help her fill her fridge . . . Giving the gift of food to those families is the best feeling throughout the food bank. Every time we are successful in finding our clients a place that they can obtain food, it's like Christmas morning."[95] Food banks and food pantries were, by design, largely ill-equipped to break the cycles of hunger, homelessness, and poverty. They tended to be very good at handing out food but essentially incapable of helping their clients get the jobs that allowed them to leave such handouts behind. Without viable pathways out of poverty, these beneficiaries kept on coming back, allowing food banks to treat each day like their very own Christmas morning.

---

[95] Benton, Angel, "Giving the Gift of Food for the Holidays," *Capital Area Food Bank*, December 13, 2012, accessed December 22, 2012, http://www.capitalareafoodbank.org/2012/12/giving-the-gift-of-food-for-the-holidays/.

Despite their differences, America's community kitchens and food banks did share a stated interest in fighting hunger. Players on both sides wanted to pursue smarter, more comprehensive partnerships that would help get the right types of food to the right people in the most cost-effective ways possible. Egger, always an advocate for enhanced partnership and efficiency, was among them. He had helped secure a million dollars from Philip Morris for the proliferation of community kitchens across the country through Food Chain, but the food banks' resources allowed them to dominate kitchens at the national level. At the time, America's leading food bank association and Food Chain claimed a combined total of 50,000 members.[96] Egger figured the much smaller Food Chain would gain newfound legitimacy by formally joining with the food bank network and gain significant new revenue through nationwide partnerships and promotions. "Food Chain was struggling. And by coming together, I thought we could facilitate a new culture of fighting hunger," Egger remembers. He supported a plan for the two groups to merge, which they did in 2001.

The merger turned out to be a mistake. "It was immediately clear that this was a hostile takeover," declares Robert. The national movement for community kitchens quickly dissolved within the much larger world of food banks. Food Chain lost its voice and its leverage. The network that absorbed them now makes no mention of community kitchens on its website or in its materials, besides asserting that 'community kitchen' is a trademarked term of the country's food banks. Fare Start's David Carleton, who had remained outside the fray, also noticed the one-sided nature of the 'merger.' "They took [Food Chain] and then dumped it. [The food banks] eventually said community

---

[96]   Poppendieck, Janet E., "Hunger," in Mink, Gwendolyn and Alice O'Connor, Ed., *Poverty in the United States: A-K, Vol. 1*, (Santa Barbara, CA: ABC-CLIO, Inc., 2004), 389.

kitchens were no longer part of their mission. Once they stopped funding those kitchens, many of them ended up closing." Today, food banks dominate the hunger-fighting landscape, especially when it comes to fundraising. Outside of a few aging hunger warriors, there is almost no one who remembers Food Chain's existence. "I led them like lambs to slaughter," Robert says, regretfully.

Egger's vision of a national network of community kitchens had been quashed by a generation of hunger-fighting professionals who had a certain view of the way things were done: food banks handed out food, hungry people ate the food, and they all waited for a better economy that would somehow provide good jobs for everybody. Robert, the tireless schemer and hater of the word 'no,' turned to his back-up plan. After all, the thing about generations is that there is always another one coming along.

During his national travels, Robert had worked in a brief stop to see his parents in Indiana. The rapid expansion of community kitchens and food banks had started weigh on him. Yes, he was glad to have more allies in the struggle against hunger, but each of these new organizations needed money for staff, supplies, equipment, and offices. Worried that every start-up would expect a significant slice of an already over-committed nonprofit pie, Egger wondered if there was a way for these groups to get started without building brand-new kitchen facilities. As he drove over a small hill en route to the Egger homestead, he spotted a new high school, its construction just completed. *"Holy shit,"* thought Robert.

"There are 60,000 school-based cafeterias across America," he would later write. "Most are closed by 3:00 p.m. In many of the high schools around the country, students are required to perform community service to graduate . . . Here in front of me was a fantastic resource—fresh kid brains, all full of interest, vigor, and youth."[97] America's colleges and high schools all have idle cafeterias, ample leftovers, and energetic young people. Robert did not need a new, professionally run community kitchen in every US city with its own executive director, paid staff, fundraising plans, and mortgages. He could use an on-campus kitchen and power it with youthful volunteers raised with a sense of civic responsibility. Instead of further dividing that nonprofit pie, he could bake a bigger one.

In 2000, one year before the Food Chain merger, Robert teamed up with the US Department of Agriculture, the Child Nutrition Foundation, and the American School Food Service Association to create a guide for 'school community kitchens.' Together, they launched 12 high school-based kitchens in places like Miami, Florida, Lawrence, Massachusetts, and Fennimore, Wisconsin. It was a good start, but, in Cynthia Rowland's words, Egger wanted "to keep the momentum going, and reach a critical mass of schools." While he liked the idea of putting high school students to work in the daily efforts of meal preparation, Robert saw even more promise in expanding his model to college campuses and training a new generation of nonprofit leaders, ones that would be more creative than their predecessors.

A year earlier, the Kitchen had hired a promising young grant writer named Karen Borchert out of Wake Forest University. While in college, Borchert had started and run a food recovery operation that partnered with the school's dining halls. That hands-on experience made her a prime candidate for the fundraising opening at DCCK, and she quickly fell in love with the organization. Before long, however, her husband found a new opportunity in Saint Louis, Missouri, and Borchert prepared to leave DC. She told Cynthia Rowland, "in jest," that when she got to Saint Louis, she might try to start a campus-based version

---

[97]   Egger, *Begging for Change*, 102.

of DCCK. Rowland seized on the concept and presented it to Robert, who had been waiting for a staffer to take up his sketch of an idea. Borchert was an ideal advocate for the program. Egger named her co-founder and director of The Campus Kitchens Project, DCCK's new national venture.

The first Campus Kitchen was founded at Saint Louis University in 2001. With Borchert in the lead, the new pilot program recruited student volunteers and worked closely with the school's dining services provider to recover and store pans of food that had gone unused and then turn them into balanced meals for nearby homeless shelters and the local Salvation Army chapter. The goal was not simply to pump out more meals. Students were enlisted to fan out across the city and find agencies and clients that specifically needed some extra food each week. No Campus Kitchen could ever out-produce a major food bank or Meals on Wheels affiliate. Instead, the program sought out small gaps in existing services and worked to fill them. Hungry clients got fed while students were inspired to leave their carefully manicured quadrangles and gain a sense of the unique needs of their surrounding community. "We could open a community kitchen anywhere," said Borchert in 2004. "The fact that we're opening at a college kitchen [reflects] our special focus: college students. We're ... providing a leadership development program."[98]

Thanks to the support of Sodexo and other corporate partners, The Campus Kitchens Project grew steadily over the next several years to include schools like Northwestern, Marquette, Gonzaga, and even Borchert's alma mater of Wake Forest. By the end of its first decade, CKP had operations at 33 schools in 20 states, enlisting 5,500 volunteers to prepare 250,000 meals annually. More importantly, the students involved were growing into real leaders. Each campus provided its own

---

[98]   Egger, *Begging for Change*, 105.

twist on the same core model, planting community gardens, planning gleaning trips to nearby farms, and instituting local food policy councils. Some schools helped install Electronic Benefit Transfer (EBT) machines at farmers' markets that allowed families to redeem their food stamps for fresh produce. Others started culinary job training programs modeled on DC Central Kitchen's. Food Chain may have been swallowed whole, but the emergence of The Campus Kitchens Project helped solidify the Kitchen's position as a primary player in America's conversation about the problem of hunger and its most promising solutions.

CKP's success wasn't bad for Egger either. As the founder and president of two respected organizations, Robert went from an iconoclast to an institution unto himself. Lifetime achievement awards began rolling in from groups like the Caring Institute, Bender Foundation, and James Beard Foundation. Oprah even had him on her show to give him an Angel Award, which came with a significant cash prize. The more he traveled, spoke, and achieved, the more people clapped their hand on Robert's shoulder and said "You really should write a book." After his time as the interim head of the local United Way chapter, Egger sat down and started to write. That same, now battered, Merriam-Webster's dictionary from his first grant proposal was still at his side. He spent three weeks sequestered in Mexico to focus on the text and returned with a new, short haircut and his now famous goatee.

Like most any conversation with its author, *Begging for Change* offers a fast-paced, ferocious bundle of principled arguments and practical ideas. It rushes from historical example to personal anecdote, rock lyric to mixed metaphor. Egger packed a lot into *Begging*'s 200 pages of accessible prose, including a history of the handout in America and a list of tips for charitable giving. The central strand of the book, however, tells the story of DC Central

Kitchen and its fundamental, even fundamentalist, opposition to so many status quos in the nonprofit sector. Egger wanted to expose the failures of existing solutions to long-standing societal crises, argue for smarter, cheaper responses, and agitate for the dissolution or destruction of do-gooder groups that were failing to make real differences. "This [book] is about killing sacred cows," he wrote. "This is about people climbing down from the cross so we can use the wood."[99]

"I was angry when I wrote *Begging*," recalls Egger. He says much of his inspiration for the book came from the misappropriation scandal at the Community for Creative Non-Violence and the battles he waged with the District in its aftermath. "That was my Mugatu moment," says Egger, citing the Will Ferrell-played villain from *Zoolander*. "Was I the one taking crazy pills? The only one seeing what was happening and what needed to be done?" Robert had taken on an alliance of entrenched interests, proposed a new vision for its shelters and social services, and hit a firm wall of intransigence and risk-aversion. "We had a chance to change the way this city approached homelessness and started to make some headway, but then complacency and fear won out," he says. That singular moment in the mid-Nineties was the closest DC came to embracing systemic change in its homelessness policies and programs. "I still am vexed by how behind the times DC is when it comes to its homeless programs and how unwilling they are to go forward," Egger told the *Washington City Paper* in 2010. "It's still big buildings full of people."[100] Through that struggle, he

---

[99]   Egger, *Begging for Change*, xix.
[100]   Cherkis, Jason, "D.C.'s Approach to Homelessness: 'It's Still Big Buildings Full of People'" *Washington City Paper*, March 11, 2010, accessed December 10, 2012, http://www.washingtoncitypaper. com/blogs/citydesk/2010/03/11/d-c-s-approach-to-homelessness-its-still-big-buildings-full-of-people/.

concluded that the nonprofit sector's commitment to consensus served, in practice, as a shield for far too many self-serving, ineffective organizations. Robert hoped the book would strike a blow against the system that protected them.

In a sector generally distinguished by its capacity for sympathy, the rough treatment received by many groups, individuals, and ideas in *Begging for Change* attracted a good deal of attention upon its release in 2004. Much of it was positive. *Begging* won the 2005 McAdam Prize for the best book on nonprofit management and provided a boon to Robert's speaking opportunities. Back in the shelter basement, the piece became the first full statement of the Kitchen's values and priorities. "It was like you sliced Robert's head open and everything came out," says current DCCK CEO Michael Curtin. "It was the first time people understood not just *what* DCCK did, but *why* we did it. Finally, there was a wider audience that began to see that we were more than a soup kitchen." Each year, Curtin sits down to reread *Begging*, checking his actions and plans against Robert's original vision. Egger intended to stir up some controversy too, though, and he certainly managed that. Some of his critics derided the book as "Begging for Attention."

As much as *Begging for Change* was about DC Central Kitchen, it also drove home the point that no one organization, not even one as plucky and pioneering as DCCK, was going to solve the looming calamities Egger spied on the horizon—the aging of the baby boomers, the decline of public sector social programs, the failure of modern philanthropy, the calcification of creativity among nonprofits, and so on. Even though Robert had wrapped up his stint at the United Way and returned to the Kitchen full-time, the manifesto he laid out in *Begging* meant he could never really go home again. "You can't solve these problems," he says, "with the extra money that's left over at the end of the year." He felt compelled to work on a national, sectoral scale.

He kept a desk at DCCK, and perhaps his heart lingered there as well, but the successful transfer of leadership from Egger to Curtin made Robert more of a mentor to the Kitchen than its manager. Egger's primary focus moved from the trenches of the war on poverty to its grand strategy. Robert refers to this division as 'the 49/51 split.' "I divide my time 49/51," he once told the influential nonprofit blog *Social Velocity*. "49 percent is spent helping colleagues at the Kitchen, or any nonprofit, work stronger, better, faster. But that's all I'll give to traditional charity, no matter how bold the effort. Why? Because grant-funded charity cannot solve the problem . . . That's why I devote 51 percent of my energy to forwarding tactics and strategies that help us as a sector (and we as a country) develop the civic courage, economic open-mindedness and political will required to finally root out root causes."[101]

After *Begging for Change* hit bookstores, Robert had some time on his hands. He decided to embark on a trip to India. The amateur historian, in his studies of Ghandi, had read a history of the subcontinent and discovered that a mere 3,000 British officers had managed to colonize and control a nation of more than three hundred million people. The stunning success and troubling implications of that divide-and-conquer strategy intrigued him, and the former military brat headed across the globe to figure out how it had been possible. On a tour of the home of India's first Prime Minister, Jawaharlal Nehru, Egger had another one of his epiphanies. "I realized we nonprofits

---

[101] Edgington, Nell, "Nonprofits as Equal Partners in the Economy: An Interview with Robert Egger," *Social Velocity*, 7 November 2011, accessed December 10, 2012, http://www.socialvelocity.net/2011/11/nonprofits-as-equal-partners-in-the-economy-an-interview-with-robert-egger/.

were like the Indians. Our problem was that we spent all of our time fighting each other for money, credit, and influence. That in-fighting made us ineffective and politically irrelevant." Egger decided that, like the early Indian nationalists, nonprofits needed a congress of their own. "We needed to find healing through unity, instead of lying and cheating in order to win donations." Robert foresaw an American future with an aging population, spiraling health costs, and foreign entanglements. Those costs would demand new revenue. "Someday soon, the government was going to come for the nonprofit sector's already limited resources, and if we remained divided, we were going to have no say in that process."

In *Begging*, Egger pleaded for his sector to call "'a national time-out' so that everyone around the country can ask themselves what the hell they've been doing and why."[102] Egger tried to enforce that time-out upon his return from India. In 2006, he co-convened the first Nonprofit Congress in Washington, DC with the head of the National Council of Nonprofit Associations, whom he had met by chance when she volunteered at the Kitchen. Five hundred people turned out, representing a wide array of nonprofit players. Egger hoped that jamming these diverse groups into the same room would help knock down some of the unnecessary barriers that divided them.

Robert knew that a more effective nonprofit sector needed more influence and a louder voice in the political realm. The traditional line between advocacy groups and direct-service organizations was undermining the sector's political potential. As he wrote on his blog, *Piece of Mind*, that separation constituted "just the kind of one-dimensional thinking that is killing us. Listen . . . change is a mush of ideas. It's not about one group advocating while another group 'feeds the poor.' It's about using media, money, volunteers, laws, votes, the power of the pen, and

---

[102] Egger, *Begging for Change*, 19.

the miracles that come from caring . . . and using them together. Divided we are weak. We all need to tilt our heads a tad and start to see the gold that lies at our feet."[103] Robert had always tried to envision system-level solutions, and he knew meaningful change had to proactively engage the public sector. Nonprofits could not afford to sit on the sidelines of major political debates and then scramble to react when those debates produced results that were bad for both nonprofits and the people they served.

Egger's focus on politics unnerved many of his peers. Nonprofits designated as 501(c)3 entities by the IRS each make a deal. They pledge to serve some community-oriented purpose in exchange for tax exemption. There is a catch, though. These groups "may not support or oppose any candidate for public office. This means 501(c)(3)s may not endorse candidates, rate candidates, contribute to candidates, or do anything else that might seem intended to help or hurt a candidate."[104] Weighing in on specific legislation is permissible, but the prohibition against working for or against candidates keeps most organizations, especially direct service nonprofits, from wading too far into uncertain political waters. In recent years, several religious leaders have made news by flouting these regulations and indicating to their congregation which candidates align with their doctrines and values. Where some mega-churches may go, however, most nonprofits fear to tread. Front-line organizations on shoe-string budgets struggle to avoid any political typecasting, lest it alienate a slice of their donor base. When a US vice presidential candidate whisked into a small soup kitchen for a photo

---

[103] Egger, Robert, "(Re)Defining Power and Influence," *Robert Egger's Piece of Mind*, August 3, 2006, accessed December 10, 2012, http://www.robertegger.org/2006/08/page/2/.

[104] Pillsbury, George, "Nonprofits, Voting, & Elections," Nonprofit Voter Engagement Network, 2012, accessed December 10, 2012, http://www.nonprofitvote.org/staying-nonpartisan.html/.

opportunity in 2012, for example, the organization's director claimed an immediate and "substantial" drop in donations.[105] When Egger organized the Nonprofit Congress, his peers were just as jittery.

The energy and enthusiasm of the weekend was high, but hard to sustain. Under DCCK's 501(c)3 status, he launched a group called the V3 Campaign, standing for voice, values, and votes. The effort was meant to educate political leaders about the economic clout and potential political power of America's nonprofit sector, which, all told, represents approximately 10 percent of the country's economy and workforce. Egger assailed the arbitrary divide between the 'dot-coms' that supposedly drove the economy and the 'dot-orgs' charged with cleaning up the messes the profit motive left behind.

As long as nonprofits dismissed their own political and economic value, Egger figured, the public and for-profit sectors had every reason to do the same. He wanted to see nonprofits creatively pool their resources, engage in hard-nosed collective bargaining, and embark on aggressive grassroots political campaigns. Robert believed he had found the antidote to traditional charity in his studies of Mahatma Ghandi, Cesar Chavez, and Martin Luther King. He found inspiration in the way they tapped "the power of small purchases" of salt, grapes, and bus rides, respectively, to effect great change. The burgeoning popularity of social enterprises affirmed, in Egger's eyes, the thirst of a nation looking to support smart solutions with their hard-earned dollars. "I'm a total capitalist, through and through," he says, with special optimism about what can be achieved through market mechanisms. In *Begging for Change*, he told readers to

---

[105] Cherkis, Paul, "Soup Kitchen in Paul Ryan Photo-Op Faces Donor Backlash," *The Huffington Post*, October 18, 2012, accessed December 10, 2012, http://www.huffingtonpost.com/2012/10/18/soup-kitchen-paul-ryan-photo-donor_n_1980541.html/.

"support businesses or products that show the link between profit and purpose. The way you spend your money—the power of capitalism—can ultimately decrease the need for charity in the first place."[106] Boycotting products was one tool, but an old and largely outdated one. Egger instead embraced 'buy-cotts,' through which people supported enterprises that shared their values. He says his goal "wasn't just to make nonprofits more like businesses. It was to make businesses more like nonprofits." He called his vision of enlightened self-interest "Capitalism 2.0."

It all made for one hell of a stump speech. Despite Egger's many profound words, however, he did not have the one thing that could really speak to politicians: money, specifically in the form of campaign contributions. As long as he ran a program under the auspices a 501(c)3 nonprofit, that was a weapon he could not add to his arsenal.

For someone who had been able to sell even hardened skeptics on one insurgent idea after another for two decades, the struggles of the Nonprofit Congress and V3 Campaign were especially disheartening. For the rest of the decade, Egger searched for his next great gig, a platform to change the way nonprofits went about their business and expressed their politics. He blogged prolifically, embraced social media, and uploaded the occasional provocative video to YouTube, including a popular response to Rush Limbaugh's claim that America's nonprofits consisted of "lazy idiots" and "rapists . . . of finance and the economy."[107] Egger continued to snag his share of headlines, but knew that pithy posts on Facebook had their limits. As he told an interviewer after the Limbaugh exchange,

---

[106]   Egger, *Begging for Change*, 183.

[107]   Perry, Suzanne, "Nonprofit Leader Takes on Rush Limbaugh," *The Chronicle of Philanthropy*, August 25, 2011, accessed December 11, 2012, http://philanthropy.com/blogs/giveandtake/ nonprofit-leader-takes-on-rush-limbaugh/26431/.

the video "got 50,000 hits and people were like, 'Dude that rocks!' And I'm like, 'Yeah it's fun,' but at the same time if I had put up a video of cute kitties flipping off Rush Limbaugh, it would have been two million hits. So let's not get carried away. Just because someone is pushing a button or sending you a tweet doesn't mean you're changing the way they think."[108] Egger needed more than re-tweets and Facebook Likes. He needed resources and a group to lead.

And so, in 2011, Robert founded a 501(c)4 called CForward. The new organization's tax designation allowed it to endorse and contribute to specific candidates. Just as importantly, he focused on a different audience of constituents. "I had been trying so hard to get nonprofit *organizations* to be political. They never would and likely never will. I realized I had to go after the *individuals* in the sector, who worked for those organizations at every level," he recounts. Egger keyed in on a series of 2012 races at the state and municipal levels to identify candidates who offered serious plans for engaging and empowering the nonprofit sector through coherent policy plans.

"Nobody keeps their job, or is hired to turn a company around, or leads an army into battle if they don't have a plan that includes and maximizes all the assets at their disposal," wrote Egger in 2012.[109] Across the political spectrum and up and down the ballot, candidates at all levels were proposing plans for economic recovery and job creation that excluded the potential value and role of nonprofits. While leaders on the left and right

---

[108] Noyes, Jesse, "Robert Egger On Why Nonprofits Need To Re-Think Marketing," *Eloqua*, May 22, 2011, accessed December 11, 2012, http://blog.eloqua.com/robert-egger-marketing/.

[109] Egger, Robert, "Nonprofits: 2012 political game changers?" *The Huffington Post*, February 6, 2012, accessed December 12, 2012, http://www.huffingtonpost.com/robert-egger/nonprofits-2012-political_b_1258538.html/.

argued the merits of providing public goods versus protecting private sector job creators by spewing dumbed-down versions of Keynes and Friedman, respectively, organizations on the front lines of America's most vital issues were dismissed. "No plan for economic recovery is viable without our work," argued Egger, "so we must compel every candidate that seeks our votes to acknowledge our collective role in the American economy."[110] Robert's rallying cry became "There are no profits without nonprofits." As he puts it, "There is a new civic mathematics in America that all leaders must acknowledge. Our sector, and the people and groups who comprise it, are and must be an essential part of the process of rebuilding our economy."

In the 2012 election cycle, CForward weighed in on eight races, providing money and messaging support to candidates of both major parties. Six of those candidates, Republican and Democrat alike, won. Despite its electoral success and the ample coverage it received from respected outlets like *The Chronicle of Philanthropy*, however, CForward struggled to raise money. The organization faced a number of structural barriers in its fundraising. Most nonprofit workers have little money to spare, and those with some limited capacity to give have been conditioned, through the 501(c)3 designation, to avoid overt displays of political activity. Egger diagnosed the problem as having "less to do with money than fear."

"I didn't want to go on this journey," Egger says of his foray into electoral politics, "but no one else would take it on, so I had to. It was the same way with the Kitchen all those years ago." Nonprofits needed a voice, but they could not be a political base in and of themselves. After more than a year of heading

---

[110] Egger, Robert, "The Most Important Word for Nonprofits: Merger," *The Huffington Post*, April 11, 2012, accessed December 12, 2012, http://www.huffingtonpost.com/robert-egger/nonprofit-mergers_b_1416178.html/.

CForward, Egger sought out a new stage, one with brighter lights. He looked to Los Angeles.

Egger had lived in southern California as a child, and the idea of opening a central kitchen in the region had intrigued him for years. Whether it was starting a west coast kitchen, designing wheelchairs with aggressive paintjobs, or using excess yak cheese to fight hunger—all actual Egger ideas—Robert wanted DCCK or CKP to embrace his latest interest with the same enthusiasm. However, the men and women charged with safeguarding and sustaining his prized creations often decided the day-to-day demands of their operations trumped the importance of responding to each new Egger epiphany. In the mid-2000s, Robert had envisioned a single organization merged with DC Central Kitchen that could bridge the east and west coasts, piloting concepts and passing programs back and forth. But when DCCK experienced spasmodic growth in 2010 and 2011 that strained its resources and organizational structure, Curtin and Egger agreed that national expansion no longer made sense. If Egger wanted a kitchen in Los Angeles, he would need to branch out on his own.

LA offered a perfect platform for his 49/51 split. As a community, the city was in dire need of creative direct service programming. LA is home to America's largest homeless population, estimated to include more than 45,000 individuals.[111] Eleven percent of the city is unemployed and 19 percent live below the poverty line. A quarter of the city is obese, even though Southern California is home to some of America's most

---

[111]   Los Angeles Homeless Services Authority, "2011 Greater Los Angeles homeless count report," August 2011, accessed December 29, 2012, http://www.lahsa.org/docs/2011-Homeless-Count/HC11-Detailed-Geography-Report-FINAL.PDF/.

prolific produce production.[112] Much of this bounty is wasted because the region's food banks cannot safely store, process, or distribute perishable fruits and vegetables. And most importantly to the gray-haired Egger, LA was at the epicenter of the country's looming aging crisis. "There are already waiting lists for Meals on Wheels," says Robert. "The next wave of homeless people is going to be older people." He had been a voice in the wilderness for more than a decade, clamoring for a strategic approach to addressing aging in America, and he needed an organization with the capacity to inspire a major shift in both practice and policy.

As he did in DC decades earlier, Egger saw a way to rearrange what Los Angeles already had in a way that would change lives and make those who were suffering stronger. The 51 percent of his time devoted to 'big picture' work also suited his new city. Image is everything in LA, and Egger was eager to test his skills in shaping optics and messaging in its dynamic, high-stakes environment. He named his new venture LA Kitchen and began fleshing out a plan for to recover tractor-trailer-sized loads of leftover produce, repurpose them into nutritionally-dense snacks and supplements for people in need, especially senior citizens, and recreate DC Central Kitchen's success in training out-of-work adults alongside eager community volunteers.

Quietly, Egger began taking the temperature of prospective funders, partners, and staffers who might support his westward expansion. As he had in the first days of DC Central Kitchen, Robert received his share of raised eyebrows and skeptical responses, but most of those he spoke to bought in quickly,

---

[112] County of Los Angeles Department of Public Health, Office of Health Assessment and Epidemiology, "Obesity and related mortality in Los Angeles County: A city and communities health report," September 2011, accessed December 29, 2012, http://publichealth.lacounty. gov/ha/reports/habriefs/2007/Obese_Cities/Obesity_2011Fs.pdf/.

partly because of his salesmanship, and partly due to his reputation. After nearly a decade of talking about politics and the power of small purchases to effect great change, Egger was getting back into the direct service arena. Some days, Robert felt encouraged by these positive reactions; "I still had it," he says. On others, however, he was troubled that these vocal supporters had gone silent when he was fighting for large-scale change. "Now that I'm back where people think I belong, feeding and training people, they can't give me enough money," he says with a sigh. "Don't get me wrong. I'm glad they're on board now. But where were they when I was starting CForward?"

Though LA Kitchen offered a new opportunity for Robert to burnish his do-gooder credentials, he never lost his focus on the larger questions that he had struggled with for years. "I could build a nice little program and be 'Robert Egger, feeder of the poor.' There are lots of people out there who will work all their lives in total obscurity, only helping others, and when they retire they'll get a plaque and it will be the best day of their lives. I got a million fucking plaques. This isn't about getting one more plaque. It's about pushing something bigger." Robert looks around and sees political, economic, and social issues that dwarf any kitchen operation he could draw up. He hopes that CForward, the buy-cott, and Capitalism 2.0 will become simple tools of great change, the way salt united India and some dimes and bus rides challenged Montgomery, Alabama. "We have a day off for Martin Luther King but our sector won't embrace one iota of his courage," he says ruefully.

Few people have had more dreams stymied than Robert Egger. The Blue Circle never found an investor. Food Chain was swallowed whole. CForward fizzled as a fundraising operation. But the man who turned simple kitchen volunteer shifts into a subversive Trojan horse always seemed to have a fallback plan that was better than his first ones. By focusing much of his LA operation on engaging older adults, Robert identified a possible solution to CForward's structural limitations. "Seniors vote," he states. "That's the future of CForward. Rather than organize 10 million nonprofit workers, I'd rather organize 70 million older people."

The streets and glitter of Los Angeles, Egger hopes, will cast his ideas in a new light and help him raise another army of better, braver nonprofit workers, philanthropists, and activists that unite young and old in new ways. In his daily life, Robert has mellowed some. He is still a fighter, but he picks the time and place of his battles now. He's more Bruce Springsteen than Zack de la Rocha. "For better or worse, a lot of my career has basically been, 'I'll show *them*," he says. There are probably plenty of fire chiefs in LA County, too. They would be wise to take him seriously.

While Egger plotted his westward move, he was not the only person unveiling a new organization based on DCCK's core model. The inexhaustible José Andrés approached Robert, Mike Curtin, and other Kitchen leaders in 2011 with an appropriately ambitious idea: World Central Kitchen.

An international culinary sensation and prolific traveler, it was almost inevitable that Andrés' philanthropic activities would ultimately move beyond his beloved DCCK. Though he was ready to lead an effort of his own creation, he also "wanted to carry the Kitchen's legacy on, to pay homage, to bring the idea of DC Central Kitchen to a bigger world." Any international project involving José was destined to revolve around food, and when a 7.0 earthquake savaged the island nation of Haiti in 2010, Andrés found his inspiration. Food aid inundated the country, which at first looked like an act of mercy. In time, however, Andrés learned that all this free food was making it impossible for local growers and vendors to sell their products. Good intentions were damaging Haiti's long-term ability to feed itself. It was Egger's epiphany translated to a new latitude. Drawing on DCCK's model of drawing from existing resources to retrofit new solutions, World Central Kitchen laid out a vision of "private investment for personal triumph." Chefs from around the globe would implement targeted initiatives geared toward job training and sustainable food system development, sidestepping clunky foreign aid mechanisms and relying instead on private donors. José and his colleagues sketched out plans involving clean cook stoves, small bakeries, and food vendor training programs. "Our goal is to change communities through the power of food," says Andrés. "Wherever food can be an agent of change, we will be there investing, instead of just throwing money at the problem."

A celebrity chef with a huge social media following launching sustainable, community-driven development projects in disaster-stricken Haiti—it is hard to imagine a sentence with more buzzwords. Successful nonprofits need more than search engine optimization, however. World Central Kitchen launched some nascent programming over the course of 2012 with a few expatriate staffers making decisions largely by committee. But Andrés needed a proven, fully dedicated leader to move the organization forward while he promoted its larger vision and tended to his growing culinary empire. He turned to his fellow Capital Food Fight mastermind, Brian MacNair, who had finally ticked off each item on the list of glaring departmental needs he had written out nearly a decade earlier.

MacNair struggled with the offer. The irrepressible energy of WCK and its focus on Latin America and the Caribbean intrigued Brian, who traveled regularly with his Panamanian wife to the foothills of her home country. Yet he had seemingly just built a department that was doing cutting-edge, creative development work. In the end, his interest in taking on new challenges bested his sense of comfort at the Kitchen. He tendered his resignation at DCCK in December 2012, looking to take the original values and mission that Robert had laid out 25 years earlier to new lands and apply them in the face of new crises.

Before he could leave, however, MacNair had one last event to plan: Robert Egger's goodbye party. In October 2012, on stage at the Capital Food Fight, Robert had announced his decision to leave DCCK and launch a new operation in Los Angeles. While he had disclosed his intentions to Curtin, MacNair, and a few other trusted Kitchen confidants, Egger tried to limit the number of people who knew of his departure until that night. The hushed crowd initially groaned in sadness at the news, but Egger's enthusiasm for his next step left them cheering. Proceeds from the event were higher than ever before, indicating a simultaneous vote of confidence in DC Central Kitchen going forward. Mike Curtin joined Robert on stage and the two men, now more like brothers than friends, demonstrated a peaceful, responsible transition of power. "Leaders don't create followers," Egger told the *National Journal* in a follow-up interview. "They create leaders. And I wanted to show that it's OK to let go."[113] Robert stepped down as President and removed himself from the DCCK board of directors. He and Claudia planned to pack their 1997 Jeep Cherokee and start their cross-country drive to LA in February 2013.

About a month before that scheduled road trip, on January 7, a collection of old do-gooders assembled at the latest ambitious creation of restaurateur Tom Meyer, a sprawling, posh spot called The Hamilton, for a nonprofit sector performance of *This is Your Life*. A team of DCCK chefs and students busied

---

113 McClane, Brianna, "After D.C. Central Kitchen," *National Journal*, December 4, 2012, accessed December 29, 2012, http://www. nationaljournal.com/domesticpolicy/robert-egger-is-taking-his-d-c-mission-to-feed-the-hungry-to-l-a-20121128/.

themselves in the kitchen, working alongside Hamilton staff to prepare a main course of braised short ribs for the 300 people in attendance. A rollicking cocktail hour transitioned into dinner, and local news anchor Jim Vance, a venerated DC institution on par with the Kennedy Center and Ben's Chili Bowl, took the stage as the night's emcee. The speakers that followed represented mishmash of policymakers, restaurateurs, punk rockers, and philanthropists. Bill Couper, former Mid-Atlantic President of Bank of America, led off. Couper recalled recruiting Robert to save the United Way of the National Capital Area at a time when it "faced an existential threat." "What were you *thinking*?" he asked Robert with a laugh. Local restaurant magnate Paul Cohn was enormously disappointed that, just before the event, he had been told that it was not a roast of Robert. He let Egger have it anyway. Glancing over Egger's bio and list of awards, Cohn paused and smiled before sneering, "I've never seen so much bullshit in my life." Robert laughed, appreciating a little levity amidst all the love.

Dan Glickman, Secretary of Agriculture under Bill Clinton, followed. The two had worked closely together on behalf of the 1996 Bill Emerson Good Samaritan Food Donation Act. "It was largely through the efforts of Robert Egger that the Congress changed the law," declared Glickman. "Robert Egger changed the world with that law." Naming Robert "one of the great humanitarian entrepreneurs," the normally blunt Glickman cited the Talmud teaching that "whoever saves a life, it is considered as if he saved an entire world." By that measure, Glickman figured, "Robert Egger has saved the world over and over and over again." Robert shifted in his seat. "*Jesus*," he whispered, with surprise in his eyes. Chef, National Geographic fellow, and Harvard lecturer Barton Seaver, a one-time protégé of José Andrés, was up next, recognizing Robert for "teaching a generation of chefs that the act of feeding is an act of principle and an act of honor."

Rockers-turned-independent-filmmakers Brendan Canty and Christoph Green were slated to talk about Egger's 'punk rock attitude.' Canty, formerly of Fugazi and now Deathfix, demurred a bit, saying the subject was "a little tough, being a father of four." He cited Robert's influence at the Childe Harold, where he was uniquely committed to providing a venue for black punk rockers and the edgy Eighties youth who discovered them at that club. Most importantly, though, Canty was amazed by Robert's ability to "talk to everybody at DC Central Kitchen but never talk down to anybody. *That's* punk rock." Green, his business partner, spoke along similar lines. A year earlier, the two had trained their cameras on one Culinary Job Training class for the entire 14 week process. "The commitment the CJT staff put into their work," he said, "was unlike anything I'd seen in my life. That comes from Robert. To him, every single person is valued and important."

Then José Andrés pulled out all the hyperbolic stops. "Thanks to your teaching and your example," the barrel-chested chef bellowed, "I know what my destiny is." Brian MacNair nodded at José from the audience, sharing an unspoken knowledge of the challenges that awaited them as they set about building World Central Kitchen. Yet, as the Founding Chair of LA Kitchen, José had a more immediate duty: welcoming Maxine Baker of the AARP Foundation to the podium. Slyly noting she was the first woman to speak, Baker, the former head of Freddie Mac's philanthropic activities, said that one of her first calls at AARP was to Robert. After years of fighting childhood hunger and poverty at Freddie Mac, she wanted an insider's take on the issues facing seniors. Robert gave her a hard-edged tour of the horizon that shaped her thinking. And that night, Baker was there to announce the AARP Foundation's biggest single gift in its history: a $1 million contribution to LA Kitchen. "Aren't you glad you answered my call, Robert?" she grinned.

Marianne Ali and Mike Curtin stepped up next. They called to the stage a short list of old Kitchen hands, each of them to read a paragraph of the city council's latest resolution. Mike went first.

"To honor and recognize Mr. Robert L.E. Egger on the 24th Anniversary of the founding of DC Central Kitchen, and to declare January 20, 2013 as 'Robert Egger Day' in the District of Columbia." Egger let out a loud, single laugh, thoroughly shocked.

Then came Chapman Todd.

"Whereas, after volunteering to feed homeless people in the District of Columbia, Mr. Egger recognized potential in the city's underprivileged and decided to develop a system that could feed the homeless and empower them at the same time." Robert hooted from the back of the room at his old "right hand brother."

"Whereas, Mr. Egger proposed a business plan that would safely collect all the surplus food from the city's restaurants, hotels, and caterers and provide food service training to people on the street who lacked job skills," said Dawain Arrington.

"Whereas, Mr. Egger founded DC Central Kitchen in 1989, which has produced over 25 million meals and empowered over 1,000 graduates to overcome addiction, homelessness, and incarceration through its culinary arts job training," declared Jerald Thomas.

"Whereas, DC Central Kitchen's School Food Program serves 4,200 healthy, locally-sourced meals to 2,000 low-income schoolchildren every day," read the raspy-voiced Phil Tyler, a CJT graduate and staple of the Kitchen's daily meal preparation efforts for the last decade.

"Whereas, every day DC Central Kitchen, through its First Helping team, provides warm meals and social services to chronically homeless residents of Wards 7 and 8," recited Cynthia Rowland.

"Whereas, DC Central Kitchen has hosted two U.S. presidents, visiting heads of state, ambassadors, senators, congressmen and women, cabinet secretaries, mayors, and other dignitaries," attested Carolyn Parham, stressing the word 'women' with a grin.

"Whereas, Mr. Egger was the founding chair of both the Mayor's Commission on Nutrition and Street Sense, the District's 'homeless' newspaper," said Crystal Nicholas, a CJT graduate now employed as the Partnership Program Manager, carrying on Chapman's vision of collaborative work.

"Whereas, Mr. Egger started the Campus Kitchens Project, which carries on hunger relief and student leadership development at 33 campuses across the country, has served over 1 million meals, and engaged over 25,000 student volunteers," stated CFO Glenda Cognevich.

"Whereas, Mr. Egger is recognized as a national leader in the field of kicking hunger's ass . . ." spouted MacNair, off script. "I mean, in the field of social enterprise and a leading voice for the nonprofit sector.'"

"Whereas, Mr. Egger has been named an Oprah Angel, a Washingtonian of the Year, a Point of Light, and one of the Ten Most Caring People in America by the Caring Institute," read his long-time assistant Annie Nash.

Marianne wrapped it up: "The Council of the District of Columbia recognizes and honors Mr. Robert L.E. Egger for his leadership and dedication to defeat hunger, poverty, and poor health in the metropolitan area, and declares January 20, 2013 as 'Robert Egger Day' in the District of Columbia."

She sang a few bars of the aptly-selected song "Ego" by Beyonce before allowing Mike Curtin to take over. The evening was running behind, so Curtin flipped past several pages of reflections and gave a truncated version of his prepared remarks. He recalled the affinity Robert and he shared for Bobby Kennedy, and summed up Egger's legacy with an excerpt from Kennedy's seminal 1966 'ripple of hope' address at the University of Cape Town. "Few will have the greatness to bend history itself," read Curtin, "but each of us can work to change a small portion of events. It is from numberless diverse acts of courage and belief that human history is shaped. Each time a man stands up for an ideal, or acts to improve the lot of others, or strikes out against injustice, he sends forth a tiny ripple of hope, and crossing each other from a million different centers of energy and daring those ripples build a current which can sweep down the mightiest walls of oppression and resistance." Mike paused, and turned to his own words.

"Robert Egger *has* bent history," he said, "but more importantly he has created ways for each of us to make our own ripples that have and will continue to break down walls of oppression and resistance." DC Central Kitchen has been many things for many people over the years: a chance at redemption, a safeguard for sobriety, or an eye-opening immersion in the wars on poverty and drugs. An organization founded on the principle of using food as a tool ultimately itself became a tool for people of all sorts, from earnest servants to devout sinners, to give back in ways that aligned with their visions, values, and interests. Ali and Curtin returned to their seats, leaving the last act to the old nightclub manager one final time.

Awash in boozy applause, Robert, once more dressed totally in black—black blazer, black button-down, black boots—headed to the microphone. All week, he had debated writing down a speech. Robert decided to play it safe and script one out. Then, when the moment came, he left it on the table and riffed instead. He gave his stump speech about starting the Kitchen, lauding his beautiful wife seated in the front row and recalling Grace Church and the Grate Patrol. Robert dropped his favorite line about charity being too much about the redemption of the giver and too little about the liberation of the receiver. He spoke briefly about LA Kitchen and his excitement for that new project.

Yet this speech was different, as he connected each point back to the streets of DC, some wealthy, some impoverished, but all of them rich with humanity. He hailed Marion Barry and the Mo' Better Man. "My birth certificate may say otherwise," said Egger, "but I will fight the man who says I wasn't born in DC. I get way too much credit. I am only a reflection of this amazing city." Of the Kitchen's unique model and tremendous success, he said only that "it was all here. All I did was move the pieces around a little bit." To definitively answer any question about his commitment to the District, Robert ended his speech by pulling off that black blazer. He had snipped off his shirt sleeves, revealing a brand-new tattoo on his left shoulder: the stars and bars of the DC flag. The crowd erupted and knocked back the tequila shots Hamilton staff had placed on each table.

The next morning was bright but chilly. Dawain Arrington ran speed racks back and forth across the Second Street kitchen, helping a team of CJT graduates turn a hefty donation of chops into a hot meal of orange glazed lamb over pasta with a side of fresh vegetables. Carolyn Parham gave group of volunteers from Saint Anselm's College a stern talking to before telling her story. The 21 students of CJT's 91st class shuffled into Ron Swanson's classroom, bracing for that day's bare-knuckled discussion about the power and value of personal expectations. At Kelly Miller Middle School in Ward 7, Miss Dorothy Bell began chopping lettuce heads into a romaine salad to accompany a main dish of baked ziti with reduced fat mozzarella. Mike Curtin sat down for a radio interview about the broader social and economic issues facing ex-offenders. Brian MacNair and José Andrés exchanged scheming texts. Jerald Thomas sipped a mug of tea, savoring his second day of retirement. At his row house in Mount Pleasant, Robert posted a picture of his giant cardboard $1 million check to Facebook before firing off a loving email to DC Central Kitchen's 140 employees.

The guard had changed. The fight continued.

Author's Note

I started this project in October of 2012, after Robert Egger and I met for shrimp po' boys and talked about his big plans for Los Angeles. We had met for many lunches over the years, starting with burgers and Cokes at the Dubliner when I was a clean-shaven DC Central Kitchen intern in the spring of 2006. In years between those sandwiches, I became the unofficial repository of DCCK memories, stories, and statistics. This is not what I set out to be.

Like many well-intentioned, but easily distracted college students, I was into politics, and writing, and philosophy, and beer. I decided to break up my sheltered collegiate existence in upstate New York with a semester 'abroad' in Washington, DC. To prepare, my father, a ferociously smart, socially conscious banker, suggested I take a potentially useful course called Proposals, Grants, and Reports.

"But Dad," I said, "I want to sign up for a class in writing my autobiography."

"You're a 19 year-old white guy from northern Maine," he replied. "No one is going to want to read that book."

Thoroughly out-debated, I took the report writing class. My father was pleased, figuring it would help me land a respectable internship at an economic policy think tank. Then Robert Egger screwed it all up.

On the first day of class, my professor, a no-bullshit blonde in a leather jacket named Patricia Spencer, declared that the course title was misleading. We would be focusing on nonprofit management and grant writing instead. Our first assignment was to read *Begging for Change*.

Robert had his hooks in me by the first time he referenced *Casablanca*, my favorite movie. We both hated the pernicious effects of pity. We were desperate for smarter solutions to old problems. We shared a testosterone-fueled confidence that bordered on arrogance.

After I finished the book, I looked up the Kitchen's website. I emailed info@dccentralkitchen.org, stating that I had read Robert's book in a grant writing class, fallen in love with the organization, and really wanted an internship.

Three days passed. Then, an email popped up from one Robert Egger. He loved the idea of a grant writing intern and set up a phone call for me with Brian MacNair. Professor Pat was thrilled and reached out to Robert directly, telling him that I could not believe he had taken the time to respond.

"Dude," he wrote back, "I can't believe someone read my book."

After Brian offered me an unpaid internship, I packed my bags for DC. I never told him that I didn't do particularly well in that grant writing class. When I arrived, MacNair walked me through the Kitchen, pointing out my new workstation. My desk was an old bookshelf. Atop it sat a computer made in a shade of beige not seen since 1998. For four months, I was on the receiving end of a fire hose of new information and jarring experiences. I began keeping a log of AIMs: Awkward Intern Moments.

If there is a spectrum of leadership models, and micromanagement is on one end of that spectrum, the light from that point will take millions of years to reach Brian MacNair. Brian was careful with me for about three weeks, checking my writing, providing background, and sending me to free workshops around town. And then he handed me DCCK's grant calendar and told me to go kick ass. In the spring of 2006, the Kitchen was primed for growth. Marianne Ali and Mike Curtin had just done a deep dive into the data and results of the Culinary Job Training program. Robert was free to roam DC and the country, making connections and elevating the organization's profile. And when DCCK reached its financial breaking point in April, prompting Curtin and Egger to publicly forego food for over a week and shame the District into paying its bills, foundation and corporate donors were ready to respond. I left town two days before their fast came to an end, becoming, I assume, one of the rare interns who leaves an organization more inspired by it than when he arrived. Along the way, I hauled in $475,000 in grants, about two-thirds of Brian's annual goal.

But, like I said, I'm easily distracted. I spent three years bouncing from one graduate program to another, struggling to shake the words of Archimedes.

Archimedes once said, apparently, that he could move the world if only he had a lever long enough and a place to stand. I too wanted to move the world—in the direction of greater justice. During my tour of three graduate schools in three years, I kept agonizing about my lever. What mechanism would allow me to make the world a more just place? International development? Humanitarian intervention? Building an army of idealistic young people, one poorly attended political science lecture at a time? Every lever I found had its drawbacks. Every tool for improving the world, it seemed, created new winners and new losers, or widened the disparity between those who were already winning and those who were not. One way or another, do-gooders all too often did wrong.

That's why, intellectually and physically, I kept coming back to DC Central Kitchen. In 2008, when I was a master's student at Georgetown, I helped put together some proposals around the organization's new focus on local farms. In 2010, I was enrolled in a Midwestern political science PhD program, and headed to DC for a humid summer vacation. Within two days, MacNair heard I was in town, called me, and said he needed a grant writer to help drum up enough funds to pay for the Nutrition Lab. I realized, after many late nights and lagers, that the lever wasn't what mattered. To move the world, I needed an ethical place to stand. And the only place I found in my many travels that created only winners and no losers, that truly walked its talk, that was genuinely committed to putting itself out of business was that basement kitchen in that shabby shelter.

When MacNair moved on to lead World Central Kitchen, I succeeded him as the Kitchen's new Development Director—or, as CJT graduate Phil Tyler calls me each day in his unmistakable gravelly voice, The Money Man. It's my job to help people fall in love with our mission and our programs. This book, however, is not part of my job.

After Robert and I finished our po' boys, I began to worry that the Kitchen would lose most of its institutional memory once he moved out to Los Angeles. I worked with him to cull through his archives and old rolodexes, tracking down yellowed newspaper articles, creased internal documents, and frayed connections to old Kitchen colleagues. I tracked down early staffers, volunteers, and even organizational rivals. I asked pointed questions about programmatic shortcomings and personal failures. I found lots of both. The griping, though, never compared to each person's sense of gratitude—to Robert, to the Kitchen, to the audacious experiments that sometimes bubbled over with financial stress and emotional strain.

As I was at the end of my internship, I am even more inspired by DC Central Kitchen than I was when I started this project. At first, the vestigial remains of my academic training told me to focus on footnotes and theories about nonprofit management, to create a pseudo-scientific textbook about one nonprofit. The more I learned and the more I wrote, however, the more I realized that the power of the Kitchen, and truly any nonprofit, is its people. The things so many of us in this sector agonize over— annual reports, financial audits, program evaluations, board dynamics—are so much less important than the human beings doing this critical work each day. When long hours and low pay force good, smart, and driven people to leave nonprofit jobs, we lose momentum, continuity, and the ability to make continuous progress. If this book is meant to say anything 'larger' it is this: nonprofit jobs are real jobs and the people who occupy them should be regarded as savvy veterans of long, complicated wars against our society's biggest problems. They deserve better than to live their professional lives pleading for donations, coddling curmudgeonly board members, and gasping for breath on that fundraising hamster wheel.

I learned enough in graduate school to know better than to wave my narrative hand at some cutesy solution in the last paragraph, so I won't do that here. Instead, let me remind you of the incredible women and men described in the chapters of this book, and ask you to think more deeply about how you can support the work of people like them where you live. Don't pity them. Invest in them, listen to them, and, when someone uses the word 'nonprofit' as code for 'unprofessional' or 'ineffective,' tell them to come visit DC Central Kitchen. We'll fix them up something special.

Alexander Justice Moore is an experienced nonprofit development professional and a recovering academic. This is his first book. Moore earned a master's degree from Georgetown University and lives in Washington, DC, with his beautiful wife and obese cat.

References

"Barry Comment Critical of Asian Business Owners," *NBC 4*, April 5, 2012, accessed January 2, 2013, http://www.nbcwashington.com/blogs/first-read-dmv/Barry-Comment-Seems-Critical-of-Asian-Business-Owners-146185485.html/.

"Our History," Western Presbyterian Church, accessed March 4, 2013, http://www.westernchurch.net/index.php/who_we_are/history/.

"Reentry trends in the U.S.," *Bureau of Justice Statistics, Department of Justice*, November 26, 2012, accessed December 29, 2012, http://bjs.ojp.usdoj.gov/content/reentry/recidivism.cfm/.

"Thanks to Egger, homeless dine well," The Associated Press, July 7, 1989.

"Unlocking Employment Opportunity for Previously Incarcerated Persons in the District of Columbia," *Center for Court Excellence*, 2011, accessed December 28, 2012, http://www.courtexcellence.org/uploads/publications/CCE_Reentry.pdf/.

Benton, Angel, "Giving the Gift of Food for the Holidays," *Capital Area Food Bank*, December 13, 2012, accessed December 22, 2012, http://www.capitalareafoodbank.org/2012/12/giving-the-gift-of-food-for-the-holidays/.

Blais, Madeleine, "A Room of Her Own," in *The Heart is an Instrument: Portraits in Journalism*, (Amherst: University of Massachusetts Press, 1994).

Bruske, Ed, "What a D.C. private school can teach us about school lunches," *Grist.org*, April 6, 2010, accessed November 24, 2012, http://grist.org/article/committed-to-better-school-food-dinner/.

Department of Justice, Bureau of Justice Statistics, "Recidivism of Prisoners Released in 1994," Langan, Patrick A., and David J. Levin, NCJ 193427 Washington, DC 2002, accessed October 29, 2013, http://www.bjs.gov/content/pub/pdf/rpr94.pdf/

Carman, Tim, "DCCK to deliver produce to D.C. food deserts," *The Washington Post*, August 17, 2012, accessed November 6, 2012, http://www.washingtonpost.com/blogs/all-we-can-eat/post/dcck-to-deliver-produce-to-dc-food-deserts/2011/08/17/gIQAZsczLJ_blog.html/.

Carman, Tim, "New Street Food Options in Washington, DC," *The Washington Post*, October 1, 2008.

Cherkis, Jason, "D.C.'s Approach to Homelessness: 'It's Still Big Buildings Full of People'" *Washington City Paper*, March 11, 2010, accessed December 10, 2012, http://www.washingtoncitypaper.com/blogs/citydesk/2010/03/11/d-c-s-approach-to-homelessness-its-still-big-buildings-full-of-people/.

Cherkis, Paul, "Soup Kitchen in Paul Ryan Photo-Op Faces Donor Backlash," *The Huffington Post*, October 18, 2012, accessed December 10, 2012, http://www.huffingtonpost.com/2012/10/18/soup-kitchen-paul-ryan-photo-donor_n_1980541.html/.

County of Los Angeles Department of Public Health, Office of Health Assessment and Epidemiology, "Obesity and related mortality in Los Angeles County: A city and communities health report," September 2011, accessed December 29, 2012, http://publichealth.lacounty.gov/ha/reports/habriefs/2007/Obese_Cities/Obesity_2011Fs.pdf/.

Craig, Tim and Mike Dibonis, "Ex-D.C. Council member Harry Thomas Jr. gets 3-year sentence," *The Washington Post*, May 3, 2012, accessed October 17, 2013, http://www.washingtonpost.com/local/dc-politics/harry-thomas-former-dc-council-member-is-sentenced-to-more-than-three-years-in-prison/2012/05/03/gIQA7X7KzT_story.html/.

Crowley, Elizabeth, "For-Profit Do-Gooder," *The Wall Street Journal*, November 29, 1999, 12.

Curtin Jr., Michael F., "Meeting of July 26, 2011—EEOC to Examine Arrest and Conviction Records as a Hiring Barrier: Written Testimony of Michael F. Curtin, Jr., President and CEO, D.C. Central Kitchen", *U.S. Equal Employment Opportunity Commission (EEOC)*, July 26, 2011, accessed December 5, 2012, http://www.eeoc.gov/eeoc/meetings/7-26-11/curtin.cfm/.

Curtin, Jr., Michael F., "We are hungry too: the fuss about healthy school food," *The Huffington Post*, October 17, 2012, accessed

25 November 2012, http://www.huffingtonpost.com/mike-curtin/healthy-school-lunch_b_1971520.html/.

Day, Paul, "Staff Profiles: William Ferrell, Culinary Job Training Class 81 Graduate," *dccentralkitchen.org*, March 20, 2012, accessed October 21, 2013, http://www.dccentralkitchen.org/staff-profiles-william-ferrell-culinary-job-training-class-81-graduate/.

DC Central Kitchen, 2006 Annual Report, March 2007.

Dobkin, Robert, "Pepco Affirms United Way Funding, Endorses New Leadership," Pepco press release, December 16, 2002, accessed 16 November 2012, http://www.pepco.com/welcome/news/releases/archives/2002/article.aspx?cid=241/.

Dym, Barry, Susan Egmont, and Laura Watkins, *Managing Leadership Transition for Nonprofits*, (Upper Saddle River, NJ: Pearson Education Inc., 2011).

Edgington, Nell, "Nonprofits as Equal Partners in the Economy: An Interview with Robert Egger," *Social Velocity*, 7 November 2011, accessed December 10, 2012, http://www.socialvelocity.net/2011/11/nonprofits-as-equal-partners-in-the-economy-an-interview-with-robert-egger/.

Egger, Robert, "(Re)Defining Power and Influence," *Robert Egger's Piece of Mind*, August 3, 2006, accessed December 10, 2012, http://www.robertegger.org/2006/08/page/2/.

Egger, Robert, "Nonprofits: 2012 political game changers?" *The Huffington Post*, February 6, 2012, accessed December

12, 2012, http://www.huffingtonpost.com/robert-egger/
nonprofits-2012-political_b_1258538.html/.

Egger, Robert, "The Most Important Word for Nonprofits: Merger,"
The Huffington Post, April 11, 2012, accessed December
12, 2012, http://www.huffingtonpost.com/robert-egger/
nonprofit-mergers_b_1416178.html/.

Egger, Robert, *Begging for Change: The Dollars and Sense of
Making Nonprofits Responsive, Efficient, and Rewarding for
All*, (New York: Harper Business, 2004).

Egger, Robert, Correspondence to Mayor Anthony Williams,
August 18, 1999.

Garner, Tracy, Daniella Trombatore, and Uzma Raza, "Obesity in the
District of Columbia," Government of the District of Columbia,
Department of Health, Center for Policy, Planning, and
Evaluation, January 2010, 18, accessed February 5, 2013, http://
newsroom.dc.gov/show.aspx?agency=doh&section=2&
release=19808&year=2010&month=5&file=file.
aspx%2frelease%2f19808%2fFINAL%2520Obesity%
25202009%2520Report.pdf/.

Goar, Carol, "His kitchen feeds dignity to D.C.'s hungry, homeless,"
The Sunday Star (Toronto, CA), June 18, 1995, A1.

Gowen, Annie, "Cupboards bare at area food pantries as
government donations drop and need rises," *The
Washington Post*, November 21, 2012.

Gowen, Annie, "D.C. food bank to open $37 million facility to combat 'growing hunger crisis,'" *The Washington Post*, July 29, 2012.

Greely, Alexandra, "Great Taste of Virginia," *The Connection*, October 13, 1993, 43.

Greenwell, Megan, "21 Regional Nonprofits Withdraw From United Way," *The Washington Post*, April 29, 2009.

Gunders, Dan, "Wasted: How America Is Losing Up to 40 Percent of Its Food from Farm to Fork to Landfill," National Resources Defense Council, August 2012, 5, accessed February 5, 2013, http://www.nrdc.org/food/files/wasted-food-IP.pdf/.

Harris, Hamil R. and Robert E. Pierre, "Internal Audit Sparked Federal Probe at D.C. Shelter," *The Washington Post*, November 4, 1996, B1.

Janet Poppendieck, *Sweet Charity? Emergency Food and the End of Entitlement* (New York: Penguin Books, Ltd., 1998.)

Johnston, David Cay, "Grand Jury Is Investigating United Way in Washington," *The New York Times*, July 17, 2002.

Johnston, David Cay, "United Way Official Knew About Abuses, Memo Says," *The New York Times*, September 3, 2002.

Killian, Erin, "DC Central Kitchen founder protests city with hunger strike," *Washington Business Journal*, May 5, 2006, accessed December 20, 2012, http://www.bizjournals.com/washington/stories/2006/05/01/daily48.html?page=all/.

Levey, Bob, "Q&A with Bob Levy," *The Washington Post*, October 8, 2002.

Levine, Susan, "A Growing Hunger for Help," *The Washington Post*, September 15, 2005, accessed December 15, 2012, http://www.washingtonpost.com/wp-dyn/content/article/2005/09/14/AR2005091400922.html/.

Los Angeles Homeless Services Authority, "2011 Greater Los Angeles homeless count report," August 2011, accessed December 29, 2012, http://www.lahsa.org/docs/2011-Homeless-Count/HC11-Detailed-Geography-Report-FINAL.PDF/.

McClane, Brianna, "After D.C. Central Kitchen," *National Journal*, December 4, 2012, accessed December 29, 2012, http://www.nationaljournal.com/domesticpolicy/robert-egger-is-taking-his-d-c-mission-to-feed-the-hungry-to-l-a-20121128/.

Merica, Dan, "Growing up in prison, coping with freedom," *American Observer*, (17: 2) October 19, 2010.

Miller, Bill, "Ex-Shelter Director Pleads Guilty to Taking Funds," *The Washington Post*, March 6, 1998, B5.

Correspondence from Milwee, Michael, General Counsel of the Department of Employment Services to Michelle D. Bernard, Esq. of Shaw, Pittman, Potts & Trowbridge, June 10, 1994.

Noyes, Jesse, "Robert Egger On Why Nonprofits Need To Re-Think Marketing," *Eloqua*, May 22, 2011, accessed December 11, 2012, http://blog.eloqua.com/robert-egger-marketing/.

O'Keefe, Ed, "Reagan Building hums along with little mention of president's 100th birthday," *The Washington Post*, February 4, 2011, accessed November 13, 2012, http://www. washingtonpost.com/wp-dyn/content/article/2011/02/03/ AR2011020303779.html/.

One Man's Hunger to Change the Way Food Charities Operate," *The Chronicle of Philanthropy* (13: 3), November 16, 2000, 29—33.

Perry, Suzanne, "Nonprofit Leader Takes on Rush Limbaugh," *The Chronicle of Philanthropy*, August 25, 2011, accessed December 11, 2012, http://philanthropy.com/blogs/giveandtake/ nonprofit-leader-takes-on-rush-limbaugh/26431/.

Pillsbury, George, "Nonprofits, Voting, & Elections," Nonprofit Voter Engagement Network, 2012, accessed December 10, 2012, http://www.nonprofitvote.org/staying-nonpartisan. html/.

Poppendieck, Janet E., "Hunger," in Mink, Gwendolyn and Alice O'Connor, Ed., *Poverty in the United States: A—K, Vol. 1*, (Santa Barbara, CA: ABC-CLIO, Inc., 2004), 389.

Rucker, Philip, "Chief's Pay Criticized as Charity Cuts Back," *The Washington Post*, July 17, 2008, accessed November 16, 2012, http://www.washingtonpost.com/wp-dyn/content/ article/2008/07/16/AR2008071602658.html?/

Sanchez, Rene, "A Leader of Homeless Who Walked the Walk; New Director Came to CCNV off Streets," *The Washington Post*, February 14, 1994, A1.

Schmitt, John, Kris Warner, and Sarika Gupta, "The high budgetary cost of incarceration," *Center for Economic and Policy Research*, June 2010, accessed December 28, 2012, http://www.cepr.net/documents/publications/incarceration-2010-06.pdf/.

Shapiro, David, "Banking on Bondage: Private Prisons and Mass Incarceration," November 2, 2011, accessed December 28, 2012, http://www.aclu.org/files/assets/bankingonbondage_20111102.pdf/.

Strom, Stephanie, "Washington United Way Names an Interim Chief," *The New York Times*, September 21, 2002.

Swantek, Josie, "Bringing School Food Home," Run Riot Films, 2010, accessed April 15, 2013, http://vimeo.com/16663471/.

Teichner, Martha, "The Cost of a Nation of Incarceration," *CBS News*, April 22, 2012, accessed December 28, 2012, http://www.cbsnews.com/8301-3445_162-57418495/the-cost-of-a-nation-of-incarceration/.

Teichner, Martha, "The Cost of a Nation of Incarceration," *CBS News*, April 22, 2012, accessed December 28, 2012, http://www.cbsnews.com/8301-3445_162-57418495/the-cost-of-a-nation-of-incarceration/.

Twomey, Steve, "The homeless are where her heart is," *The Washington Post*, January 20, 1994, B1.

Vance, Danielle L. "Government Funding and Failure in Nonprofit Organizations," MA Thesis, Department of Philanthropic Studies, Indiana University, (Bloomington, IN: IUPUI Scholar

Works, 2010), accessed October 15, 2013, http://hdl.handle.net/1805/2502/.

Wilhelm, Ian, "A Maverick's Defense," *The Chronicle of Philanthropy*, December 11, 2008, accessed November 16, 2012, http://philanthropy.com/article/A-Mavericks-Defense/57518/.

Wolverton, Brad, "What Went Wrong?" *The Chronicle of Philanthropy*, September 4, 2003.

Yates, Clinton, "Yes Organic Market needs more than a name change," *The Washington Post (The Root DC)*, December 14, 2012, accessed December 18, 2012, http://www.washingtonpost.com/blogs/therootdc/post/yes-organic-market-needs-more-than-a-name-change/2012/12/14/4acbc230-45e6-11e2-8e70-e1993528222d_blog.html/.

CPSIA information can be obtained at www.ICGtesting.com
Printed in the USA
BVOW03s0645150414

350627BV00001B/1/P

9 781491 727911